Be Afraid

Be Afraid

How Horror and Faith
Can Change the World

Joseph Haward

Foreword by John E. Colwell

WIPF *&* STOCK · Eugene, Oregon

Wipf & Stock
An Imprint of Wipf and Stock Publishers
199 W. 8th Ave., Suite 3
Eugene, OR 97401

www.wipfandstock.com

PAPERBACK ISBN: 978-1-5326-3200-6
HARDCOVER ISBN: 978-1-5326-3202-0
EBOOK ISBN: 978-1-5326-3201-3

Manufactured in the U.S.A.   SEPTEMBER 18, 2018

For Sarah, Grace, and Lizzie.

Always my hope whatever horror fills the world.

Contents

Foreword

S OME YEARS AGO, STANLEY Hauerwas wrote an essay titled "McInerny Did It: Or, Should a Pacifist Read Murder Mysteries?"[1] One could readily ask a similar question of the author of this present book: should a Christian, committed to nonviolence, read horror stories? Joe Haward's response, as the following pages reveal, is that one should read horror stories because they confront us with truth, uncomfortable truth perhaps, disturbing truth certainly, but truth nonetheless.

One could object, of course, that horror stories, like future fiction (and the two genres often overlap), are wholly fictitious, works of imagination, creations of an author. But Joe Haward has been sufficiently immersed in the Christian Scriptures to know that truth is often best expressed in parable, metaphor, or poetry—indeed, the paucity of literalism is its blinkered refusal to recognize the imaginative power of story to convey that which is most deeply true.

One could similarly object that, if art imitates life, it is also true that life imitates art: if the horror genre reflects the violence and self-absorption of contemporary society it may also serve to promote that violence and self-absorption. At very least there is a symbiotic relationship here that is as potentially corrupting as it is revealing. But this is a poor excuse for failing to face-up to the horror that surrounds us—and maybe we need such shock tactics to initiate such self-awareness of a disturbing reality.

On more than one occasion I have come to the end of a book (or a film) pondering the warped and disturbed mind that could frame such a story. (It's taken many years to develop the courage to discard a poor book after the first chapter or to walk out after the first ten minutes of a pointless film—I'm getting old and don't know how many hours I have left to waste on the uninteresting.) I guess there may be some who write horror stories simply to thrill and to make money. But those who have ever tried writing in any serious way will know that it is impossible to write anything without

1. Hauerwas, "McInerny Did It," 201–10.

conveying something of yourself within the text. Indeed, it can prove a quite disturbing experience to re-read that which you've written and to realize that which it reveals. Inevitably that which the author shares in this book reveals as much about him as it does about the genre with which he is engaging. What is it that prompts the parallels that he draws? Why do these stories affect him in the manner that they do? Joe Haward is aware of such questions and, to some degree, discloses something of himself and his background that may go some way toward identifying the context of his own reading. In particular, as I have already mentioned, Joe Haward comes to these stories as one primarily immersed in the stories of the Christian Scriptures: it is these stories and the One they render to us that shapes the author's life and reading, at least in part determining that he engages with other stories in the manner that he does.

But if this is true of the writing of books and of the engaging with stories by this present author, then it is similarly true of our engagement with stories in general and with the book that follows in particular. Texts are read and heard, films are seen and heard; they only truly exist in our engagement with them. And, as with the present author's engagement with these stories, so too with our engagement with them and with this book, such engagement says at least as much about us as about that with which we are engaging. If this present book makes you angry, ask yourself why this is so. If you find yourself disagreeing with the author's analysis of these books and films, or (more likely) disagreeing with the parallels he draws and the conclusions he suggests, again ask yourself what this tells you—not so much about him, as about you. It may be possible to engage with horror simply for the adrenalin rush, but if these stories provoke terror what does this tell us about ourselves and our deeper fears?

As I get older, shaving becomes an uncomfortable experience (ironically, when I was younger, I didn't bother to shave). I suppose I could just focus on the act of lathering and scraping my face, but I cannot but be distracted by the increasing baldness, the tired eyes, the wrinkles, the skin blemishes—sometimes, when looking at photos, I find myself asking whether that really is me.

In the same way horror can prove an uncomfortable experience, whether it is through engaging with horror directly, as looking at yourself in a mirror, and seeing disturbing truths about yourself and the society we all inhabit, or whether it is engaging with the imaging of horror as presented here, rather like observing a photograph taken by another—either way we are confronted with truths we might rather choose to ignore. But ignorance here is far from bliss. To ignore the horrific cycle of violence is, by default, to perpetuate it. We might feel powerless to change things, powerless to confront violence other than violently, but we have the choice to live differently, to break the cycle, to live as peaceable men and women. And this, albeit idealistically, is what the Church is called to be, the body of Christ, the embodiment by the Spirit of the one who confronted violence and horror peaceably, without retaliation and thereby overcame it. As you read this book, ask yourself the question of whether you have the courage to follow after him, taking up a cross in all its horror, and thereby embracing hope and peacefulness.

John E. Colwell
Budleigh Salterton
Lent 2018

Preface

THE SIGHT OF A priest in a horror film or present within a horror story is common place, from Pastor Jacob Fuller killing vampires in *From Dusk Till Dawn*, Father Karras battling demons in *The Exorcist*, Graham Hess fighting aliens in *Signs*, to the small-town preacher Jesse Custer who literally goes searching for an absent God in *Preacher*—the priest or preacher as a symbol of faith within horror is not a jarring nor an unusual occurrence. Sometimes they are a symbol of weakness, or a figure of evil, possessed by the very forces they were commissioned to battle against. They are often flawed, people of doubt and fear who struggle with a God who is silent or vengeful, people who have demons to battle, suffering to endure, pasts that haunt them, that cause them to "contemplate the moment in the garden; the idea of allowing your own crucifixion."[1] The priest Emilio Sandoz in *Children of God* unflinchingly describes his own faith,

> I made a cloister of my body and a garden of my soul . . . I made a garden that I left open to heaven, and I invited God to walk there. And God came to me . . . God filled me, and the rapture of those moments was so pure and so powerful that the cloister walls were leveled. I had no more need for walls . . . God was my protection . . . And now the garden is laid waste . . .[2]

For a reverend such as myself to write a book about horror should be of little surprise. Our vocation is one where we see the very best and the very worst in our common humanity, where the doubt, bravery, fear, beauty, violence, depression, atheism, faith, honor, and vengeance expressed through priestly characters within horror are simply a projection of what humanity is like, summed up in these symbolic personalities. I imagine that horror would be of familiar territory for those in my profession, but I am not sure that it is. I have regularly met Christians for whom horror is seen as a "no-go

1. Rust Cohle, Episode 1, Season 1, *True Detective* (2014).
2. Russell, *Children of God*, 85.

area," ministers who regard it as an unsuitable genre for Christians to engage with, and, as a result, there is a total rejection and nonengagement with it. I understand the uneasiness. Horror deals with dark and uncomfortable themes, themes that can plumb the depths of our own capacity for evil, as well as the reality of chaos within our world; so within the context of church communities where people are encouraged to ponder on whatever is right, pure, and lovely (Phil 4:8–9), to engage with horror seems the antithesis of what people of faith are called to pursue. It is of little surprise that ministers of churches have not only avoided horror but have not even begun to positively reflect on what horror is saying to us.

When I studied theology at college, we spent no time whatsoever dissecting horror nor asking questions as to horror's popularity within contemporary culture. At the time this was something of which I paid no attention to, something of which I did not even consider. Now, after studying horror and all that can be discovered through it, this is a huge surprise to me. Of course I am not the only minister to write or reflect on horror, but there are not many of us doing it, even though our "professional presence" in the horror genre is a common phenomenon. The theological depth, the cultural analysis, and the human reality that emerges through horror is of such wonderful depth that I would suggest that theological colleges, at the very least, consider incorporating into their courses studies in horror. Faith and spirituality figure with regularity within horror, but more than that, the deep questions that surround our humanity, our identity, our culture, our ethics, our history, and our place within the universe offer such remarkable incisiveness, it seemed to me that a book that explored the themes within horror, that drew from the deep well of faith expressed through the life of Jesus of Nazareth, was a natural and obvious project, one that I hope will benefit not only those who love horror, but others from many and varied walks of life, studies, and knowledge. I hope that more ministers will begin to consider what horror is saying in order that they might be able to speak positively into their church and local communities.

I want to be clear from the very outset that this is *not* a book that criticizes horror, but nor is it a book that encourages people to embrace horror who hate it, for I fully recognize that horror will never be to everyone's taste for a variety of reasons; rather, through this book I hope that people will grow a love and appreciation of *what horror is saying* because of the depth of insight it offers us into our humanity. So I am not in any way suggesting that everyone should watch or read horror, nor grow a love for it if you hate it, but what I am saying is that, even if you hate it, horror provides surprising and deep revelations as to who we are. I hope this book is something that both horror lovers and horror haters will enjoy because of the ideas it offers.

When I was writing my first book, *The Ghost of Perfection*, I was exploring a theme that I had observed within the zombie genre. Whilst researching, I struggled to find anything written that offered a theological perspective of what was happening within zombie stories, even though it seemed obvious to me that there was significant themes within that offered not only insights into the mystery of faith and spirituality, but also into the gritty reality of our human experiences. As I reflected on the horror genre I consistently saw powerful examples and insights that I believed were too important not to say something about. Not only that, but because horror continues to be immensely popular—enjoying a stellar performance at the cinema in 2017, a huge popularity across streaming platforms, and a plethora of books to choose from—then it seemed to me that writing a book exploring horror and *what it is saying to us* was an important and valuable task. So what you hold in your hands is my attempt to celebrate horror and all that it brings to our creativity and understandings, but not only that, to ask questions as to the way it is able to tell us far more than we perhaps could ever have imagined, as well as reveal how we might live well in a world where it is easy to be afraid. Humanity has always emerged through trials and tribulations, threats and rumors of wars, political instability, tensions between us, fear of what tomorrow may bring, and so in many ways we live in a time like any other, a time when fear is real. Yet I want to argue throughout this book that it is by facing our fears full on, by turning to confront them, we then have the capacity to live according to love and not terror. I believe that it is a love witnessed through the life and person of Jesus, through his humanity, that we discover those remarkable ways we can live where we flourish, a flourishing that does not hide from the monsters that seek us but is able and willing to pursue those ways that enable and directly ensure our betterment.

Horror is a wide and far-reaching genre, and so my intention is in no way to even attempt to say everything that could be said about horror; my apologies to you if I fail to address an element of horror that you, the reader, are passionate about or interested in. Perhaps one day I will attempt a second edition where I pick up on the themes that are not explored within this book if this project proves to say something worthwhile, and that is my hope, that what is said here is of value and importance—a value that reaches beyond the horror genre and into many other areas of society, of humanity, of faith, and of ourselves.

My thanks to Wipf and Stock for its willingness to continue to allow space for voices such as mine to be heard. I hope this, my latest offering, reveals a voice that is worth hearing. Thank you to everyone who read through my manuscript and helped make it better, especially my twin brother, Tom; I hope to return the favor soon enough. Many thanks to John Colwell for writing the foreword to this controversial and provocative outing. I appreciate all that you continue to give into my life by way of gently helping me recognize my own fear and anger. You are a good friend.

Thank you to my Facebook friends for the help in choosing the title for this book. I always am amazed at how difficult I find it, even after writing the whole book, to think of a title that will work. I provided a variety of suggestions to my friends on social media, and they offered their thoughts and perspectives, the result being what we now have. I am grateful to those of This Hope, the small community that I am part of who explore faith, build relationships, and never shy away from the gritty reality of life. They will never be fully aware of the depth of love and gratitude I have for them and the way they continue to shape my thinking; this book is, in so many ways, a reflection of the conversations and relationships I have with them. And once again thank you to my three beautiful girls: my wife, Sarah, and our two daughters, Grace and Lizzie. I fully recognize that when I am writing a book it is not always easy, as I am consumed in my own thoughts, anxieties, and fears of failure. So for all your continued support and patience, thank you; I love you.

To you, the reader, thank you for reading this book. I hope that through it you discover unexpected things about yourself, in the unexpected place of horror, and unexpectedly discover something about the world, about faith, and about others, that has the potential to literally change the world.

Rev. Joseph Haward
Newton Abbot, UK
Lent, 2018

Abbreviation

Throughout this book the following abbreviation is used:

ANF *Ante-Nicene Fathers of the Christian Church, 10 vols.*, eds. Alexander Roberts and James Donaldson (Edinburgh: T. & T. Clark/Grand Rapids, MI: Eerdmans, 1993–97 [1885–96]).

Introduction

The Power of Horror

Tawny: I'm afraid.

Seth Brundle: Don't be afraid.

Ronnie: No. Be afraid. Be very afraid.

— THE FLY[1]

HORROR IS POPULAR. FROM books, to cinema, to television, there is little doubt that vampires, psychopaths, zombies, and demons from the pit of hell continue to fascinate, terrify, and entertain us in a variety of ways, and for a variety of reasons. Not only that, but horror has a power to get right into the heart of our psyche, challenging our grasp on reality, and at times disturbing us to the point that what we have experienced as entertainment stays with us long after the film has ended or the book has been closed. A few years ago, a woman came and spoke to me about a horror film she had seen the night before. She knew I was a reverend and wanted to specifically ask me about the film she had watched called *The Exorcism of Emily Rose*. She told me that the film really scared her, that she could not stop thinking about it, and that after watching the film she was frightened that she too could be possessed by demons. So, she wanted to know what I thought, whether I believed in demons and was she right to be afraid. She was not a "religious" person as such, nor someone who gave much attention to "spiritual things," and yet, after watching this film, she was fascinated and

1. *The Fly*, David Cronenberg, SLM Production Group, 1986.

xix

horrified by what she had watched. What was most interesting about this hour-long conversation was not actually the conversation about demons (although that was interesting enough), but how powerful the horror genre is in evoking emotions, fears, and feelings within us.

Horror has for some time now sought to push the boundaries of the human condition, asking questions about our place in the cosmos and what we are capable of, both for good and for evil. Within each generation there are the horror films that go down in folklore because of the power they have to shock us, to terrify us, to challenge us as to our place in the world, and what it is we are capable of. In part, these questions are directed straight toward the filmmakers, to the minds of those who have created what we are witnessing. How, we might ask, can someone even conceive of the terror we have just experienced? Such a question, however, if asked with brutal honesty, can only highlight that it is quite easy to imagine and create these horror stories, for humanity has always been capable of truly horrific things. The twentieth century alone should be evidence enough that human beings each have the line of good and evil drawn directly down them, each of us holding the potential to inflict untold pain and suffering upon our fellow humanity. The horror of the Soviet Gulag, the Nazi Concentration camps, and Pol Pot's "Security Prison 21"[2] are all evidence enough of the brutality and evil we are capable of. Not only that, but these examples prove to us the power of evil to actually dehumanize us and pull away from us our humanity and the ability we have of no longer seeing others as human; to inflict that level of torture upon another person, by our own hands, can only mean that we no longer see the person before us as a person and have ceased to regard them as anything other than a thing that needs eliminating. These examples from our recent history should be enough to convince us of our own capacity for evil, but if we go back through the centuries it is abundantly clear that we have committed terrible crimes of horror against one another, engaged in deplorable acts of sadism and violence with little or no regard for its impact upon the people we are brutalizing.

The North African Christian theologian of the second century, Tertullian (c. 155—c. 230), wrote of the *De Spectaculis* or "The Shows" that were common within the Roman empire, a popular form of entertainment that, among other things, were displays of extreme violence, where "men were

---

2. A survivor of Pol Pot's Tuol Sleng prison describes what it was like, "After beating me for five or six days, they pulled out my toenails. A few days later they put electric shocks through my ears. I passed out . . . For 12 days and 12 nights they interrogated me and tortured me each day from 7–11 am, then from 1–5 pm, and 7–10 pm." See http://www.phnompenhpost.com/national/tuol-sleng-survivor-tells-his-story.

torn to pieces by wind beasts,"[3] where fathers took their virgin daughters to watch "bodies all mangled and torn and smeared with their own blood," and shows of gladiators who killed with "rods and scourges."[4] These "shows" of pain and cruelty were incredibly popular, and such displays of violence have, in one form or another throughout the centuries, been a type of spectacle that attracted the attention, curiosity, and dark amusement of crowds, transcending culture and empire. The Persian, Roman, and British empires are all examples of how to master the act of killing in public displays of barbarity, and such displays of violence, and the "creativity" employed throughout the centuries of ways to kill one another are so imbedded within the collective human consciousness that little imagination is needed by today's horror writers. Some filmmakers, such as Lars von Triar (*The AntiChrist*) and Tom Six (*The Human Centipede*), have created films whose impact often leave audiences in a state of shock and bewilderment long after the movie has ended; yet films such as this are simply a projection, an extension of the cruelty humanity has been capable of since the dawn of time, with ancient culture filled with stories of human sacrifice, of the gods who kill one another, of rivalry and public shows of death—a mixture of reality and myth, stories that tell us something of what has occurred, and myths that shape the culture of any given time.

And so, with "torture porn" films, some filmmakers are seeking to push audiences to the limit and beyond of what we can stomach, quite literally because, deep down, we remember what we have come from as a species committed to violence and brutality. Certainly, the shock factor can be an audience draw, a way of creating excitement and rumors that increase the profile of the film. But those films that endure, those stories that last long after the initial buzz are those that have something meaningful to say, that speak to us a truth of who we are and the kind of world in which we live. *The Exorcist*, for instance, as both book and film, continues to appeal to us, not purely because of its enduring power to shock us, but also because of its ability to bring to the surface issues of faith, relationships, and matters of mental illness.

There are those horror films and books that address something of the human nature, a creative art form that exposes the dehumanizing power of violence, that asks questions about the nature of evil, that plumbs the depths of the human consciousness and asks profound and sometimes prophetic[5]

3. Tertullian, *De Spectaculis*, xii.

4. Tertullian, *De Spectaculis*, xxi.

5. By *prophetic* I mean the ability to interpret our culture and get behind what is being presented and challenge the narrative with insights that enable us to understand the "why" beyond the words and actions.

questions about the cultural narrative that we live in and the people that we are; we are not simply violent, untamable beasts whose only history is one of violence—rather, throughout human history we see, mixed in with the violence, our capacity for greatness and good, our ability to do remarkable things. This is where the true power of horror lies, for these stories reveal our duel nature, the line that is drawn down each of us, of our capacity for good and evil. Horror, as a genuine story of the struggle of our humanity, of that which damages and destroys us, it is these approaches that I will seek to explore throughout this book. Whilst much could be said about "torture porn" films and books of extreme violence and sadism, the reality is that, in my opinion, these works have little to actually say themselves. Movies and literature of this nature are quite often works of exploitation and shock value, created to make a stir, purely for mind-numbing entertainment, made by opportunists who know that works of real shock create a curiosity that many people want to satisfy. These works are not the focus of this book; rather, throughout I will explore some of the major sub-genres within the horror realm: those characters, films, books, and television shows that continue to capture our attention and captivate us with their ability to shock, terrify, and inspire us. Horror does not exist to purely frighten us and shred our nerves, for its enduring presence within our cultural framework lie in its ability to say something of deep significance and lasting worth. Dracula has continued to captivate our imagination not simply because he is a great character, but rather because Bram Stoker's novel profoundly speaks to us about the human condition; Ridley Scott's *Alien* films are not only great sci-fi horror films, but they are a lasting commentary on the power of identity; *Jaws* is not just a great monster film, but a powerful reminder of how desperate we are to preserve our way of life; and so on. Horror speaks to us because it has something to say.

This is why I believe we continue to give our attention, time, and energy to the consumption of horror, for within its diverse narratives we instinctively know that something of importance is being shared with us, something that speaks into who we are as human beings, both to inspire us, but also to terrify us. Of course, we also simply love to be entertained, and horror can provide a remarkable spectacle for our viewing pleasure. A fellow Baptist minister has written a book called *The Frighteners* that explores *why* we love horror, and what it is that continues to fascinate us and draw our attention.[6]

I am post-modern enough to believe that everything can be interpreted, that all things have meaning, a meaning that might not have been

---

6. Laws, Peter, *The Frighteners: Why We Love Monsters, Ghosts, Death, and Gore.* London: Icon, 2018.

the author's original intention, and yet, because of the world in which we currently live, the text has taken upon itself a meaning it might never have previously owned. This is the great challenge of hermeneutics, of how we interpret texts, especially ancient ones, for we each bring meaning to every text—written, spoken, seen—and apply who we are to that text, bringing ourselves to that which we are interpreting. As a result, the text is an extension of us, our interpretation a reflection of who we are, the life and backstory we own becoming part of the very thing we are seeking to give meaning to. This should not worry us, nor shock us. Contrary to certain models of biblical interpretation, for instance, there is no such thing as "the plain text," no way of reading anything in a vacuum whereby we can hear the original voice of Paul, or the writer of Genesis, and nor should we desire this as our ultimate goal. Certainly modern scholarship and science enable us to better understand the various cultures out of which ancient texts emerge, and as a result help us to hear these texts better; but we will never be in a position whereby we do not bring ourselves and our culture to the text, no matter how much we try. We are children of our time, and to embrace this frees us from the absurdity of inerrancy. The Bible did not fall from heaven; rather, it is a text of beautiful complexity because it was written by beautifully complex people, living in different times and cultures, bringing who they were to the words they wrote down. Not only that, but every person who has sought to translate these ancient words into the language of their own culture was also a beautifully complex person, themselves living in a different time and culture, often speaking a different language, bringing who they were, the differences in what words mean, and how they are understood to the translation of the text. Then there are those who read it in our own language, each of us beautifully complex, bringing our own meaning to words and phrases, living with the reality of our own traditions, understandings, and prejudices. So we see, meaning and interpretation is a tricky and challenging process, but that does not mean nothing of any importance can be said, far from it. Rather, we can approach any text with a self-awareness that is honest about what we bring, and in doing so, can ensure we interpret with humility, aware that we could be wrong, but unashamed in our attempts to search out meaning because we know we have done the hard work of understanding the text as best we can through the knowledge we now have, conscious of our own prejudices, as much as we can be, and humble enough to hold lightly to the interpretation we bring.

This is what I hope to bring to this book, an exploration of horror, *that might be wrong*, but, I believe, says enough well enough to convince you that horror speaks in a depth and value beyond the simple act of enjoyment. Indeed, I would like this attempt of interpreting horror to help the reader gain more enjoyment out of horror, to find a deeper fascination with this genre, and to discover new insights about their favorite horror stories because of the work I have sought to do in these pages. The meaning then that I bring to these horror texts are not the only words that could be said, and are most definitely not the final word that could be said about these texts; filmmakers will continue to repel us with flesh eating zombies, novelists will pursue our darkest nightmares through apocalyptic visions, television producers will haunt us with demonic houses, but I am convinced however that what I do say now about horror will open up meaning for tomorrow's horror. So from monsters to zombies, vampires to aliens, apocalypse to demons, you are invited to discover the depth of possibilities that horror presents to us, the ways in which it speaks of more than terror, is of more powerful significance than pain, and can reveal, through all the darkness that it presents, the possibility of hope. This is where I seek to take you on each and every chapter, that through these horror themes we can see hope emerge, a hope that is encountered in the Gospel of Jesus Christ.

Theology and horror are not an obvious pair, but I am convinced that such was the revolutionary life, character and message of Jesus, and such was the scope of his work, that into every possible part of human culture we can trace the "Christ element," the way that Jesus' life of unconditionality, peace, hope, and love, infuses all things and can never be extinguished no matter how strong the evil is. Horror invites us to a face-to-face contact with the worst, a truthful revealing of humanity's capacity for great evil and great good, of the deep and unconscious fears within us all, and into that God beckons us to confront this horror, challenge it head on, and pursue the power of hope. Horror is a remarkable genre that offers us glimpses and gateways into our human reality, into the "space between spaces" that we might also call faith, into the great mystery of that which we call "God."[7] It is through this lens of our humanness that I will be exploring horror, asking questions that surround our humanity, faith, spirituality, and more specifically, our capacity for violence. There is a thread throughout our human history, a thread we see throughout the horror genre, a thread of violence and our ability to be violent, at times, in the most "creative" ways.[8] Theology

7. The word "God" is increasingly unhelpful nowadays because of how fluid and subjective a word it is. We could be engaged in an enthralling discussion about God, only to discover that what I mean when I say "God," and what you mean, could be completely different. Care is needed with language, for meaning and purpose can be quite different for each of us.

8. I hesitate using the word creative for violence, for, as we will explore, violence directly impedes our imagination, whereby we often struggle to pursue or imagine other possibilities to violence. Horror, however, is wonderfully creative for it offers us remarkable alternatives when we are convinced that violence is the only option, as well

offers us the possibility to get to "what lies beneath" within the horror genre, giving us insights and opportunity to understand ourselves, and the world in which we live, and the history that we are part of.

Many years ago, when I was a young and zealous new Christian, I believed that horror films, books, and stories should be totally avoided, for they were a symptom of depraved minds and sinful natures. Yet as I have grown in many different ways, I truly believe horror is a unique and important voice that we will do well to listen to, if we are given the tools to interpret what is being said. For those that want the pure entertainment of horror and nothing more, I believe this book will do nothing to diminish that entertainment and will indeed add to it. For those that love horror and are searching for meaning and depth within this genre they hold so dear, then I hope I have served you well. For those who hate horror and have perhaps picked this book up out of curiosity, then perhaps you will be surprised by how much you enjoy this book, for it is more than a horror book, but a work of hopeful expectation of what might be, of what *we might be* if we are willing to pay attention. As an unashamed follower of Jesus, I believe his life offers us a vision of True Humanity, the Way to live for our betterment and flourishing, and it is within this context, through his life, that I believe all things can be examined and interpreted with a penetration his life offers us, but also a generosity that flows out of who he is. This penetration and generosity provides us with the all that we need as we begin this journey through horror, as we explore the hidden corners of our haunted minds, and peel back the mask of our fears, stare into the horror before us, and search for the answer to what drives us in our deepest desires.

Throughout this book we will explore one of the oldest stories, asking along the way what part we play in this story, and how we might change the story into something of indescribable beauty. What is this story?

". . . the oldest . . . Light verses dark."[9]

As we journey together through horror, we will ask questions and explore themes that speak directly into our deepest humanness, things whereby we recognize how often we can be afraid, and yet, what I hope will emerge are ideas and ways we can live by that can quite literally change the world.

---

as highlighting the violence within us that can be obscured or ignored.

9. Rust Cohle, *True Detective*, Season 1, Episode 8, "Form and Void," Cary Joji Fukunaga, Parliament of Owls (2014).

Monsters

The Horror of Compassion

MacReady: Somebody in this camp ain't what he appears to be. Right now that may be one or two of us. By spring, it could be all of us.

Childs: So, how do we know who's human? If I was an imitation, a perfect imitation, how would you know if it was really me?

—THE THING[1]

JAWS REMAINS A FILM of enduring significance. While the scenes with the shark may appear at times clunky and unrealistic, the power of the film lies in its ability to keep the shark monster off the screen while the threat of the monster remains very real. Whenever someone is even near water, we feel a sense of dread, an uncertainty and fear that we cannot shake off. We know that the best outcome for everyone is to simply stay out of the water! And yet the draw of the water, the skepticism that a killer shark actually exists, is too powerful to stop people from diving into the crystal waves. The constant sense of apprehension that you feel as a viewer while people are in the water is a credit to the genius of Steven Spielberg.

Jaws is a film for our time, for it speaks into a Western culture whose narrative is one of fear of what lurks beyond us. It is a monster that we glimpse that needs to be destroyed, that we know is not everywhere, that

1. *The Thing*, John Carpenter, Universal Pictures, 1982.

is very specifically in one place, albeit a vast and expansive space, and yet at the same time the media and government make us feel like the threat lies potentially everywhere. Since 9/11, the American and UK governments have committed themselves to the "war on terror." We have spent billions on war, sending troops on the ground, dropping bombs from the air, and increasing our ability for monitoring and surveillance of our own citizens— all to combat and defeat the threat of "terror." We have been fed a narrative through the media and government that there is a specific threat that needs to be dealt with, and our energy and money needs to be given to the eradication of this threat, a threat that we should be afraid of. In one scene in *Jaws* the beach is packed full of people, all sunbathing and playing on the sand, but no one has gone into the sea. A boy has already died earlier in the film, eaten by the underwater monster that results in a massive search for the killer shark, with seemingly the whole town out in their boats looking for the shark to kill it. One boat finds and kills a massive tiger shark, and the whole town celebrates, yet, paradoxically, uncertainty remains. The visiting shark expert, Matt Hooper, tells Chief Brody that the shark that has been caught is not the shark they are looking for, that it's too small, but the mayor will have none of it, fearing any talk of a killer shark still on the loose will damage the town's summer economy. The townspeople and summer visitors seem to have an enduring sense of fear, unsure whether it is actually safe to go back in the water, so that on the Fourth of July weekend everyone is on the beach but not in the sea. The mayor throughout the film is deeply concerned by lost profits and revenue. A beach where no one is swimming is not good advertising. He walks up and down the beach ordering the locals to get in the water, which they eventually do. Once one person starts swimming many others join them, and fears of a killer shark soon disappear. But of course the threat remains, and another shark attack leads Chief Brody, Hooper, the marine specialist, and Quint, the hardened, skilled, and battle-worn fisherman, to go in search of the underwater monster. At the climax of the film Quint has been killed by the shark, the war veteran devoured by the relentless, sleepless killing machine. The hero, it turns out, is Brody, the middle-class, hard-working, white, all-American, saving the all-American town, preserving its middle-class beauty. Brody, having jammed a pressurized scuba tank in the shark's mouth, climbs the mast of the sinking boat, and starts shooting at the tank. He then utters the immortal line, "Smile, you son of a bitch,"[2] and shoots the tank and destroys the shark. What then, you might ask, has this to do with "the war on terror"?

2. *Jaws*, Steven Spielberg, Universal Pictures, 1975.

Fear is a great motivator, and fear of the unknown, the unusual, or "other" can result in our desire for security and protection, whatever the cost. The "war on terror" has cost a lot: money and lives. What we seek is a resolution, for the unseen enemy to be destroyed. We want our way of life to be preserved, indeed, to remember how things used to be and reclaim our country, in order to have a better life that has been eroded and disturbed by forces out of our control. The narrative from both media and successive governments is that there is a terrorist threat that needs destroying, so we send our "all-American heroes" or "British heroes"; these regular, hardworking people, we send them out to hunt and destroy the terrorists who are killing us and terrorizing our way of life. The only way to defeat the enemy is though violence, through bullets ripping through the enemy's territory, much like Brody's bullets tearing through the water. The scuba tank in the shark's mouth is perhaps a modern-day symbolism of our own weapons in the hands of terrorists, sold to Saudi Arabia, resold to terrorist groups. *Jaws*, then, is that classic monster tale—a story of fear, of peace disrupted, a monster out to destroy our way of life—and the only way to overcome it is through our violence, a violence that will preserve our way of life. But not all monster stories follow this pattern; *The Babadook* is a different monster story altogether that offers us another way to handle the fear that the unseen terror evokes within us.

Babadookian Fear

The Babadook tells the story of Amelia, a depressed and troubled widow, who is struggling to raise her six-year-old son, Sam. Amelia's husband, Oskar, was killed in a car accident while Amelia was in labor with Sam. Throughout the film we discover the strain this has caused on Amelia's ability to bond with Sam, a simmering and sometimes overt resentment to her son. One night, Amelia reads to Sam a pop-up storybook called Mister Babadook, a mysterious man/monster with a top hat and pointed fingers, dressed in black with a pale face, who torments his victims once they become aware of his existence. She doesn't finish the story, but the first few pages are enough to terrorize Sam.
The poem of Mister Babadook goes like this,

> If it's in a word
> or in a look,
> you can't get rid of the Babadook.

If you're really a clever one
and you know what it is to see,
then you can make friends with a special one,
a friend of you and me.

A rumbling sound
then three sharp knocks,
"A Baba-dook-dook-dook"
Let me in.

This is what he wears on top,
He's funny don't you think?
That's when you know he's around
you'll see him if you look.

See him in your room at night
and you won't sleep a wink.
I'll soon take off my funny disguise.

Take heed of what you read.
Once you see what's underneath,
You're going to wish you were dead.

I'll wager with you
I'll make you a bet,
The more you deny the stronger I get.
You start to change when I get in,
the Babadook growing right under your skin.[3]

The book, understandably, gives Sam nightmares, and so he climbs into his mum's bed. Once Sam is asleep, Amelia moves across the bed as far from her son as possible, a look of revulsion written over her face.

As the film progresses the unseen presence of the Babadook grows, as does Amelia's paranoia and fear that something is lurking in the shadows, hunting her and her son. Eventually Amelia is literally possessed by the Babadook, but Sam manages to tie her up in the basement. He pleads with his mum to admit to herself that the Babadook is inside of her otherwise she can never get rid of him. Sam goes to her and strokes her face, at which she

3. *The Babadook*, Jennifer Kent, Screen Australia, 2014.

manages to get her hands free and begin to strangle her son. He once again strokes her face, showing her compassion, not fear, and with that she lets go and vomits a black oily substance. Suddenly there is a terrible shriek and Sam is dragged upstairs by an invisible presence. Amelia runs upstairs to see her son being thrown around the room by this unseen monster. She grabs him, holds him close, and kisses him. The Babadook finally appears from the shadows and Amelia screams at Mister Babadook, "You are nothing. You're nothing! This is my house! You are trespassing in my house! If you touch my son again, I'll fucking kill you!"[4] The Babadook screams and flies down the stairs into the basement and Amelia holds her son close.

The final scene of the film is of Sam's birthday party, Amelia and her son finally united in love. Amelia takes a bowl of earthworms down into the basement where the monster now lives. The Babadook invisibly grabs her around the throat and begins to strangle her at which she gently touches its unseen face and shows the monster compassion. At this it shrieks and retreats to the shadows. The fascinating twist to this film is that the monster is defeated, not through violence, but through compassion. Whether the Babadook is simply a projection of Amelia's fears and resentment toward her son in light of his survival and her husband's death, or a monster that feeds off such resentment, is not clear; what matters is the way this monster is overcome—overcome through compassion. The light of compassion shines into the darkness and will not be overcome.

Jaws and *The Babadook* are similar in that they are both monster films dealing with an elusive creature that draws out our fear and anxiety, beyond our control and grasp.

Yet they are also profoundly different.

Jaws is the violent overcoming of an unseen monster that seeks to disrupt our middle-class, manageable lives, whereas *The Babadook* is the compassionate overcoming of an unseen monster that has highlighted the reality of our fears and resentments. Both of these films fit the typical monster horror genre: lurking in the shadows, occasionally seen, bringing terror, feeding off our fears and panic. Both then can be a commentary of our modern culture, one highlighting our fear of disruption to our way of life and the other our fear of facing up to our bitterness and unforgiveness. In the world of the film *Jaws*, the only thing wrong to begin with is the monster; destroy the monster or odious "other" and everything goes back to normal and peace is restored. Yet in the discovery of the monster the tranquility and peacefulness of the

4. *The Babadook*, 2014.

small community is disrupted, and this small town begins to fight with one another. Soon it becomes apparent to the town that the only way to restore peace is to destroy the monster. This is the classic sacrificial mechanism; something monstrous has visited us and we need to destroy it or we might destroy ourselves, for we are, after all, "children of wrath" (Eph 2:3 NRSV).

Destroy the Monster

René Girard argues that as a species we were religious before we formed communities. Indeed, archaeology seems to confirm his theories. Göbekli Tepe, in the highlands of Turkey near the Iraqi and Syrian borders, has been discovered to be a place that was constructed specifically as a sacrificial site. It has no evidence of habitation and therefore appears to have been used purely as a sacrificial site by early humans in around the time of 10,000 BC. This is a remarkable discovery. It reveals how humanity has for thousands of years used sacrifice. Girard argues that humanity has always used sacrifice to placate their anger and violence, the community united against the scapegoat in order to restore peace to a people bound in rivalry and violence against one another. Humanity has believed for thousands of years that if we offer a sacrifice to the gods the gods will visit us with blessing and peace, an economy of exchange. In many ways we see this process being played out in *Jaws*, a community disrupted by a monstrous other, its destruction the only way peace can be restored. However, in the world of the film *The Babadook*, the monster is a sign and a symptom of how wrong things actually are, and what needs to be destroyed is not the monster but our own fear, bitterness, unforgiveness, and hate. What needs overthrowing is our resentment toward the "other," to be able to look with compassion upon those who have hurt us, who are unlike us, who we feel repulsion toward. Jean Vanier says,

> We can only truly love people who are different, we can only discover that difference is a treasure and not a threat, if in some way our hearts are becoming enfolded in the heart of the Father, if somewhere God is putting into our broken hearts that love that is in God's own heart for each and every human being. For God is truly in love with people, and with every individual human being. This healing power in us will not come from our capacities and our riches, but in and through our poverty. We are called to discover that God can bring peace, compassion and love through our wounds.[5]

---

5. Vanier, *From Brokenness to Community*, 20–21.

Oliver O'Donovan says that compassion today is often motivated by our desire to answer the question, "what needs to be done?" as a form of strong pragmatism that is motivated to *practice*, to what we can do, and not to *thought*, and how do we understand this.[6] Yet what the church needs today more than ever is a compassion that comes from the theological and not the pragmatic. The lure of modern Western culture is pragmatism, the desire to always act. Theresa May, in her keynote speech at the 2016 Conservative Party conference, said, "That's what government's about: action. It's about doing something, not being someone." Orthodox Christian theology, however, has consistently sought to root itself in *ontology*, in who we are in the Person of Jesus Christ and his grace. Indeed, according to the gospels, the works of our hands are determined by our character and motivation, by who we are, and so such language by Theresa May separating action and being is thoroughly un-Christian. But more than that, it does nothing to bring out our humanness, a humanness that transcends Christian faith and theology, but that the church should have something to say if it takes seriously how Jesus lived.

Dietrich Bonhoeffer (1906–45) understood that for the church the first task was theological, and it is from this place of theology that we might know what it means for us to be a people of compassion, a people who renounce violence and power and stand up for the weak and vulnerable. Bonhoeffer says,

> Christianity stands or falls with its revolutionary protest against violence, arbitrariness and pride of power and with its apologia for the weak. I feel that Christianity is rather doing too little in showing these points than doing too much. Christianity has adjusted itself much too easily to the worship of power. It should give much more offense, more shock to the world, than it is doing. Christianity should . . . take a much more definite stand for the weak than to consider the potential moral right of the strong.[7]

In other words, we must seek other ways than violence to rid ourselves of monsters. In *Jaws* the monster is overcome through violence, until, that is, another shark returns to terrorize in *Jaws 2*, *Jaws 3*, and *Jaws: The Revenge*. Since the dawn of time we have sought to eradicate our monsters through violence, only to find another violent monster emerges from the shadows.

6. O' Donovan, *Begotten or Made?*, 11.

7. Bonhoeffer, *London*, 347.

Breaking the Cycle

In Shakespeare's *The Tempest*, Prospero, having discovered the plot against him to see him murdered, decides to forgive his brother Antonio. Prospero declares,

> Though with their high wrongs I am struck to the quick,
> Yet with my nobler reason 'gaitist my fury
> Do I take part: the rarer action is
> In virtue than in vengeance . . .[8]

In this action Prospero breaks the cycle of vengeance and violence.

There must be, then, another way.

God is compassionate in that he moves toward us, *makes movement toward us*, is present with us and empties God's own self in order to redeem, transform, and heal the cosmos. Compassion, however, is a terrifying thing, and our desire to see our enemies destroyed is far greater than our belief in the power of redemption,

> Now the word of the Lord came to Jonah son of Amittai, saying, "Go at once to Nineveh, that great city, and cry out against it; for their wickedness has come up before me." But Jonah set out to flee to Tarshish from the presence of the Lord. He went down to Joppa and found a ship going to Tarshish; so he paid his fare and went on board, to go with them to Tarshish, away from the presence of the Lord. (Jonah 1:1–3 NRSV)

The story of Jonah is a remarkable tale, this brief journey of the reluctant prophet, called by God to go and deliver judgment upon a people whose wickedness has escalated to such a degree that they are obvious and visible from the heights of the heavens. Jonah's response to God's call on his life is to run away. His desire to flee is perhaps through fear of going to Nineveh and telling them the truth, that if they continue in their actions the consequences will be of their own destruction; but more likely, in light of the ending and Jonah's bitterness to Nineveh's survival, it is that Jonah simply does not want to warn them so that they would destroy themselves. Religious jealousy and holiness codes lead us to desire the destruction of others, a hope that people will indeed continue in their path of destruction; why should they have all the fun, while those of us committed to a holy life have to suffer through denial and demand? Jonah lacks compassion and jealously

8. Shakespeare, *The Tempest*, Act V, Scene I.

guards his life with God (which, because of his jealousy and desire to hoard this relationship, is, in fact, no relationship at all), desiring his own survival above anyone else. Indeed, for Jonah, his desire to protect what he has and not share it with anyone else reminds us of classical dragon tales, whereby the dragon is the keeper of a great hoard of gold and treasure, closely guarding it from thieves.

In the enduring tale *Beowulf*, the dragon has "a treasure-trove of astonishing richness"[9] with "glittering gold spread across the ground."[10] Any who seek to steal the treasure are eaten, unable to claim the treasure for themselves. So the dragon sits on its treasure, down in a cave of darkness and away from any who would desire the gold for themselves. The parallels of this to what we read in the biblical story of Jonah are striking; Jonah finds himself in the belly of a giant fish, down in the "belly of Sheol," cast "down into the deep" and, as a result, joins those who "worship vain idols."[11] The story of Jonah resembles the mythological dragon, storing treasure in the depths, grasping onto something of great worth, with no desire to share this treasure with others. Any claim to the treasure is met with fire and destruction in classical dragon mythology, and so in the story of Jonah the desire of the reluctant prophet is to see fire rain down on the those for whom the treasure—in this case the treasure is God's grace and compassion rather than gold—is being offered to; Jonah does not want others to share in his wealth regardless of the inexhaustible depths of this treasure. This is the horror of compassion, for its depths are inexhaustible, its power utterly transforming, and in a world of retribution, such movement of love can move us toward anger.

Compassion not only transforms through its rejection of vengeance, it transforms through its ability to name reality for what it is, it refuses to allow deceit to narrate events, and demands that we stand and take notice of what is really happening. It is not about slaying the monster, but confronting our own violence, fear, and anxiety, confronting the reality of our sin, and becoming aware of the compassion of God. It is a frightening prospect. That God would move with such self-giving, self-emptying love toward us and the whole of creation is remarkable and horrifying! How could God possibly be that gracious, that loving, that compassionate? Where is justice? That we, as children of wrath, who are bound up in our violent, wrathful ways, can be overcome and redeemed by this One of Unconditionality, is a tidal wave of glory often too much for us to handle. The evil and deadly dance of

9. Heaney, *Beowulf*, 87.

10. Heaney, *Beowulf*, 87.

11. Jonah 2:2, 3, 8 NRSV.

violence and death has been overcome through the horror of compassion, the compassion of the Triune Dance, exposing every Babadookian terror, releasing us from every Babadookian grip, defeating it through the cross, and leading us out in the dance of resurrection. Luke 1:78–79 declares,

> Through our God's inmost mercy,
> whereby a dawning from on high will visit us,
>
> To shine upon those sitting in darkness and death's shadow,
> so to guide our feet into the path of peace.

There is a sense in the Scriptures that mercy and compassion come from a deep place within God, a passionate and powerful place within God's own nature. His desire for us, his compassionate love for us, is striking and shocking. It is a white-hot love that will not be overcome, will not be defeated. It is a powerful and emotive love. In other words, I can almost imagine God saying, when speaking of his creation, saying to all the principalities and powers, to the power of sin and death, to all the powers that would seek to strip us of our humanity, that would desire to grip us in fear, "You are nothing. You're nothing! This is my house! You are trespassing in my house! I'll fucking end you!"

2

Vampires

The Horror of Identity

Of course. You have to invite them inside. He knew that from
his monster magazines, the ones his mother was afraid might
damage or warp him in some way.

He got out of bed and almost fell down. It was only then
that he realized fright was too mild a word for this. Even terror
did not express what he felt . . . Yet if you looked in the eyes, it
wasn't so bad.

If you looked in the eyes, you weren't afraid anymore and you
saw that all you had to do was open the window and say, 'C'mon
in, Danny,' and then you wouldn't be afraid at all because you'd be
at one with Danny and all of them and at one with *him*.[1]

— *'SALEM'S LOT*

THERE IS, PERHAPS, NO more powerful an image within the horror genre
than that of the vampire—that soulless creature, forever young, full of
vitality, strength, and sophistication, sustained by blood. Of course, vampires
have been depicted in a variety of ways throughout the last two hundred years,
from brutal warrior and terrorizer, rustic and earthy, to teenage heartthrob
with a conscience,[2] and yet the image that remains, the one that is most en-

1. King, *'Salem's Lot*, 257.
2. The variation and variety of vampire representation with film and literature is

during, is of class and elegance, wrath and fury, terror and cunning, decadent, sensual, the ultimate hunter. The true horror of the vampire is that it looks like us but is wholly other than us, able to perform acts and feats way beyond human capabilities, and yet so like us in outward appearance. Vampires are often portrayed as beautiful and sensual beings, their gaze able to draw us in, inviting us into their other worldliness, beckoning us to join them in their descent into darkness, a darkness of pure bloodlust and gratification. The ability of vampires to strike terror into our hearts stems from their similarity to us, yet their profound differences from us which is also intimately linked to their fascination and attraction; for a vampire also represents immortality, the gift and curse of eternal life, never getting old, revealing the reality of our own mortality, humanity trapped in the decay of time, vampires released into the freedom of a body that never decays. This is perhaps summed up most strikingly in their lack of a mirror image. Vampires are not like us, yet they retain much of what makes them look like us. As Žižek highlights, "a dead person loses the predicates of a living being, yet he or she remains the same person. An undead, on the contrary, retains all the predicates of a living being without being one."[3] Is this not the very challenge many face within our Western culture? To become a new person without death? To be the living dead?

Consider the staggering rise within current Western culture surrounding body image, identity, and self-worth. People are determined to transform themselves into something other than they currently are. The ability to #filter every #selfie, to master the art of a "perfect" photo, and

significant. For instance, we have the story from 1727 of Arnod Paole, a Serbian soldier, who returned from war in Turkey, died, and then rose again as a vampire, terrorizing his village. Then we have "Carmilla," the lesbian vampire stories from *In a Glass Darkly*, published toward the latter part of the nineteenth century, written by J. Sheridan Le Fanu. There is the enduring image of Max Schreck as Count Orlok in the 1922 film *Nosferatu* directed by F. W. Murnau, the tall, bald, long-nailed figure, climbing the stairs. In more recent times we have Luke Goss's savage mutant vampire in Guillermo del Toro's 2002 film *Blade II*, to teenage vampires with a desire to love and be loved like Angel in the television series, *Buffy the Vampire Slayer* and Edward from the *Twilight* saga. The concept of a vampire with a conscience perhaps first appears in James Robinson Planché's *The Vampire* from 1820. Planché introduces remorse and revulsion from the vampire Lord Ruthven over his state of being, "Demon as I am, that walks the earth to slaughter and devour! The little that remains of heart within this wizard frame, sustained alone by human blood, shrinks from the appalling act of planting misery in the bosom of this veteran chieftain. Still must the fearful sacrifice be made, and suddenly, for the approaching night will find my wretched frame exhausted—and darkness— worse than death—annihilation is my lot! Margaret! Unhappy maid! Thou art my destined prey! Thy blood must feed a vampire's life, and prove the food of his disgusting banquet." *The Vampire*, Act I, Scene II, https://sites.google.com/site/vampyresite/ vampires/the-vampire-or-the-bride-of-the-isles/act-1-scene-2.

3. Žižek, "A Hair of the Dog That Bit You," 275.

assess it before you post it to social media, is a symptom of the desire to be transformed into something "other," someone other. Over the last few years books providing the answers to a transformed lifestyle continue to be the biggest sellers, with people desiring answers to the ancient questions surrounding our human identity. It is of no surprise then that the *Twilight* saga proved to be so popular to teenagers and young adults. Although the books and films were roundly slated for their one-dimensional characters, their popularity spoke into an unconscious demand for answers to our low self-worth and identity crisis. Edward Cullen, the lead character in the *Twilight* series, possesses immense beauty, strength, and powers of attraction. What more could we desire? Vampires offer us a life without living, a truly #filtered reality, an ability to "retain all the predicates of a living being without being one," and yet seems to offer more; beauty, strength, immortality. The rise of the #selfie highlights an example of our craving to be beautiful, to reclaim and embrace our self-worth (which we will come back to), to regain our inner strength, and to etch our name in history and thus become immortal. Vampires do not have this dilemma, for they exude the confidence and assurance of their living deadness, that what they are is so powerful and attractive, and herein lie their modern fascination, a fascination that means tales of Dracula continue to hold us.

In Bram Stoker's *Dracula* we encounter the Count, a rich, aristocratic vampire, who is powerful and sophisticated, holding an immense influence upon all whom he meets, striking fear and terror into the peasants who live near his castle in Transylvania. When Jonathan Harker arrives at the Carpathians he is warned off going to stay with Count Dracula by the landlord's wife of the hotel he is staying in,

> Must you go? Oh! Young Herr, must you go?' She was in such an excited state . . . 'Do you know where you are going, and what you are going to?' She was in such evident distress that I tried to comfort her, but without effect. Finally she went down on her knees and implored me not to go . . . She then rose and dried her eyes, and taking a crucifix from her neck offered it to me.[4]

Stoker's *Dracula*, written near the end of the nineteenth century, surely invites us to consider the rise of capitalism, the growing disparity between rich and poor, and the very real injustice that the lower classes endured. Karl Marx, writing in *Capital*, says, "Capital is dead labor which, vampire-like, lives only by sucking living labor, and lives the more, the more it sucks."[5] The proletariat (the industrial working class) had only their labor, taken by

4. Stoker, *Dracula*, 6.
5. Marx, *Capital*, 242.

the capitalist bourgeois (the property owning class) and used to generate greater wealth and profit, and, like Count Dracula who is led by the desire for blood, the need to satisfy his thirst, so the bourgeois, according to Marx's stinging critique, use the proletariat to satisfy their desire for greater wealth. In the book and the film adaptation of *Interview with the Vampire*, humanity are a background noise, merely a form of cattle, useful only for our blood and to sustain the lavish lifestyle of the vampire, with the character Lestat feeding off humans in his opulent dining room like one would dine on oysters or lobsters. The echoes here to Marx and Engels should not be ignored,

> The bourgeoisie has stripped of its halo every occupation hitherto honored and looked upon with reverent awe. It has converted the physician, the lawyer, the priest, the poet, the man of science, into its paid wage-laborer.[6]

They go on,

> These laborers, who must sell themselves piecemeal, are a commodity, like every other article of commerce, and are consequently exposed to all the vicissitudes of competition, to all fluctuations of the market.[7]

Not only this, but vampires are comfortable in their own skin and desires, regardless of the cost to the lives of others—much like Marx's understanding of the bourgeois—vampires are also remarkably self-aware.

Imagine Me

Stoker's Count is self-aware; his desire for Mina Harker is a mix between powerful nostalgia for his dead wife and a need to satisfy his lust and human craving,

> "You yourself never loved; you never love!" On this the other woman joined, and such a mirthless, hard, soulless laughter rang through the room that it almost made me faint to hear; it seemed like the pleasure of fiends. The Count turned, after looking at my face attentively, and said in a soft whisper: "Yes, I too can love; you yourselves can tell it from the past. Is it not so?"[8]

The challenge that moderns face today is the continual bombardment of images—images that directly impact and influence the way we see and imagine

6. Engels and Marx, *The Communist Manifesto*, 222.
7. Engels and Marx, *The Communist Manifesto*, 227.
8. Stoker, *Dracula*, 34.

ourselves, and can, in many ways, impede our ability to be self-aware. It is, in Lacanian terms, the Imaginary, the image of self somewhere between what is internalized and that which is seen. Our self-worth and identity are often projections made up from the images given to us, the words spoken over us, the actions done to us. How we perceive ourselves is often different to the way others view us. It is like hearing the sound of our own voice; the internalized sound of our voice is different to the way others hear us, so much so, that it can be a shock to hear a recording of ourselves.[9] We project upon ourselves our imagined selves, a version of who we are that can challenge our own sense of self-worth made by distorted and disorientated narratives fed to us through the media and social network lens.

The mirror then raises all kinds of questions surrounding self-projection and understandings of who we are as opposed to our imaginary and symbolic self.[10] According to Lacan, the mirror is the first time we connect the dots of our identity, recognizing, unconsciously, that we are not a disjointed, fragmented self, but whole. Think about how the world and our own selves look by simply gazing through our own eyes. We "see in part" aware that we have a face, alert to the reality that we make facial expressions, but unable to see our face as others see us. Now, of course, the way we "see" another person's face carries with it symbolism, whereby we attach emotion and meaning, and, if we are someone who is blind or partially sighted, how we see a face is again transformed,

9. I have an identical twin brother. Whenever we speak to one another I am convinced our voices are acutely different, and yet people always tell us that our voices are virtually identical, so much so that on the phone people often cannot tell the difference between us. I realized this myself one day when I left a message for my wife on the home answer phone. When I returned home later that same day I saw the answer phone light blinking and, forgetting that I had left a message, played the message. I was really confused as I could hear my brother speaking but his message didn't make any sense to me (why was he saying "babe" and telling us he was going to be home later than usual?). It was only then that I suddenly realized it was me speaking and how similar my voice was to my brother's.

10. By the Symbolic self I mean the identity of ourselves that we mediate meaning through, images of ourselves that give an interpretation beyond our reflection. For instance, when we look at our image and see a laughter line by our eyes, what we see is a wrinkle, a sign that we are aging and getting older. Why do we attach this meaning to that line on our faces? Why do we not see it as a fruit of enjoyment, as a sign that we have laughed through life, experienced pleasure and satisfaction? Because the dominant media narrative is of skin perfection, any blemishes photoshopped out, wrinkles a hindrance to the gleaming, glowing, seductive, and imitative power of a face free from the forceful onslaught of time. Is this not part of the wonder of the vampire? Gleaming, pale, smooth, and seductive skin?

> In chapter 5 of *The Tactile Heart*, John Hull explores the theme
> of the image of God and in particular the face. In terms of image
> he rightly asserts that most Christians project onto God what
> they consider to be the human norm, but a bit better. What
> hope do the abnormal have? I didn't realise how important face
> is in terms of embodiment and the gateway to the mind and the
> spirit of a person. Other than the tactile memory of faces I have
> touched, face is meaningless. To look like isn't a category I have.
> It is impossible to get a decent tactile memory of eyes.[11]

My friend Glen, who has been blind from birth, is here helping us create different categories of how we see, a mode of seeing beyond eyes and gaze and mirrors, but through the relationship, touch, voice, and presence of another. The act of seeing oneself then goes beyond the reflection of the mirror—it is internalized; the mirror is simply a means through which we attach ever more layers to our symbolized selves. The #selfie creates further layers of meaning and confusion as we struggle to recognize where our humanity begins and ends, and in what ways our lives are dehumanized, where our humanity is marred and masked. For vampires, our humanity is the problem and is what we need releasing from; but for us, it is how we can reclaim our humanness. Keanu Reeves stars in the 2005 film *Constantine*, a loose adaptation of the comic book character John Constantine created by Alan Moore and Stephen R. Bissette, and the DC Comics series *Hellblazer*, which had many and various contributors during its time. At the beginning of the film we are introduced to Reeves's character going to the apartment of a family whose daughter is possessed by a demon. On arrival Constantine is confronted with, what appears to be, a standard exorcism. While he is performing the exorcism ritual in, again, what appears to be the usual way, the solider demon suddenly tries to burst through the stomach of the girl and gain access to the world, something that is impossible due to the ban of angels and demons on earth by God and Lucifer. Constantine hooks a full-size mirror up above the girl, and her reflection is of the demon that then starts to try and smash through the mirror and gain access to Earth before Constantine smashes the mirror, thus releasing the girl from her demonic possession.

To look in the mirror is a frightening act, for in that moment we are confronted with a version of ourselves that is distorted, and yet points us to our image. What I mean by this is that when we look in a mirror we never see our true form, for every mirror reflects our image back to us in slightly different ways according to the surface of the mirror, the atmosphere between us and the mirror, and the way the light is absorbed or scattered after making contact

---

11. Reverend Glen Graham, email conversation, April, 14, 2017.

with the surface. Not only that, but our eyes receive the image in different ways, thus creating differences in how our image is received. And further to this, there is the process of interpretation that our brains make for an image we see is always a virtual image, a representation that is not quite reality because vision is mediated—it happens *through* other things. We are always interpreting what we see because we already have an expectation of what we will see when we look. You never simply look at an object; rather, you unconsciously bring interpretation to that object—added with the light refracting presenting photons, impacted by our distance and position to that object or from the mirror, the reception of the image into our eyes, an expectation of what that object is (and thus, what it isn't), a further expectation of what we will see—all coming together to make sight possible. We do not simply "look" at something or ourselves. This is why there are those who look in the mirror and "see" someone completely different to how others see them,

> Body Dysmorphic Disorder (BDD) is characterized by a pre-occupation with one or more perceived defects or flaws in appearance, which is unnoticeable to others. Sometimes the flaw is noticeable but is a normal variation (e.g., male pattern baldness) or is not as prominent as the sufferer believes. The older term for BDD is "dysmorphophobia," which is sometimes still used. The media sometimes refer to BDD as "Imagined Ugliness Syndrome." This isn't particularly helpful as the ugliness is very real to the individual concerned, and does not reflect the severe distress that BDD can cause. As well as the excessive self-consciousness, individuals with BDD often feel defined by their flaw. They often experience an image of their perceived defect associated with memories, emotions and bodily sensations—as if seeing the flaw through the eyes of an onlooker, even though what they "see" may be very different to their appearance observed by others. Sufferers tend repeatedly to check on how bad their flaw is (for example in mirrors and reflective surfaces), attempt to camouflage or alter the perceived defect and avoid public or social situations or triggers that increase distress. They may at times be housebound or have needless cosmetic and dermatological treatments. There is no doubt that the symptoms cause significant distress or handicap and there is an increased risk of suicide and attempted suicide.[12]

There is a reality in modern Western society whereby we are unable to look at ourselves truthfully, for we see something that causes us pain, distress, and a sense of shame. To look in the mirror in modern society can be a painful

---

12. http://bddfoundation.org/helping-you/about-bdd/.

and difficult act. Selfies enable us to look in the mirror and radically change what we see, and the image that we believe others will see. With the help of endless retakes, different angles, various lighting, makeup, and an array of filters, we can post pictures of ourselves online that help project something that is closer to the image and identity that we are searching for. And yet, in truth, we do not know what it is we are actually searching for—an image that does not exist, the ghost of perfection. For some, the image they see of themselves as they look in the mirror brings pain and distress, a vision that evokes negativity and even disgust. It is not a case of ego or narcissism for those who suffer with BDD, but genuine emotional and spiritual suffering as to what they are perceiving their appearance to be. As we have already stated, when we look at an image there are multiple processes occurring in order to make sight possible, one of which is our interpretive function within the unconscious that operates whenever we observe anything because of our own lives and stories. Let's think about this a little more deeply with something trivial to help us grasp what it is that is happening.

Look at a cup. Go get one if you do not have one near you. Got one? Good. Hold the cup in your hand. If you have sight, what do you see? If you are blind, what can you feel? Is it a good cup in your opinion? Is it big enough for what you would like in the size of a cup? Or is it small enough for your desired cup? Do you even drink out of cups? If not, why not? If you do, what is your favorite drink to have in a cup? Did someone make you the cup, like one of your children or a friend? Can you remember where your cup came from? How much did you spend on the cup? Does it have sentimental value? Why are you reading a book that is asking you about a cup? Here is the thing: that cup that you are holding in your hands is more than simply a cup, because it represents other things beyond its own purpose. In my own house for instance, a cup represents drinking tea (we are Brits after all!) and not just drinking tea, but picking up a cup of tea only to discover it has gone cold because we have been distracted by some other event (children needing something, putting the bins out, checking our phones, cooking dinner) before we even got to drink the cup of tea. I always joke to my wife that if confronted with an alien invasion similar to the film *Signs*, then we will be absolutely fine.[13] We also have various cups that hold significance for us as they have been painted or made by our children, or represent a significant anniversary or special occasion. There are also our favorite cups that we like to drink out of because of size, shape, and ability to keep the tea hotter for longer. So, what

13. One of the main characters in the film is a young girl who only ever drinks half her cups of water and leaves them all around the house, much to her father's annoyance. The end of the film, however, shows how useful this half-full cups of water actually are when dealing with the alien invasion.

is my point with all of this about cups? That whenever I make a cup of tea and pick a cup up, what I see in the picking up of that cup is more than simply a cup—I unconsciously, and sometimes consciously, look at that cup through interpretation, and therefore "see" something more than simply a cup. My own life and story has created a way, a lens if you will, through which I see a cup, and in the moment of looking there is the act of interpretation. This act happens all the time in various ways according to what it is we are looking at. So it is with image and the act of looking in the mirror. I recognize here that the blind community do not approach reflections in the same way as sighted people, and therefore, how mirrors are understood here needs to be handled in such a way that makes sense to sighted and blind people. So it is that for some there is a huge amount of negative interpretation that is associated with their own image. The rise in muscle dysmorphic disorder among men is a further sign that we live in a time when anxiety and shame over the way we see ourselves transcends gender. Many men in the West are struggling with self-image, with the sense of who they are because of how they look. It is not simply that men want to have muscular and lean physiques, but that men are struggling with the onset of age, and to look in the mirror is to see how time is relentless, and like King Canute (Cnut) unable to stop the tide, so we are unable to halt our rising age.

To gaze then is to imagine our lives as something other than they actually are. Žižek makes the point that when it comes to jealousy we imagine and create a utopian world that we are witnesses to, that we are able to gaze upon, yet are excluded from.[14] In gazing upon others we imagine their lives as better than ours (and worse than ours),[15] as something of greater satisfaction and fulfillment. This is the curse of social media and the #filtered lives we encounter every day, staring back at us through the screen, a constant beckoning toward a life that can never found. In the gaze we have desire, a longing for that which we cannot have, or have yet to acquire. And here is the paradox: if we do actually acquire that which we have gazed at, it never is the thing we imagined, for its form changes the moment we lay hold of it and possess it.[16] The ancients understood only too well the power of the gaze, and its ability to create rivalry, conflict and violence,

14. "In jealousy, the subject *creates/imagines a paradise* (a utopia of full *jouissance*) *from which he is excluded.*" Žižek, *Living in the End Times*, 81.

15. Do we not feel better when we are witnesses to lives that appear worse than ours? We imagine how superior our lives are compared to those we deem to be beneath us. There has, in the UK at least, been a great surge of "poverty porn" programs, whereby we gaze upon the lives of people who have no money, no power, no social status, and we imagine how much better our own lives are. And yet there has also been a surge of programs dedicated to the "superrich," those of whom we can be jealous of.

16. Consider the way you feel when you wait for the newest iPhone or car or

> Now Abel was a keeper of sheep, and Cain a tiller of the ground.
> In the course of time Cain brought to the LORD an offering of
> the fruit of the ground, and Abel for his part brought of the first-
> lings of his flock, their fat portions. And the LORD had regard
> for Abel and his offering, but for Cain and his offering he had
> no regard. So Cain was very angry, and his countenance fell.
> The LORD said to Cain, "Why are you angry, and why has your
> countenance fallen? If you do well, will you not be accepted?
> And if you of not do well, sin is lurking at the door; its desire is
> for you, but you must master it." (Gen 4:2–7 NRSV)

Cain's gaze is upon the favor Abel has with the divinity. Abel is gazed upon
by the divinity with regard, and Cain is encouraged by this divinity to not
let his gaze drop, "Why has your countenance fallen?" In other words, "Keep
looking! Keep desiring!" The LORD is here, a representation of the gaze,
the demand of the gaze to keep looking at what you do not have, to stir
within you greater desire for that which you are missing. This gaze leads to
rivalrous relationships, to the increase in the violent pursuit of what others possess. Herein lies the importance of the final commandment in the
Decalogue, "You shall not covet your neighbor's house; you shall not covet
your neighbor's wife, or male or female slave, or ox, or donkey, or anything
that belongs to your neighbor" (Exod 20:17 NRSV). To covet is to desire to
be our neighbor, to imitate in rivalistic ways who our neighbor is, a desire to
be like them and thus take violently their lives. It is a life, however, that we
gaze at, that we desire through the lens of exclusion and utopianism, a life
that simply does not exist.

The Gaze

The gaze is a powerful motif within the vampire myth. In Stoker's *Dracula*, the
Count has a gaze of intensity and fury: "Never did I imagine such wrath and
fury even in the demons of the pit. His eyes were positively blazing. The red

---

consumeristic object, how, in anticipation you imagine what it will be like. In the moment of acquisition the object changes, loses its imagined beauty, and becomes, moment by moment, a disappointment. The same is true for people who have affairs; the
anticipation and symbolic imagining of this secret encounter becomes, over time, a
thing of anguish and resentment, for it can never be that which we gazed upon and
desired, for in our gaze we have imagined and given meaning in the mirror of our
own lives, seeking to increase our own self-worth, seeking to repair our own identity
through the desire of an object. The spell is always broken once we have taken hold of
our desire, because we recognize that our desires are a projection of our own pain, and
our pain needs healing not feeding.

light in them was lurid, as if the flames of hell-fire blazed behind them."[17] It is a gaze of power, able to hypnotize and paralyze: "There lay the Count. . . . A terrible desire came upon me to rid the world of such a monster. There was no lethal weapon at hand, but I seized a shovel which the workmen had been using to fill the cases, and lifting it high struck, with the edge downward, at the hateful face. But as I did so the head turned, and the eyes fell full upon me, with all their blaze of basilisk horror. The sight seemed to paralyze me."[18] The Count's "looking" brings paralysis to Harker, a gaze that is able to immobilize him and bring great fear, to make him question his very actions, and this is our own horror. To look in the mirror is to ask questions about our very identity, to ask whether what we are gazing at reflects who we really are. To stand and look at our image, and then to ask questions as to our identity and place within the universe is unique to humanity. As Jesuit scientist Pierre Teilhard de Chardin describes, inner reflection is,

> . . . the power acquired by a consciousness of turning in on itself and taking possession of itself as an object endowed with its own particular consistency and value; no longer only to know something—but to know itself; no longer only to know, but to know that it knows.[19]

Humanity and its ability to "know that it knows" is both wonderful and terrifying, identified in our ability to not only stare at our reflection, but to ask questions beyond our gaze at the mirror, questions surrounding our gaze within the mirror, within the image that stares back at us. More than that, each time we look into the mirror we are confronted with our own mortality, the ongoing assault of age, a reminder that our time is fleeting. Even with hair dye and plastic surgery, the image that stares back at us has aged, has noticeably aged, and there is nothing that we can do about it. The vampire, however, transcends the assault of time upon our bodies, transforming our decay into something beautiful;

> Mike's lashes lay cleanly against his cheeks. His hair was tousled loosely across his brow, and Ben thought that in the first delicate light he was more than handsome; he was as beautiful as the profile of a Greek statue.[20]

The vampire has no need for their reflection, for they have transcended humanity and its continued descent into decay and death. The image in the

17. Stoker, *Dracula*, 34.
18. Stoker, *Dracula*, 44–45.
19. Chardin, *The Future of Man*, 90.
20. King, *'Salem's Lot*, 249.

mirror no longer stares back; it has disappeared as the vampire enters a different reality, no longer competing with onset of time, no longer in competition with their own image and the ever-transforming image that continually stares back at us each morning with the rising of the sun, a signal of a new day, but a reminder that we have aged in our sleep. But here vampires and humans share a common enemy: the new dawn as a signifier of death. Humanity steps into its rays, another day onward into the grasp of death, the vampire steps into the sun's rays and disintegrates, the inevitability of death that each new dawn brings with it, rushing in all at once on the vampire who steps into the light. The vampire then avoids the rising of a new dawn and lives in the darkness, each new dawn blocked out and avoided. Here vampires represent humanity's deepest fears, the sudden extinguishing of life in the brightness of the sun, the dawn a signifier of new beginnings and hope,[21] having now become a source of terror. The West predominantly struggles with death, hidden away behind closed coffins and curtains, language of "sleep," "passing away," and "rest"—unconscious strategies to enable us to avoid the power of death over our lives.

The pursuit of eternal youth, then, has long been a fascination within human consciousness, and the vampire genre has continued to bring this idea to us through film and literature. The attractive and beautiful creatures who never age and carry a dark and sensual vitality are a powerful and popular image in a time where image and identity and sex are carried close together through the power of social media. Indeed, our ability to filter and transform every photo of ourselves before putting it online, as well as using selfies to promote and increase our identity and popularity, speaks of a culture that is determined to be masters of our own destinies, who will seek ways to hold on to our youth, and be seen as beautiful by those who gaze at us. In many ways the selfie has replaced the mirror, for we no longer need to gaze back at our image, rather we invite others to gaze at us, to notice that we, like vampires, are as beautiful as the profile of a Greek statue. However, our image, whether it is gazing back at us through a mirror, or #filtered through a #selfie, reminds us of what we are not, of what we will never be.[22] There is a very real sense, although often unconscious and rarely named, that we are

---

21. ". . . the sun of righteousness shall rise, with healing in its wings." Mal 4:2 NRSV.

22. "Imagine spending three hours of your life taking photographs of yourself at different angles to get that ever-elusive 'perfect shot' to post online, only to remove it seconds later because it didn't get enough 'likes.' This sorry tale of the social-media age—a fruitless and time-sucking quest for self-validation—was shared with activist, author, and broadcaster Gemma Cairney by a girl in a year nine class (13- to 14-year-olds)." Read more at https://www.campaignlive.co.uk/article/beware-snaplash-social-media-faces-true-self-conundrum/1448993#9aGZBy9hLYrtCsKh.99.

trapped in some kind of symbolic network, images of who we desire to be, reflections reminding us who we are not, mirror images inviting us to ask questions about our very identity, all creating a symbolism of who we are and humanity's goal and purpose; answers about what it means to be human hidden by layers of the imaginary, struggling to find their way to the surface of our egos. We then, bound in the layers of imaginary, not only struggle to name who we are because of our own mortality, we create God in our own image, gazing toward a version of God that represents our own fear of what we are not, rather than what we are *becoming*. And vampires represent the power to become something greater than we are presently, an invitation to be transformed into a being that does not age, is powerful in ways beyond our comprehension, and to cast off the limitations of humanity, the weakness and fear that impede us from all that we desire. Yet such a vision of becoming is no becoming at all, but a regression into that which inhibits us from *true becoming*; as my friend Glen notes above, becoming is *not* about the "human norm being made a bit better."

Becoming

Vampires represent this very image of a humanity that is just "a bit better" than what we are prejudiced to believe is the "normal." Rather, the gospel invites us to imagine a humanity that is being shaped by the God who is revealed in Christ, a humanity that is not defined by the gaze and prejudices of another, a humanity that is not defined by the impossibility of our own gaze, the levels of obscurity we attach to ourselves through the power of the #selfie. Who we are becoming *in Christ* is our *true selves*, a humanity where our identity, our whole person, is redeemed and enabled to become who we truly are, where our personhood, our humanity, our very self, fully *becomes*, without hindrance, without damage, beyond all dehumanizing structures and behaviors. It is not simply a general "superhuman" that all will be like; rather, it will be who we are, *in fullness*—our individual selves, who we are now, becoming even more ourselves into eternity. This is truly good news, especially for the disabled community, for it makes no able-bodied judgments as to what perfected humanity looks like or will become; rather, it embraces the beauty of our humanity in all its rich diversity and complexity, and imagines a future whereby God is determined to bring each human being into their true likeness, into who they truly are. In part, the power of sin upon humanity is how much it distorts our God-given identity, how, because of sin, we can pursue behaviors and beliefs that directly contradict our humanity and mar the image of God within us. Vampires are a desire, a pursuit of a humanity that is somehow freed from our limitations, and yet, as we have discussed, vampires are actually a poorer version of humanity, a step backwards in our pursuit of a humanity that is actually free. Freedom thus defined is a freedom of simple love, not a freedom that casts off all that inhibits our desires from being fulfilled. Indeed, we live in a time when who we freely are is a maze and puzzle of meanings, projections, symbolism, and prejudices that have been divorced from the simplicity of unconditional love, a love for God, for others, and for ourselves. To love oneself is again not the pursuit of narcissism, a lust for our own image, believing none to match up to the image we see in our reflection; rather, it is a love that recognizes we have first been loved by God, that we are precious to the Creator of all things, and that this very Creator is also Redeemer, and desires that all enter into the Divine rest of knowing God fully and being fully known. This is a depth of love, a depth of humanity, a depth of divinity, a depth of knowing that vampires could only dream of, if, of course, they were ever able to dream.

3

Cannibalism

The Horror of Forgiveness

There was a barber and his wife, and she was beautiful. A foolish barber and his wife. She was his reason and his life, and she was beautiful. And she was virtuous. And he was . . .[1]

—*SWEENEY TODD:*
THE DEMON BARBER OF FLEET STREET

I N SOME VERSIONS OF Greek mythology, Zagreus was the son of Zeus, ruler of the Greek gods of Mount Olympus. Hera, the Queen of the gods, directs the Titans to tear into pieces, cook, and eat the infant Zagreus. In fury and rage, Zeus strikes the Titans with lightning, whereby they are consumed with wrath and fire. Out of the ashes and smoking ruins of the Titans the first humans are created, possessing both the evil nature of the Titans and the divine nature of the gods. It is no surprise that within Greek mythology there is a reference to the emergence of humanity closely tied in with cannibalism, for throughout human history there has always been a close link with cannibalism and the origin of our species, our evolution and the development of who we are out of our desire to physically consume one another. Archaeological evidence has shown us "the frequency of cannibalistic practices in a very large number of archaic cultures and not a few

1. *Sweeney Todd: The Demon Barber of Fleet Street*, Tim Burton, DreamWorks, 2007.

25

ancient historical cultures,"[2] confirming how embedded within our human history is our desire to eat one another.

Whenever we think of cannibalism today it is likely that the figure and presence of Hannibal Lecter swiftly follows us like a haunting nightmare. When we meet Lecter for the first time in the 1991 film *The Silence of the Lambs* he is behind bars, caged, locked up, away from us, yet still terrifying, carrying an almost fallen angel quality; we believe that Lecter can still get to us even though he is trapped in a prison cell. Indeed, our belief that Lecter can still "get us" even when seemingly restrained, is confirmed in a passage in the book, *The Silence of the Lambs,* when Lecter simply speaks to the prisoner, Miggs, in the adjacent cell. Jack Crawford phones Clarice Starling to tell her what happened,

> " Miggs is dead," Crawford said . . .
>
> "How?" She felt numb and she had to handle it.
>
> "Swallowed his tongue sometime before daylight. Lecter suggested it to him . . . The overnight orderly heard Lecter talking softly to Miggs. Lecter knew a lot about Miggs. He talked to him for a little while, but the overnight couldn't hear what Lecter said. Miggs was crying for a while, and then he stopped . . . Lecter did it to amuse himself."[3]

Anthony Hopkins's portrayal of Lecter in the film adaptation has firmly embedded itself within the consciousness of popular culture, fascinating and horrifying us in equal measure. What horrified us, both with Hopkins's portrayal, but more widely with the character itself, was the sheer level of intellect and violence that Lecter possesses, able to escape from high-security prisons, kill people by simply whispering to them, and recounting his kills with joy and flippancy,

> "A census taker tried to quantify me once. I ate his liver with some fava beans and a big Amarone."[4]

Indeed, Lecter enjoys the ability he has to baffle others as to not only who he is, but *what* he is,

---

2. Pierpaolo, *How We Became Human,* 200.

3. Harris, *Silence of the Lambs,* 426–427.

4. Harris, *Silence of the Lambs,* 412. In the film adaptation Hopkins delivers the line as, "A census taker once tried to test me. I ate his liver with some fava beans and a nice chianti."

"Nothing happened to me, Officer Starling. *I* happened. You can't reduce me to a set of influences."[5]

More recently, Brian Fuller brought to our television screens the program, *Hannibal*, with Mads Mikkelsen playing Lecter, and Hugh Dancy in the role of Will Graham. The show centers upon the relationship between Lecter and Graham, one that evolves from colleagues (before Lecter is discovered as a mass murderer, he is regarded as a brilliant psychologist who is asked to work with Graham to help solve gruesome murders) to those who become strange friends, and then to enemies, to potential lovers. Graham has the ability to deconstruct a murder scene and the events that unfolded there by inhabiting the psyche of the murderer. In the opening scene of episode one Will Graham arrives at the house of a woman who has been shot dead. He stands in the middle of the crime scene and closes his eyes. The screen fades to black, and then we see the crime scene return to normal before the murder has occurred. Will Graham is now in the psyche of the murderer and walks through in his mind what happened, with us the viewer able to see how it occurred; for this moment Graham is the murderer and we witness how it happened, step by step. The FBI call Graham in because of his incredible ability to solve murder crimes, an ability that is a real gift but also a terrible curse, revealing Graham's mental instability and emotional turmoil; there are only so many murder scenes you can inhabit before you become part of the scene itself;

> "What he has is pure empathy. He can assume your point of view, or mine—and maybe some other points of view that scare him. It's an uncomfortable gift, Jack. Perception's a tool that's pointed on both ends."[6]

Lecter sees in Graham someone who he can sculpt and transform into his own image. Graham's gift to inhabit the world of someone else, his genius and tortured existence, intrigues Lecter, and so little by little Lecter manipulates Will Graham, changing him to be like him,

> **Hannibal Lecter [to Will]**: "You just came here to look at me. Came to get the old scent again. Why don't you just smell yourself?"[7]

What Hannibal wants is for Graham to embrace the love of killing, to merge with him in his desire to kill and eat others, to find wonder, awe, and beauty

5. Harris, *Silence of the Lambs,* 409.

6. Hannibal Lecter to Jack Crawford, *Hannibal,* Season 1, Episode 1, "Apéritif," Bryan Fuller, NBC, 2013.

7. *Hannibal,* Season 3, Episode 10, ". . . And the Woman Clothed in the Sun," 2015.

in the act of taking another's life, another who is viewed as lesser, and inferior. This is why Lecter does not kill Graham, because he sees in Graham someone who is in some way like him, who sees the world and humanity differently. Whenever Graham steps into the psyche of the murderer he always utters, "This is my design," highlighting the sense of power and mastery the killer feels, but also an insight into Graham's psyche, a growing sense that these moments are indeed the desired design of Graham. The final scene of Season 3 is of Graham and Lecter in an embrace, covered in the blood of Francis Dolahyde, a serial killer of incredible strength who they have just killed,

> **Hannibal:** "This is all I ever wanted for you, Will. For both of us."

> **Will:** "It's beautiful."[8]

The transformation is complete. Lecter and Graham become one.

Lecter desires to become one with Graham through the sharing of this act, for their desires to merge. For Lecter, this journey toward coming together is sacred, for in this joint act Lecter is seen for who he really is. Only those who Lecter kills and eats see him for who he really is, and so Graham is invited to the supreme sacred relationship of knowing, where all pretense falls away, where Lecter invites Graham in, to become part of him, not through eating him, but through sharing in the ritual of killing another. The transformation is complete: Lecter and Graham are now at peace with one another.

This relationship between Lecter and Graham gives us a profound insight into our contemporary human condition. As we have already noted, humanity has always been cannibalistic, eating the "other" as a result of their sacrifice. René Girard says, "The eating of sacrificial flesh . . . can be seen in light of mimetic desire as a veritable cannibalism of the human spirit in which the violence of others is ritually devoured." He goes on to say that, through this sacrifice and cannibalistic act, a sense of "peace, strength, and fecundity" are restored to the community.[9] Lecter devours others in order to live, and the act of eating the sacrificial flesh in ancient communities is believed to be an act that brings life. Lecter "eats the rude" and any who he deems unfit, useless, or uninteresting. At the end of *The Silence of the Lambs*, Lecter pens a letter to Clarice Starling, saying, "I have no plans to call on you, Clarice, the world being more interesting with you in it."[10] Lecter has an inner code of who he eats, and Starling in *Silence*,

---

8. *Hannibal*, Season 3, Episode 13, "The Wrath of the Lamb" 2015.

9. Girard, *Violence and the Sacred*, 277.

10. Harris, *Silence of the Lambs*, 741.

and Graham in Fuller's *Hannibal*, are far too interesting for Lecter to kill and eat. Lecter could then, in light of all that we have just said, represent our current Western culture, in that we will consume and devour others in order to live, sacrificing them on our altar of consumerism in order to deal with the violence and instability all around us. We know we are in trouble—we see it all around as we tear the planet apart through forced farming of animals, through global warming and our insatiable need for fossil fuels, and through forced cheap labor to provide the lifestyles we are desperately seeking to hold on to. Our desires for what the other person has are incredibly powerful. Advertisers are well aware of this phenomenon and so use the most beautiful and attractive people in order to tap into those inner desires that each of us has. We see these gleaming and gorgeous people, with gleaming and gorgeous products, and—convinced not only of their ability to make our lives better, but also how they make us more like the people we desire to be like—we do all that we can in order to obtain the product, whatever it might be. This is "mediated desire," a longing for what the other already has, or is perceived to have.

From here rivalries break out, for in mediated desire there is always competition. So, the more we desire what the other has, the more we desire to be who the other is. So, our lust for the greatest and best product drives the market and the companies and producers of products to see the best way to ensure we receive the products, even if that means through violence to others. This desire for the supreme object, based upon our belief that we can become the supreme person, has led us into a sense of transcendence, whereby we believe that we are the gods now. Such is our capabilities, skills, and strength; we are convinced by our own power. Yet this desire and this rivalry leads us into "undifferentiation" whereby we become the same, desiring *for* the same thing, desiring *to be* the same thing, rivals seeking to be our own masters. Now this does not mean everyone is specifically desiring to be the next superstar, or millionaire, or sportsperson; rather, it is to highlight how collectively in the West we seek to hold on to some perceived sense of individuality, where we are masters of our own destiny, protecting what we have acquired ourselves. This is a desire for security, whether that be material, economic, or physical, and we do whatever we can in order to secure it; security has produced sameness in the West. So we need sacrifice in order to secure our security, in order to live, much like the ancients believed. It is no secret that people across the majority world are paid very poorly by large companies in order to keep costs down for Western consumers. Indeed, the economic inequality between the richest and poorest are at levels potentially never seen before, with the richest eight billionaires in the world owning more wealth than the poorest half of the world's population. There is an estimated 3 billion people who earn less than $2.50 a day, with 1 billion children living in poverty.[11] These are staggering levels of inequality. Yet so bound up in this sacrificial consumer matrix are we, so desperate to protect what we have in our own little worlds, there is little we want to do or feel able to do in order to change things. When big companies tell us that 1 percent of the cost of our coffee or pair of shoes will go to a child trapped in poverty somewhere in the world, it makes us feel better about our consumerism, convincing us that we can be materialistic and charitable, all at the same time.

We sacrifice others and feed on them in order to maintain our own existence.

In the act of sacrifice, ancient communities transferred their violence and aggression upon the victim, the one who is scapegoated in order to maintain peace. This was always an unconscious act of murder, a belief that this person really is the cause of the trouble, violence, and instability within the community, and so the justification of their death, and the myth of their guilt would remain; humanity continue to be blinded in our need to place collective violence upon someone in order to bring a fragile peace. And we continue to do violence to the poorest, sacrificing them to the god of Mammon with purchase after purchase. Like Lecter, we feed on them because we do not feel anything for them; they simply do not matter, "It's only cannibalism if we're equals."[12]

In cannibalism, the person is eaten because they are sacrificed, the consuming of the flesh is part of the sacred act where the person murdered goes from demonized to divinized; the one who is blamed for the escalating conflict within the community, and so killed by the collective, is then held to be divine for the miracle of peace that occurs through their death; the gods have visited us! Sacrifice has been part of human history since our beginnings, and our ability to blame an odious other for our suffering and so offer them to the gods in order to woo the gods into favor is a sacrificial process long embedded within our collective consciousness. This sacrificial heart of ours did not die with our atheistic stake when we stopped believing in monsters who demanded a virgin, or the gods who demanded an offering; we continue to offer to the god of the market our poorest in order that we might sustain the lives we desire or acquire the lives we aspire to. And in this whole sacrificial process the poor go from demonized to divinized, held as both at the same time.

11. https://www.dosomething.org/us/facts/11-facts-about-global-poverty.
12. *Hannibal*, Season 3, Episode 1, "Antipasto."

Think of how we view the poor,

"If they worked harder . . ."

"If they managed their money better . . ."

"If they weren't scroungers . . ."

"They are drug addicts and alcoholics . . ."

"If they didn't have so many children . . ."

Yet we also hold them up as people to aspire to, as those who show us a more truthful humanity,

"They are always so happy . . ."

"They are so generous with so little . . ."

"Look how wonderfully simple their lives are . . ."

"If only we could live in that kind of close community . . ."

"It is amazing how content they are . . ."

The dehumanizing of the poor through our demonization, sacrifice, and divinization of them highlights how powerful the god of the market is upon us here in the West. These bullshit platitudes of how wonderfully the poor are living in such simplicity, alongside how easily we blame the poor for their poverty, deify them in their poverty ("they have discovered how to live beyond material things"). Our sacrifice of them for our greed through cheap labor reveals how like the ancients we really are in our sacrificial DNA. When Jesus calls us to feed, water, and clothe the poor, as well as challenging the injustices that are making people poor, we would rather buy another cup of coffee and give a little bit of that purchase to some child somewhere beyond our sight and consciousness.

Hannibal Lecter represents how easily we will consume those we think are inferior to us. And yet, like Lecter's relationship with Graham, we assimilate and bring into our existence those whom we can mold more into our consumeristic likeness. And as we symbolically stand covered in the blood of the poor, much like the sacrificial priests of old, holding our latest iPhone like the sacrificial knife, we see nothing but its beauty. For us, like the ancients, to be able to consume the victim there must a sacred otherness to them, they must incarnate some kind of divine transcendence in order for us to feel like their sacrifice is going to change us; we devour them, and whatever they are, whatever they represent becomes part of us as we absorb them into ourselves. Like Lecter, those who are less than us the market kills (with our materialist, consumerist help), and those who are willing to be shaped and transformed into the likeness of the market are embraced and shaped more into the market's desires.

Eat Well

The meal instituted by Jesus is that which should wake us up out of our cannibalistic consumerist desires and bring us to our senses. In John's gospel, the writer puts upon the lips of Jesus these words,

> So Jesus said to them, "Very truly, I tell you, unless you eat the flesh of the Son of Man and drink his blood, you have no life in you. Those who eat my flesh and drink my blood have eternal life, and I will raise them up on the last day; for my flesh is true food and my blood is true drink. Those who eat my flesh and drink my blood abide in me, and I in them. Just as the living Father sent me, and I live because of the Father, so whoever eats me will live because of me. This is the bread that came down from heaven, not like that which your ancestors ate, and they died. But the one who eats this bread will live forever." (John 6:53–58)

Jesus invites us to this meal, to recognize our own desires to break one another apart, our desire to tear the flesh off each other and drink the life force out of our victims. Michael Hardin puts it like this,

> In the Eucharist, we come as a killing mob, breaking our victims in order to consume them, to suck the life-force out of them. This is why victims were eventually divinized or made into gods: we sought divine and eternal life in our victims, life beyond death.[13]

In our lust for technological advancement, to discover the roots of our death, to etch ourselves into eternity through the work of our own hands, we are willing to sacrifice workers in the majority world in order that we might gain immortality; we continue to seek eternal life through our victims. Hardin goes on,

---

13. Hardin, *Mimetic Theory*, 102.

... we think we derive life from our victims ... Yes, we derive life from our victims, but it is the pseudo life of the Lie, the Lie that we are just and right in what we do when scapegoating others and creating distinctions between us and them. In Jesus' meal ... we are bringing nonviolence—life-giving, life affirming nonviolence—right into the core of our very being ... taking into our deepest being the one who would restore all our relationships.[14]

The invitation on the lips of Jesus to share in his flesh and blood is to recognize our inherent violence as a human species, to see how, like Cain, we are willing to kill our brothers and sisters in our unconscious desire to have what they have, to be like them; how, like Abraham, we are willing to kill our children at the whim of the "gods of exchange" who demand blood and sacrifice—with approximately 200,000 civilians killed directly from the war in Iraq, Afghanistan, and Pakistan, as well as the approximately 800,000 who have died indirectly from these wars since October 2001, and the bombs sold by the British government to Saudi Arabia that have been used in Yemen contributing to the deaths of more than 10,000 civilians, it is safe to say that the gods of war and money are receiving child and adult sacrifice with a religious regularity and a holy zeal. Like the blood of Abel crying out, it would appear that we demand vengeance and more violence to bring peace, to secure our own security. Yet the blood of Jesus "bespeaks something better than that of Abel" (Heb 12:24). Jesus speaks peace, "Peace I leave you, my peace I give to you; I give to you not as the cosmos gives" (John 14:27a). Jesus speaks forgiveness, "Father, forgive them; for they do not know what they are doing" (Luke 23:34). The act of forgiveness is the pathway to peace. In the Eucharist, this meal of bread and wine, we symbolically tear Jesus apart, the mob joining in the collective murder of the innocent victim, united in this act like in every era of human history where we have scapegoated and killed another, pouring our wrath and violence and disharmony upon the victim in order that they might absorb it and in doing so, create an uneasy peace. And yet, unlike the blood of Abel, unlike the wrath of Zeus upon the Titans, Jesus speaks peace and forgiveness.

This meal is to us an act of grace, a means through which God mediates God's own presence, by the Holy Spirit, joining us together in the power of forgiveness. This is why it is vitally important that we share in this meal together regularly, not in sterilized environments, but incorporated into the act of eating food together in one another's homes. In these moments of a shared table we share lives and hearts and push apart those social dynamics that prevent us from being our true selves. In the laughter and messiness

14. Hardin, *Mimetic Theory*, 108.

and conversations we get in touch with ourselves and recognize one another for who we really are; we see the beauty in each. And in this meal we come to recognize that "while we were still sinners, Christ died for us." We are the mob, and yet God's position toward us is one of forgiveness, an everlasting movement of peace, transforming us, by the Spirit, into the likeness of the True Human, Jesus, the Son of God. In this meal we are invited into Jesus' own story, his story becoming our history and story, the Spirit breathing life, love, and grace, opportunities to be shaped by peace. When Jesus speaks peace to the disciples, and calls out forgiveness from the cross, this reveals the very heart and nature of God toward all of creation, and to the whole of humanity, for Jesus is the One,

> "Who is the image of the invisible God . . ." (Col 1:15a)

In Jesus we encounter the fullness of God, of who God is and what God is eternally like in character and nature. When Jesus calls forgiveness, the Trinitarian Life is calling our forgiveness. When Jesus speaks peace, the Trinity is speaking peace; this is what God is like.

Hannibal Lecter's desire for Will Graham is to consume him onto his own likeness, to find life in death, beauty in blood, transcendence in murder. In the Greek myth story of Zagreus that is cited at the beginning of this chapter, humanity is birthed out of cannibalism and wrath. In ancient practice, as we have discovered, humanity evolves through violence, sacrifice, and cannibalism. And today we continue to practice sacrifice on the altar of Mammon. Yet Jesus beckons us toward another Way, one of hope, whereby we discover our humanity through the most difficult practice of all: forgiveness. If we continue to be locked into mimetic rivalry, desiring to violently consume one another, then we will continue the path of descent with Lecter and Graham, locked in a blood-soaked violent embrace, falling off a cliff into the treacherous waters of hate. Yet if we follow the One who is Peace, then we are beckoned into a Resurrection embrace, to discover our "divine nature," and follow the Way of Truthful Life as communities who know how to practice forgiving love.

4

Apocalypse

The Horror of Nostalgia

Oh God, thank God, Larry thought. *I will fear no evil, I will f—*

Silent white light filled the world.

And the righteous and the unrighteous alike were consumed in that holy fire.[1]

—THE STAND

THE END OF THE world is a "popular" concept, with regular predictions by (predominantly) religious fundamentalists of impending judgment and destruction upon the world. Indeed, it seems that with every solar eclipse, Mayan calendar date, revised Western calendar date, or some other natural phenomenon, an end-time warning is delivered. And such is the fascination of end-of-the-world predictions, the theme of apocalypse is popular within fiction and the horror genre,

> He walked out in the gray light and stood and he saw for a brief moment the absolute truth of the world. The cold relentless circling of the intestate earth. Darkness implacable. The blind dogs of the sun in their running. The crushing black vacuum of the universe. And somewhere two hunted animals trembling

---

1. King, *The Stand*, 1244.

like ground-foxes in their cover. Borrowed time and borrowed
world and borrowed eyes with which to sorrow it.[2]

The apocalypse genre is fascinating in how it depicts humanity, our ability
to survive or otherwise, the reasons for the apocalypse, and how the human
species responds as a result. In the 1998 blockbuster *Armageddon*, starring
Bruce Willis, the heroes are deep-sea oil drillers.[3] This gang of men (why
is it usually men?) are the best deep-core drillers in the world, drafted in
by NASA to fly into space, land on the asteroid heading toward earth, drill
down 240 meters, and plant a nuclear bomb. Once safely off the asteroid
they will detonate the bomb and save the world. The motley crew of oil
drillers assembled to join NASA to save the world are your classic stereo-
typed working-class hero, prone to violent outbursts, run-ins with the law,
but have hearts of gold and a heroic, loyal, patriotic character. And this is
what we love about apocalyptic films—the strength of the human spirit, the
inherent goodness that eventually shines though, our ability to overcome
even in the face of total annihilation, and the common person rising up to
take their place as a significant hero in this brave new world. In the film *2012*
it is the common man—poor, dysfunctional, a nobody—who becomes the
hero. And there is something deeply attractive about the common person
becoming the hero, someone who has little influence, and seen as a failure in
the beginning, going on to win the day. The hero who emerges is so deeply
popular in Western consciousness that TV producers make programs out
of it, guaranteeing significant viewing figures. Shows like *The X-Factor* and
America's/Britain's Got Talent are successful, not simply because of the talent, but because of the stories behind the talent; we love people and their
stories, and we especially love people whose stories capture the underdog
spirit, who have had to fight their whole lives, or who have experienced deep
tragedy and trauma, and this moment on this stage is perhaps their chance
at redemption and new beginnings.

There is no doubt that the rise and eventual success of the underdog
has captured our modern imaginations; the *Rocky* films with Sylvester

---

2. McCarthy, *Road*, 130.

3. The choice of deep-sea oil drillers should be of no surprise. Our dependence on
fossil fuels has grown into unsustainable and staggering proportions. We do not know
how to wean ourselves off oil, and it is the eventual impact of fossil fuels on our climate,
as well as our inability to drill enough oil the scarcer it gets, that may well bring about
monumental shifts in migration, and significant destruction to our human species.
Although *Armageddon* is a film about an outside asteroid the size of Texas (at one time
the oil drilling center of the USA) on collision course with the earth, it is actually a film
about our oil dependency and how we really do not have a plan B for energy, and our
disregard for the planet we are called to care for.

Stallone have endured because it is the fighter from the streets, fighting not just in the ring, but in life, who captures our hearts and support, and provide an inspiring story. This is the reason people find quotes from the film a genuine source of inspiration, because most of us can relate to the person who is "on the ropes" and needs a break, needs a way out,

> Let me tell you something you already know. The world ain't all sunshine and rainbows. It's a very mean and nasty place, and I don't care how tough you are, it will beat you to your knees and keep you there permanently if you let it. You, me, or nobody is gonna hit as hard as life. But it ain't about how hard you hit, it's about how hard you can get hit and keep moving forward; how much you can take and keep moving forward. That's how winning is done! Now, if you know what you're worth, then go out and get what you're worth. But you gotta be willing to take the hits, and not pointing fingers saying you ain't where you wanna be because of him, or her, or anybody. Cowards do that and that ain't you. You're better than that! I'm always gonna love you, no matter what. No matter what happens. You're my son and you're my blood. You're the best thing in my life. But until you start believing in yourself, you ain't gonna have a life.[4]

Apocalypse films, then, are the ultimate underdog story—humanity against chaos and catastrophe on a monumental scale, a chaos and catastrophe that provide seemingly impossible odds in overcoming, yet from the brink of extinction, humanity endures, survives, and provides the hope to thrive. This is in part why we love a good end-of-the-world drama; we want to be the underdog who wins and thrives. *Armageddon*, *Deep Impact*, *The Day After Tomorrow*, and *2012* all portray humanity's fight for survival in these terms, and all end with humanity overcoming, of a new dawn rising in our journey,

> We watched as the bombs shattered the second comet into a million pieces of ice and rocks that burned harmlessly in our atmosphere, and lit up the sky for an hour. Still, we were left with the devastation of the first. The waters reached as far inland as the Ohio and Tennessee Valleys. It washed away farms and towns, forests and skyscrapers, but the water receded. The wave hit Europe and Africa, too. Millions were lost, countless more left homeless, but the waters receded. Cities fall, but they are rebuilt. And heroes die, but they are remembered. We honor them with every brick we lay, with every field we sow, with every

4. Rocky Balboa, *Rocky Balboa*, Sylvester Stallone, MGM, 2007.

child we comfort and then teach to rejoice in what we have been re-given. Our planet, our home. So now, let us begin.[5]

This kind of speech in *Deep Impact* is present in many apocalypse tales; the honor of the hero remembered in every brick laid, every seed planted, is the hero of the every person who lost their life to the apocalyptic enemy, an enemy who has not won or overcome humanity and its ability to survive our greatest threats. It appears that in many of these large-scale apocalypse Hollywood films it often falls to the American president to deliver these lines of defiance against this outside enemy, lines of hope and inspiration, lines of belief in the capacity of the human will and spirit. So, whether we are battling comets,[6] global warming,[7] or catastrophic alien invasion,[8] the president delivers a speech highlighting our common humanity, united in

5. President Tom Beck, *Deep Impact,* Mimi Leder, Paramount Pictures, 1998.

6. "I address you tonight not as the President of the United States, not as the leader of a country, but as a citizen of humanity. We are faced with the very gravest of challenges. The Bible calls this day "Armageddon"—the end of all things. And yet, for the first time in the history of the planet, a species has the technology to prevent its own extinction. All of you praying with us need to know that everything that can be done to prevent this disaster is being called into service. The human thirst for excellence, knowledge; every step up the ladder of science; every adventurous reach into space; all of our combined modern technologies and imaginations; even the wars that we've fought have provided us the tools to wage this terrible battle. Through all of the chaos that is our history; through all of the wrongs and the discord; through all of the pain and suffering; through all of our times, there is one thing that has nourished our souls, and elevated our species above its origins, and that is our courage. The dreams of an entire planet are focused tonight on those fourteen brave souls traveling into the heavens. And may we all, citizens the world over, see these events through. God speed, and good luck to you." President, *Armageddon* (1998).

7. "My fellow Americans. This will be the last time I will address you. As you know, catastrophe has struck our nation, has struck the world. I wish I could tell you we could prevent the coming destruction. We cannot. Today, none of us are strangers. Today, we are one family, stepping into the darkness together. We are a nation of many religions, but I believe these words reflect the spirit of all our faiths. 'The Lord is my Shepherd, I shall . . .'" [signal cut]. President Thomas Wilson, *2012* (2009).

8. "Good morning. In less than an hour, aircraft from here will join others from around the world. And you will be launching the largest aerial battle in the history of mankind. 'Mankind.' That word should have new meaning for all of us today. We can't be consumed by our petty differences anymore. We will be united in our common interests. Perhaps it's fate that today is the Fourth of July, and you will once again be fighting for our freedom . . . Not from tyranny, oppression, or persecution . . . but from annihilation. We are fighting for our right to live. To exist. And should we win the day, the Fourth of July will no longer be known as an American holiday, but as the day the world declared in one voice: We will not go quietly into the night! We will not vanish without a fight! We're going to live on! We're going to survive! Today we celebrate our Independence Day!" President Thomas Whitmore, *Independence Day* (1996).

our will to continue in our existence. And with each line of soaring rhetoric, nostalgia rings bolding and unashamedly out.

Remember

We are a society drenched in nostalgia, longing for a moment in a yesterday that we gaze at through sentimental eyes and hazy memories. Although Donald Trump's speeches throughout his presidential campaign never got close to the rhetoric and inspirational language of the fictional presidents in these apocalyptic films, or the remarkable oratory excellence of Barack Obama—and note how similar in tone Obama's inaugural speech is to those made by American presidents in apocalyptic films, mainly in part because of the financial crisis that hit the world in 2008[9]—Trump's language tapped directly into the nostalgic consciousness of many Americans, a nostalgia bound together in patriotism and religious craving. In his campaign announcement speech at Trump Tower he spoke in terms of America losing, saying, "We don't have victories anymore" when speaking about America's place in the global market; so, in part his promises were to make America the unrivaled, global trading superpower. He also used language of winning and losing in regard to foreign policy, declaring that, "Nobody would be tougher on ISIS than Donald Trump." And to finish he said that he would bring back the American dream, "and make America great again." In his inaugural speech, Trump declared, "When you open your heart to patriotism, there is no room for prejudice. The Bible tells us, "how good and pleasant it is when God's people live together in unity" . . . We will make America

9. "So let us mark this day with remembrance of who we are and how far we have traveled. In the year of America's birth, in the coldest of months, a small band of patriots huddled by dying campfires on the shores of an icy river. The capital was abandoned. The enemy was advancing. The snow was stained with blood. At the moment when the outcome of our revolution was most in doubt, the father of our nation ordered these words to be read to the people:

'Let it be told to the future world . . . that in the depth of winter, when nothing but hope and virtue could survive . . . that the city and the country, alarmed at one common danger, came forth to meet [it].'

America: In the face of our common dangers, in this winter of our hardship, let us remember these timeless words. With hope and virtue, let us brave once more the icy currents, and endure what storms may come. Let it be said by our children's children that when we were tested we refused to let this journey end, that we did not turn back nor did we falter; and with eyes fixed on the horizon and God's grace upon us, we carried forth that great gift of freedom and delivered it safely to future generations.

Thank you. God bless you. And God bless the United States of America." https://www.aol.com/article/news/2017/01/19/president-barack-obamas-first-inauguration-speech-full-text/21657532/.

great again."[10] Trump deliberately combines a love of America with the Bible, of Christianity, and unity. What this does is create in the minds of the religiously devote that true unity is found in everyone being Christian, Bible-believing, and lovers of America. Those, therefore, who question at least one of these precepts are in danger of exclusion.

"Make America Great Again" created the idea that there was a time when America was strong, powerful, proud, and envied as a nation to aspire to. Trump and his campaign team recognized a patriotic longing within many Americans, disenfranchised by economic hardship, and a powerful media rhetoric that convinced many that the country they grew up in no longer represented them, or belonged to them, or held to the values that they associated with what it meant to be American. The effectiveness of Trump's campaign meant that people nostalgically looked back to a time and desired, through Trump, to bring that lost time once again into the present reality. The same thing happened in the United Kingdom with the European Union referendum. A significant percentage of the population in Britain voted to leave the European Union, with a desire from some to reclaim their country, to make Britain great again. Some within the Leave campaign used the same type of language as Trump, vowing that Britain would reclaim its sovereignty, be in charge of its own borders, make its own laws, and become a great and proud nation once again. Now the arguments to stay or leave the European Union were, of course, much more complex than that, and people who voted either way had their own reasons,[11] but it cannot be ignored that the same nostalgic longing that swayed the American vote caught the imagination of many in the British public. It should therefore be of no surprise that Trump and Brexit happened when you consider how deeply nostalgic we are in the West. Advertisers have known this mood of the population for quite some time, highlighted by the resurgence within the clothing industry of fashion styles that belonged in the eighties and nineties, of old computer games and the characters within those games re-emerging, the games not evolving to

10. https://www.whitehouse.gov/inaugural-address.

11. I think there are legitimate concerns that need to be addressed regarding the European Union and the way democratic nations govern themselves today. It is my belief that true democracy gives power to the common person and seeks to ensure that the way a nation is governed ensures that the most vulnerable are cared for properly, and heard, their voice reflected in the decisions that are made. Big government stops this process from happening and ensures the richest and most powerful grow in influence and wealth and the detriment of the poorest. The problem with the EU Referendum was that the Leave vote was not framed in this way, and the true complexity and impact of Britain leaving the European Union was not given the time, energy, and serious research the public deserved to hear and know about. The narrative on both sides of the debate was thus often skewed into pithy sayings and one-liners, much to the intellectual poverty of everyone.

the next level of technological capability but re-released on the brand of their original appearance, *Mario*, *Street Fighter*, and *Sonic* all being marketed on their original platforms. Nokia recently released their original mobile phone, widely held to be the most popular cell phone ever produced. Everything then, from car adverts to perfume, seeks to remind us of a time that once existed, with companies selling their products according to our nostalgic longings.

Religion is discovering this same revival. Books on spirituality have seen increases in sales over the last few years, and while some commentators might put it down to a spiritual fad, it seems to me that it is a result of nostalgia, searching for a time when we were more in tune with our spiritual side. In the UK there has been a significant increase in church attendance at Christmastime; if you go to most Anglican churches in Britain around the time of Advent, they will probably be standing-room only.[12] Anecdotally, the small Anglican Church my mom attends every week, with a regular congregation of about thirty people, sees about three hundred people fill the pews at the Christmas Eve carol service. To my North American readers, a church congregation of three hundred people will probably seem pretty small, but when British regular church attendance is at about 8 percent of the population, then this is significant in a tiny community where people do not travel any great distance to go to church. Cathedrals in Britain have reported a significant rise in attendance at Christmas,[13] with people seemingly wanting Christmas to "feel like Christmas," in other words, Christmas carols, Bible readings, and baby Jesus. Richard Dawkins, one of the fiercest critics (not necessarily the best, though) of Christianity and religion over the last ten years, has himself commented on how much he enjoys singing Christmas carols and celebrating the Christmas spirit.[14]

---

12. "Last year attendance on Christmas itself jumped almost five per cent to just over 2.5 million people . . . In addition 2.3 million people attended advent services in churches while civic carol services attracted 2.7 million. Although there will be some overlap, the combined attendance at Christmas and advent services adds up to 7.5 million people." http://www.telegraph.co.uk/news/2016/10/27/british-families-only-attend-church-at-christmas-new-figures-sug/.

13. "Christmas attendance was 125,200 in 2015, the highest figure since 2011. There were 33,100 communicants at Christmas in 2015. Services during Advent, the period leading up to Christmas, attracted an attendance of 824,300 in 2015, the highest figure for the past decade. All events and services from the beginning of Advent to 23 December are captured in the Advent total." https://www.churchofengland.org/media-centre/news/2016/09/cathedral-statistics-2015-show-continued-growth.aspx.

14. "Christmas belongs to anyone who wants it, and just because I gave up believing in a god doesn't mean I gave up believing in the love and joy of family. I did not give up the joy of celebration with my abandonment of the absurd. So to my religious and non-religious friends, I wish them all a Merry Christmas or a Happy Hanukkah from the heart and I hope they take it with the true spirit with which I give it—that of the spirit of

What does all this tell us? Nostalgia looms large in every sphere of Western culture, the belief that there was once a time when things were better, when we lived happier, more fulfilled, and comfortable lives, indeed a time when we were perhaps wealthier and doing better in our jobs. Nostalgia convinces us that there were better times in the past that can be reclaimed in our today. Yet does our nostalgic longing create with it distorted memories of our own power and dangerous delusions of what we are capable of?

Memory Remembered

In apocalyptic stories the theme of memory always figures large, and rightly so, for memory is who we are. Augustine said that, "If I find you beyond my memory, then I shall be without memory of you. And how will I find you without memory of you?"[15] So stories are told of how things used to be, the knowledge of that which we once shared and used, and what it was like to live in times now destroyed. Yet the apocalypse has also brought with it a reality to the human condition, a recognition that we are not always all we think we are,

> Looking down at Peter he thought: *Maybe if we tell him what happened, he'll tell his own children. Warn them. Dear children, toys are death—they're flash burns and radiation sickness and black, choking plague. These toys are dangerous; the devil in men's brains guided the hands of God when they were made. Don't play with these toys, dear children, please, not ever. Not ever again. Please . . . please learn the lesson. Let this empty world be your copybook.*"[16]

Here in Stephen King's *The Stand*, Stu acknowledges humanity's capacity to fuck things up when given the power and capabilities of creating plagues, and disease, and nuclear weapons. In ancient times we attributed to God the power to wipe out humanity with plagues, or flood, or fire, yet now we are the gods of wrath and war, living in a time where we can unleash chemical warfare upon one another, with nuclear power capable of global extinction. Most versions of apocalypse in film and literature, like here in *The Stand*, leave us with the chance of a new beginning, learning from past mistakes of moral recklessness, and power run amok, an anticipation of a new beginning, a brutal lesson learned from past mistakes. The Greek word *apokalupsis*

---

humanity—something we can all celebrate." Richard Dawkins, https://richarddawkins. net/2012/12/a-very-atheist-christmas/

15. Augustine, *Confessions*, 10.17.26.

16. King, *Stand*, 1320.

carries with it meaning of revelation, unveiling, uncovering, a discovery of truth, unknown things being made known; humanity as a whole is invited to learn from their stupidity, greed, temerity, and pride. In apocalypse the few discover salvation—the few who enter through the narrow gate, those who have remembered how things were, learned from the mistakes that we have made, discovered the truth of our recklessness, while the rest of humanity burns or become a zombie, the memory of them extinguished.

Over the last fifty years the nuclear threat has felt extremely real and viable. The world has no need for nuclear weapons, and the visions of nuclear holocaust that *The Matrix* and *Terminator* portray, although fiction, highlight the deeply troubling times we live in when unstable people have such power. The enduring significance of both those films is that it is artificial intelligence that rules the world after we try and destroy them with our nuclear capabilities; the creators become the slaves. No doubt these films could speak to us about the rise in technology and how addicted to it we are, how enslaved we are to our gadgets.[17] More interestingly though, these films recognize our desire to be gods, forging our own future, freed from the superstition, shackles, and rules of religion. In *The Matrix* and *Terminator,* humans start as the creators, and become the slaves, and this is an analogy for our own existence with God, a desire for God to become the slave, the One we use to do our will; in these films humanity represent God, and the machines represent humanity. The fascinating thing in the big-budget apocalypse films is how atheistic they are, despite the religious language used. In *Armageddon* it is not God who saves the world, it is us. In *2012* we build "arks" to rescue humanity. The same is true for *Independence Day, The Day After Tomorrow,* and *The Matrix*; humanity rescues humanity; there is no God saving the day. In ancient stories God's hand is upon those he has chosen, directly intervening, winning battles, raining down fire, holding back water. Yet this is not true in our modern tales. We see a hint of a sense of divine help in *The Stand,* but this divine help is seen as death, the mercy of dying before something even worse than death comes. Otherwise, these modern tales of global catastrophe are absent of divine help or presence, and this should be celebrated by those who take seriously a theology shaped by the cross of Jesus of Nazareth.

17. My good friend Rob made a point that we are so early into our discovery of smartphones and social media that this time is surely us simply exploring, and in time it will even out as we learn better how to manage it.

God of the Machine

Dietrich Bonhoeffer highlighted the disaster of the *deus ex machina* god.
Before we unpack that, let us hear an extended quote from him:

> So our coming of age leads us to a true recognition of our situa-
> tion before God. God would have us know that we must live as
> men who manage our lives without him. The God who is with us
> is the God who forsakes us (Mark 15:34). The God who lets us
> live in the world without the working hypothesis of God is the
> God before whom we stand continually. Before God and with
> God we live without God. God let's himself be pushed out of the
> world on to the cross. He is weak and powerless in the world,
> and that is precisely the way, the only way, in which he helps us,
> Matt. 8:17 makes it quite clear that Christ helps us, not by virtue
> of his omnipotence, but by virtue of his weakness and suffer-
> ing. Here is the decisive difference between Christianity and all
> religions. Man's religiosity makes him look in his distress to the
> power of God in the world: God is the *deus ex machina*. The
> Bible directs man to God's powerlessness and suffering; only
> the suffering God can help. To that extent we may say that the
> development toward the world's coming of age outlines above,
> which has done away with a false conception of God, opens up
> a way of seeing the God of the Bible, who wins power and space
> in the world by his weakness.[18]

The *deus ex machina* that Bonhoeffer speaks of is the *god of the machine*. In
ancient Greek and Roman plays, a machine was used to lower into the play
a person who represented a god or some figure who would come and rescue
someone from a seemingly impossible situation. The person playing the god
or rescuer would get in a basket and be lowered onto the stage just in the
nick of time—the hero, the rescuer, the god. We see this in modern characters like Superman, who is the archetype *deus ex machina*. Read any graphic
novel or watch any film with Superman and you will notice how often he
arrives just in time to rescue a person falling from a building or save a plane
from crashing and killing all inside. This is the god who rescues us when we
are convinced we are doomed, the god who swoops in and saves us when all
hope has gone. The fascinating thing about the 2016 film *Batman vs. Superman* was how un-Superman Superman was. In a court scene where Superman is on trial, he fails to save everyone in it from a bomb that explodes—he
simply stands there in the midst of the fire and death recognizing his own
limitations; it is brilliant Christian theology. Why? The cross of Christ, as

18. Bonhoeffer, *Letters*, 196-97.

Bonhoeffer comments above, reveals a weak and suffering God who is not a *deus ex machina* who does not swoop in at the last minute and rescue us. So, whether consciously or unconsciously, many of the Hollywood apocalyptic blockbusters have done away with the god of the machine and asks whether humanity can rescue themselves.

In Cormac McCarthy's *The Road*, there is a bleakness, that humanity has lost its senses, a continued sense of loss, that the world has lost beauty, burnt away in the horror of what gripped it, the long-lasting winter of desolation: "There were times when he sat watching the boy sleep that he would begin to sob uncontrollably but it wasn't about death. He wasn't sure what it was about but he thought it was about beauty or goodness. Things that he'd no longer any way to think about at all."[19] Throughout *The Road* we are confronted with human savagery, or at least the consistent threat of human savagery, sometimes acted out with brutality, when the world has lost itself, humanity lost in its appetites, distorted desires for anything that will satisfy. A few like the Man and his Son remain, but their journey is perilous as beyond every corner, over every hill, the potential to encounter another human who has lost all compassion and empathy, is real. These stories, films like *Mad Max: Fury Road* and *The Purge*, reveal the truth that, while our capability for tremendous good and beauty is evident, we are also capable of great evil. The horror of the Jewish Shoah demonstrated how the everyday person can commit acts of unimaginable cruelty, all because they are ordered to do it.[20] In the twentieth century alone, human ideology, displayed

---

19. McCarthy, *Road*, 129–30.

20. Adolf Eichmann sought to use "superior orders" as his defense for his involvement in the murder of the Jews during the Second World War. In his trial he said,

"I have heard the Court's severe verdict of guilty. I see myself disappointed in my hopes for justice. I cannot recognize the verdict of guilty. I understand the demand for atonement for the crimes which were perpetrated against the Jews. The witnesses' statements here in the Court made my limbs go numb once again, just as they went numb when once, acting on orders, I had to look at the atrocities. It was my misfortune to become entangled in these atrocities. But these misdeeds did not happen according to my wishes. It was not my wish to slay people. The guilt for the mass murder is solely that of the political leaders. I did try to leave my position, to leave for the front, for honest battle. But I was held fast in those dark duties. Once again I would stress that I am guilty of having been obedient, having subordinated myself to my official duties and the obligations of war service and my oath of allegiance and my oath of office, and in addition, once the war started, there was also martial law. This obedience was not easy. And again, anyone who has to give orders and has to obey orders knows what one can demand of people. I did not persecute Jews with avidity and passion. That is what the government did. Nor could the persecution be carried out other than by a government . . . I accuse the leaders of abusing my obedience. At that time obedience was demanded, just as in the future it will also be demanded of the subordinate. Obedience is commended as a virtue. May I therefore ask that consideration be given to the

through secularist despotic regimes, led by those such Stalin, Pol Pot, and
Mao, led to the murder and death of some estimated 150 million people,

> . . . by the end of the 20th century, wars had been waged on a
> scale never before imagined, and a number of Utopian, strictly
> secularist ideologies—each in its own way the inheritor both of
> the Enlightenment project to remake society on a more ratio-
> nal model and of the late 19th-century project to 'correct' hu-
> man nature through the mechanisms of a provided state—had
> together managed to kill perhaps 150 million persons . . . By
> century's end, all certainties had been shattered: the power of
> 'organized religion' in the West had been largely subdued, but
> organized irreligion had proved a far more despotic, capricious
> and murderous historical force.[21]

So, in many ways the supposedly hopeful vision of the future mapped out
in films like *2012* actually unveils a Utopian ideology like those pursued by
dictators in the twentieth century, an ideology that, as we have just heard,
leads to a murderous and brutal imposition upon society, one that is ruthless in achieving its end.

Lessons Learned?

On August 2, 1934, President Paul von Hindenburg died and, with his death,
Adolf Hitler, as Reich Chancellor and Führer, took virtual dictatorial control
of the public affairs of Germany. His influence and intimidation were immense, so much so that privately no one dared confront or challenge him,
meaning his decisions were largely unopposed within the government. Hitler wanted to establish the pride of Germany and the German *Volk*. World
War I had brought a sense of great shame to Germany as a nation, and there
were many still emotionally (and physically) wounded from the war itself
and the tight restrictions placed upon Germany as a result. Germany was
struggling through shame, economic devastation, and international restrictions. Hitler appealed to a national identity—to restore pride to the nation,
a pride that, according to Hitler and Nazi ideology, had been threatened by
Communists, Jews, and the powers at Versailles. With Hitler's rise to power

---

fact that I obeyed, and not whom I obeyed. I have already said that the top echelons,
to which I did not belong, gave the orders, and they rightly, in my opinion, deserved
punishment for the atrocities which were perpetrated on the victims on their orders.
But the subordinates are now also victims. I am one of such victims." http://remember.
org/eichmann/ownwords Lines 4–23.

21. Hart, *Story of Christianity*, 329–30.

Germany felt a sense of pride and hope again, the promise to restore the nation to its former glory. Part of his plan was to evoke Christian language, so much so that many people in Germany would have seen Hitler as an ally of the German church. In a speech in February 1933 Hitler declared,

> We want to fill our culture again with the Christian spirit, not just theoretically. No, we want to burn out the rotten develop-ments in literature, in the theatre, in the press—in short, burn out this poison which has entered our whole life and culture during the past fourteen years.[22]

There was a desire among many German Christians for Hitler to bring to-gether the church and the state and so anchor Christian identity in German "race and . . . cultural heritage."[23] To bring back the pride of the Volk was an immensely powerful message that not only large segments of German Christians got behind, but something that the nation got behind. Dietrich Bonhoeffer (1906–1945) did not get behind Hitler's message. He was a fierce critic of Hitler's political ideology and warned the German church of its path toward wholehearted acceptance of a Nazi State,

> Whether or not we want to see it, whether or not we think it is right, the churches are caught up in a struggle for their faith such as we have not seen for hundreds of years. This is a strug-gle-whether or not we agree-over our confession of Jesus Christ alone as Lord and Redeemer of the world.[24]

Whereas for Bonhoeffer Jesus Christ alone was Lord, Hitler sought to es-tablish unquestioning allegiance, an allegiance that would see realized his vision for a future and a time, "when a nation of citizens would arise which would be welded together through a common love and a common pride that would be invincible and indestructible forever."[25] Such allegiance did arise within the German church whereby, in 1938, the director of the Ger-man Evangelical Church ordered all pastors to "take the oath of allegiance to the Führer."[26] Such an order might seem absurd to our ears today, yet Bonhoeffer recalls in that same year a cross replaced by a floodlit swasti-ka—a sure sign that Christian identity and nationalism had been merged together. Indeed, nationalism, identity, and military service were to become so closely aligned, submerged in totality into Nazi ideology, that critiquing

22. Quoted in Helmreich, *German Churches Under Hitler*, 128–29.
23. Matheson, "New Guiding Principles," 23.
24. Bonhoeffer, *London*, 376.
25. Hitler, *Mein Kampf*, 387.
26. Bethge, *Dietrich Bonhoeffer*, 599.

one was to be seen to critique them all, resulting in punishment, prison, and even death. On April 7, 1933, the Law for the Reconstitution of the Professional Civil Service was passed. This contained what came to be known as the "Aryan paragraph" in which all "non-Aryans" (i.e., Jews) could not hold civil service jobs. This overt anti-Semitism and oppression toward Jewish people would feed itself into the consciousness of the people, resulting eventually in the night that has come to be called *Kristallnacht*; on November 9, 1938, synagogues throughout Germany were set on fire, Jewish homes and businesses were destroyed, one hundred Jewish people were murdered, and over thirty thousand were sent to concentration camps. In March 1933 Hitler managed to get the "enabling act" passed by the Reichstag, which gave virtually unlimited power to himself, effectively removing parliamentary democracy. Hitler had also managed to curtail freedom of the press and the freedom to assemble, ensuring that his message was not subverted on the ground amongst the common person. On October 14, 1933, Germany left the League of Nations, a move applauded by the majority of people, but not by Bonhoeffer. Hitler broke the Treaty of Versailles and built his army in secret. He reintroduced conscription on March 16, 1935, and pumped huge amounts of money into the military service. There was a very positive and high view of military service among German people at this time, including German Christians. Even with Hitler's rise to power, many saw serving in the military as a sign of patriotism. Conscientious objectors were few and far between in 1930's Germany and, much like in Britain during World War I, such views were seen as unpatriotic and against the common good of the country. Bonhoeffer, however, was a pacifist and therefore a "voice crying out in the wilderness" in regard to violence and military service as there were so few who were conscientious objectors. In August 1934 he addressed the Ecumenical Council of Churches,

> Nationalism and internationalism have to do with political necessities and possibilities. The ecumenical Church, however, does not concern itself with these things, but with the commandments of God . . . For the members of the ecumenical Church . . . His commandment of peace is more holy, more inviolable than the most revered words and works of the natural world . . . They cannot take up arms against Christ himself—yet this is what they do if they take up arms against one another! Even in anguish and distress of conscience there is for them no escape from the commandment of Christ that there shall be peace. How does this peace come about? Through a system of political treaties? Through the investment of international capital in different countries? Through the big banks, through

money? Or through universal peaceful rearmament in order to guarantee peace? Through none of these, for the single reason that in all of them peace is confused with safety. There is no way to peace along the way of safety. For peace must be dared. It is the great venture.[27]

For Bonhoeffer, the Sermon on the Mount was the "pure doctrine,"[28] something that must not be "discussed as an ideal"[29] but a calling to participate in the life of Christ, to recognize that what Jesus teaches in the Sermon is something "he really means us to get on with."[30] Bonhoeffer did not expect the world to live according the Sermon, and argued against the call of Jesus to nonviolence and nonresistance as an "ethical blueprint for general application," for in doing so we would be "indulging in idealistic dreams."[31] No, according to Bonhoeffer, the Sermon is for the church, a calling for the church to live out because it is the church who has been called to follow Jesus in the way of the cross, a Way that Bonhoeffer believes will change the world. He says,

> . . . the cross is the only justification for the precept of nonviolence, for it alone can kindle a faith in the victory over evil which will enable men to obey that precept . . . The passion of Christ is the victory of divine love over the powers of evil, and therefore it is the only supportable basis for Christian obedience . . . The cross is the only power in the world which proves that suffering love can avenge and vanquish evil.[32]

According to nostalgic apocalyptic visions, the world is transformed through our power to overcome, the human capacity to violently start again and impose utopian ideals that will correct the mistakes of the past. Yet Bonhoeffer offers us something remarkably different from the life of Jesus: suffering love.

So, in Germany there was a rise in nationalism, a national crying out to reclaim the nation's former glory, a sense of shame and stripping away of identity that Hitler sought to restore. There was deep recession and poverty, a return to the pride of the military, a fear of immigrants and non-

27. Bonhoeffer, "Church and the Peoples," 307–09.

28. Bonhoeffer, "Church and the Peoples," 217.

29. Bonhoeffer, Cost of Discipleship, 138.

30. Bonhoeffer, Cost of Discipleship, 138.

31. Bonhoeffer, Cost of Discipleship, 93.

32. Bonhoeffer, Cost of Discipleship, 94.

Germans, a distrust of Europe and the shame that had come through the
Treaty of Versailles and the loss of sovereignty. Bonhoeffer, writing in
1935, said,

> Under the onslaught of new nationalism, the fact that the church
> of Christ does not stop at national and racial boundaries but
> reaches beyond them, so powerfully attested in the New Testa-
> ment and in the confessional writings, has far too easily been
> forgotten and denied.[33]

The German church was largely silent—silent through fear, silent through
a lack of understanding, silent through theological ineptness. Eberhard
Bethge, Bonhoeffer's closest friend, said that Bonhoeffer "was ashamed of
the Confessing Church"[34] in its German nationalism and would thus distance himself further from them. Bonhoeffer, through theological study
that led to a cultural and political insight, spoke out and saw early on the
reality of where Germany was heading under the rule of Hitler and why
such ideology was opposed to the Way of Jesus. Nationalism, militarism, recession, pride, rejecting Europe and demanding we reclaim our sovereignty,
a fear of immigrants and refugees—these were all a stark reality in Germany
during the 1920's and 30's, and they are all present today. Perhaps we are in
similar days where our nostalgic longings and our fear of what the world is
becoming might lead us into dark and terrible places.

Modern-Day Parallels?

Martin Luther King Jr. said there were three evils of society: racism, poverty,
and militarism. In an address to the National Conference on New Politics
on August 31, 1967, King said, "When machines and computers, profit mo-
tives and property rights are considered more important than people the
giant triplets of racism, economic exploitation and militarism are incapable
of being conquered."[35] The language of Western governments for the past
forty years has consistently been one of "growth," whereby the means to better our society will be through growing our own economy. David Cameron,

---

33. Bonhoeffer, "Confessing Church," 140. Consider then how different the language of Bonhoeffer is from Theresa May who, in her keynote speech to the Conservative Party Conference in October 2016, said, "But if you believe you're a citizen of the
world, you're a citizen of nowhere. You don't understand what the very word 'citizenship' means." http://www.independent.co.uk/news/uk/politics/theresa-may-speech-
tory-conference-2016-in-full-transcripta7346171.html.

34. Bethge, *Dietrich Bonhoeffer*, 603.

35. https://www.youtube.com/watch?v=6sT9HjhocHM.

speaking at the G8 summit on June 15, 2013, said that the issues of poverty needed to be dealt through "the benefits of growth" confirming then how Mammon continues to be served unquestionably. Think too of the rise in military pride. Remembrance Day in the UK has grown considerably over recent years, a newfound sense of pride in the armed forces and an unquestioning loyalty demanded of society to support our troops. In such a climate, it is difficult to even ask questions of the legitimacy of the military and the ethics of war without coming under fierce criticism and being seen as unpatriotic. Indeed, the conversation is shut down before it has begun in such a climate. And then there is the fear of "other"—people who are not like us. After the European Referendum in the UK there were increasing reports of hate crimes toward ethnic minorities and the Muslim community. Theresa May was reckless and inflammatory in her keynote speech at the Conservative Party conference in 2016 when she used the language of "low-skilled immigration" taking the jobs of British people. Such language creates and escalates the climate of fear and hate toward people who have arrived in the UK from other countries. Donald Trump's comments and political actions toward the Muslim community have furthered fear and resentment toward ethnic minorities, highlighting the power of language to generate violence. And such language instinctively brings dehumanization and further exasperates the very problems Martin Luther King Jr. spoke about fifty years ago.

October 2–5, 2016, the UK Conservative Party held its annual conference. The Prime Minister Theresa May, along with her cabinet, spoke in stark terms of nationalism, Britishness, and highlighting "foreign workers." In her keynote speech she said,

> . . . if you're one of those people who lost their job, who stayed in work but on reduced hours, took a pay cut as household bills rocketed, or, and I know a lot of people don't like to admit this, someone who finds themselves out of work or on lower wages because of low-skilled immigration, life simply doesn't seem fair.[36]

Throughout the speech she speaks of "citizenship," "nationalism," how, in leaving the EU we will "become, once more, a fully sovereign and independent country" and how "we should employ the power of the government for the good of the people." She goes on to say, "That's what government's about: action. It's about doing something, not being someone."[37] Yet Bonhoeffer

36. http://www.independent.co.uk/news/uk/politics/theresa-may-speech-tory-conference-215016-in-full-transcripta7346171.html.

37. http://www.independent.co.uk/news/uk/politics/theresa-may-speech-tory-conference-215016-in-full-transcripta7346171.html.

saw within his own context how dangerous and misguided such language is: "human authorities who sought to build peace upon a political foundation find themselves shipwrecked."[38] Furthermore, orthodox Christian theology has consistently sought to root itself in *ontology*, in *who we are in the Person of Jesus Christ* and his grace. Indeed, according to the gospels, the works of our hands are determined by our character and motivation, by who we are, and so such language by Theresa May, separating action and being, is thoroughly un-Christian and a false dichotomy.

The Conservatives also plan to introduce a "British bill of rights" rooted in "British values" that will replace the Human Rights Act set up in 1998. The act protects fifteen fundamental rights and freedoms, including the right to life, privacy, and free speech, which are all based on articles of the European Convention on Human Rights. The freedoms must be upheld by all public bodies, and British courts and tribunals must interpret legislation in a way that is compatible with the rights enshrined in the convention. A "British bill of rights" based on "British values" is a frightening prospect. Who determines what "Britishness" even is? What will be the measure to which someone is judged to be acting according to "British values?" The ideology and language of this Conservative government is consistently of "other," of "the good the government can do" and "center ground," language that seeks to restore faith in the political system and restore pride in British politics, British pride and British identity, yet can actually work as a means through which alternative views are suppressed and demonized. In Britain the biggest-selling newspapers are overtly politically "right-wing" and look for ways to make such views the new "center ground." In reality, it is neo-liberalism pushed ever more to its extremes. When such political ideology becomes the norm it is common for socialism and politically left ideas to be ridiculed and feared as "Marxist" or "communist." When that happens, it is incredibly difficult to have a different voice in the political arena.

Theresa May and this current Conservative government, in seeking to revoke the European Human Rights Act and install a "British" version—alongside a determination to establish a set of "British values" that people, especially those seeking residence here must abide by in order to combat this so-called "war on terror," together with new laws that enable extreme snooping of our electronic communication, alongside language of nationalism, fear of immigrants, and economic hardship—create a potentially dangerous sociological atmosphere, one that has the potential to be brutal and unforgiving. Here the church's theological task is vital and necessary. The church must not allow itself to be swept up in any kind of nationalism,

38. Bonhoeffer, "Christ and Peace," 258.

in language and support of war or any kind of segregational or oppressive practice. It must seek the distinctiveness of Christ, a peculiar people defined through Jesus' teaching, a people who follow the Way forged by the cross of Christ. The church must be a Beatitude people, a Sermon on the Mount revolution, a Philippians 2 *kenosis* people who declare Jesus and not Caesar is Lord. Bonhoeffer says,

> Christianity stands or falls with its revolutionary protest against violence, arbitrariness and pride of power and with its apologia for the weak. I feel that Christianity is rather doing too little in showing these points than doing too much. Christianity has adjusted itself much too easily to the worship of power. It should give much more offense, more shock to the world, than it is doing. Christianity should . . . take a much more definite stand for the weak than to consider the potential moral right of the strong.[39]

We must, all of us if the time comes, speak out. We must take a stand and recognize the dark path that is potentially being trod. We must stand in solidarity with the oppressed. We must not be bound up in fear, for perfect love casts out fear. We must recognize our common humanity in every face, opening our hearts and our homes to all, walking in the Unconditionality and grace of God. We must reject all forms of violence and all calls to strengthen our military might. We must lay down our swords and follow the path of peace shown to us by Jesus Christ, modeled by many throughout the last two thousand years. We must think theologically if we are to have any kind of voice that is distinct to the culture around us.

> It is as though all the powers of the earth had sworn themselves against peace; money, the economy, the drive to power, yes even love for the fatherland - all have been pulled into the service of hate, the hatred of the people, the hate of compatriots to their own compatriots.[40]

Apocalypse Now?

Perhaps then, in light of all that we have explored, apocalyptic films like *Mad Max*, a world of chaos, destruction, death, and human savagery, are the logical sequel to films like *2012*, the obvious reality to the Utopian visions so often portrayed within mainstream apocalyptic Hollywood blockbusters. At

39. Bonhoeffer, *London*, 347.
40. Bonhoeffer, "The Church Is Dead," 378.

the end of *The Day After Tomorrow*, astronauts look down from space at a frozen earth, now free from pollution (and most of the human population), an earth ready to be reborn; *Deep Impact* ends with the crew on the spaceship *Messiah* engaging in a suicide mission, unable to stop the smaller comet that causes a mega-tsunami, blowing themselves and the larger comet up on course to destroy the world with nuclear warheads, with the president of America urging the world to rebuild after the blessing of a second chance; *2012* ends with a very small selection of humanity rescued on arks (the vast majority of those rescued are those with money), sailing toward the Cape of Good Hope as the sun rises on the horizon. All of these films imagine a world reborn in ice, water, and fire, humanity now destined for a new Utopian future where we have learned from the mistakes of our past and will rebuild a brighter tomorrow. Yet each of these films are entrenched within despotic Utopian ideology, whereby, according to this ideology, millions of people have to die in order for a more rational and enlightened humanity to emerge, a humanity that has been corrected from its flaws and mistakes so that a perfect society can be created. Apparently, someone who served under Stalin once said, "When the state becomes everything, it will become nothing!" In other words, the Utopian vision will be all-consuming, all doctrine, ethics, thought, belief, and behavior determined in entirety by the state until the people of the state no longer recognize their un-freedom, no longer aware of a prison without walls. The evil committed by and under Stalin and Hitler and Mao and Pol Pot were in order for a so-called new society to emerge, one where people "will become really free" as Stalin once said, a Utopian vision for humanity. The *Mad Max* films and *The Road* then, as stated above, are the obvious sequels to the apocalyptic disaster stories that grip our imagination today, for in these visions of a post-apocalyptic future, there is a bleakness and harsh realism to the human condition, an unveiling of our propensity to commit acts of great violence against one another, the awareness that history continually repeats itself. So how do we learn from our past, how do we resist the horrors that we are drawn to, the ability to inflict untold violence upon our fellow humans, our desire to wipe out and start again?

Perhaps the answer rests in living lives according to the Prince of Peace, refusing the way of fear and hate, resisting the push of nostalgia to reclaim an idealistic vision of the past that has, in truth, never existed. Rather, let us collectively pursue the way of resistant love that will not be overcome by Utopianism that inevitably leads to scapegoating and death. The "Yes" and "Amen" of God's grace and love is greater than the "No" of our hate and fear.

> For the Son of God, Jesus the Anointed, who was proclaimed
> among you by us . . . did not become a "Yes" and also a "No";
> rather, in him came "Yes." For, however many God's promises
> may be, in him there is the "Yes"; therefore, through him there is
> also our "Amen" to God. (2 Cor 1:19–20)

The vision then of a world reborn happens not through fire and blood, but through the refusal of our own violent desires, the pursuit of the Way of forgiveness, the casting off of the nostalgic memories that imagine how things used to be, and the embrace of today in authenticity, refusing to pursue some kind of ideological utopianism, but to name the world as it really is. And it is this pursuit of authentic speech that we now turn to.

5

<h1 style="text-align: center">It</h1>

The Horror of Authentic Speech

Creepy as hell. You ever see that TV movie about the clown in the sewer?[1]

—*MR. MERCEDES*

I T DWELLS IN THE depths of the sewers of Derry, a monster who feeds off the children of this small town, its lair the place where It feeds and sustains Itself, killing and feasting off children for centuries. The monster, simply known as It, has "spent Its long, long existence inflicting pain, feeding on it,"[2] providing fear and terror to the children and people of Derry for hundreds of years, returning in cycles of twenty-seven to thirty years when an act of significant violence happens in Derry—these acts somehow a means through which this ancient monster awakens from hibernation. The most common way It manifests Itself to children is as Pennywise the Dancing Clown, yet Its powers mean that the monster can shape-shift, becoming anything it wants to be, usually in a form that represents the child's worst fear or nightmares.

---

1. King, *Mr. Mercedes*, 14.
2. King, *It*, 1280.

"Kill you all!" The clown was laughing and screaming. *"Try to stop me and I'll kill you all! Drive you crazy and then kill you all. You can't stop me! I'm the Gingerbread Man! I'm the Teenage Werewolf!"*

And for a moment It was the Teenage Werewolf, the moon-silvered face of the lycanthrope peering out at them from over the collar of the silver suit, white teeth bared.

"Can't stop me, I'm the leper!"

Now the leper's face, haunted and peeling, rotting with sores, stared at them with eyes of the living dead.

"Can't stop me, I'm the mummy!"

The leper's face aged and ran with sterile cracks. Ancient bandages swam halfway out of its skin and solidified there. Ben turned away, his face white as curds, one hand plastered over his neck and ear.

"Can't stop me, I'm the dead boys!"

"No!" Stan Iris screamed.[3]

According to a vision that two of the main characters, Richie and Mike, had, It descended from space to earth millions of years ago, "a burning, falling object," "gigantic," and "too bright to look at." As Richie and Mike look at this falling object, they know that whatever It is, It "came down on that long-ago day . . . from a place much farther away than another star or another galaxy."[4] Having settled underground in the place that Derry would eventually be built upon, It simply waited for humans to settle, and then began Its reign of terror on a town that would stay under Its curse. This terrible monster brings "an ecstasy of terror" that for some, even gazing at It causes insanity and death,

> Richie saw another body . . . Blood had run from both of the stranger's eyes and caked in a foam around his mouth and on his chin.[5]

Its shape is so horrific that the human mind is unable to fully grasp what It actually is, as Mike observes when confronted with It in its lair,

> *But It's something else, there's some final shape, one that I can almost see the way you might see the shape of a man moving behind a movie screen while the show is on, some other shape, but I don't want to see It, please God, don't let me see It . . .*[6]

3. King, *It*, 881.
4. King, *It*, 913.
5. King, *It*, 1286–87.
6. King, *It*, 1270.

It feeds on the flesh and blood of children. This is It's existence and purpose, "It wanted only to eat and sleep and dream and eat again."[7] This is the horrifying reality of It; a predator, not simply of the natural world that eats in order to survive, but a predator whose existence is to bring terror in order that It might eat. In Derry, "It had created a place in Its own image, and It looked upon this place with favor from the deadlights which were Its eyes. Derry was Its killing-pen, the people of Derry Its sheep."[8] There is a raw terror and evil to It that cannot be reasoned with, and will never grow tired of, for It exists in order to bring terror and death; there is no placating, no way of making a creature such as this cease in its horror. As Alfred says in the film *The Dark Knight*, "Some men just want to watch the world burn."[9] But It is not a man—is not a human at all—and we are confronted with Its terror right at the beginning of King's novel as we witness the death of young George Denbrough, just six years old.

> The terror, which would not end for another twenty-eight years— if it ever did end—began, so far as I know or can tell, with a boat made from a sheet of newspaper floating down a gutter swollen with rain.[10]

Having been given a paper boat made by his older brother Bill to float on the running water in the streets due to torrential rain, George goes outside in his yellow slicker and sails his boat down the street, only to watch it run into a storm drain. Running over, he peers in to be greeted by a clown.

> George blinked and looked again. He could barely credit what he saw; it was like something from a made-up story, or a movie where you know the animals will talk and dance. If he had been ten years older, he would not have believed what he was seeing, but he was not sixteen. He was six.
> There was a clown in the storm-drain.[11]

And the clown is holding his boat, "'Want your boat, Georgie?" The clown smiled. With this smiling clown in the storm drain, there is the smell of the circus rising up, cotton candy, popcorn, and the "cheery aroma of midway sawdust."[12] And then there are the balloons. Balloons of many different

---

7. King, *It*, 1221.

8. King, *It*, 1220.

9. The *Dark Knight*, Christopher Nolan, Warner Bros., 2008.

10. King, *It*, 3.

11. King, *It*, 15.

12. King, *It*, 16.

colors, bright, shiny, and beautiful, "like gorgeous ripe fruit."[13] As strange a
sight the clown is down the storm drain, George is caught up in wonder, because he is six years old and here before him is a clown, holding balloons in
one hand, his boat in the other, the smell of the circus rising up like incense
to greet his childhood wishes. Even when there is a hint of rot, a background
stench floating past the smell of the circus coming up out of the storm drain,
George is not going to run away, because, as a child, the fear of monsters in
the dark, hiding in storm drains, vanishes quickly when a clown offers you
a balloon.

> "Do they float?"
> "Float?" The clown's grin widened. "Oh yes, indeed they do.
> They float! And there's cotton candy . . ."[14]

So George reaches in to get a balloon and his boat back from Pennywise.

> The clown seized his arm.
> And George saw the clown's face change.
> What he saw was terrible enough to make his worst imag-
> inings of the thing in the cellar look like sweet dreams; what he
> saw destroyed his sanity in one clawing stroke.[15]

George is killed by It. "They *float*," It growled, "they *float*, Georgie, and when
you're down here with me, you'll float, too . . ."[16] The death of six-year-old
George Denbrough sets into motion the tale of It, the coming together of
an unlikely group of heroes, the so-called Losers Club, who together will
seek to destroy whatever It is, and so end the terror inflicted upon this small
town in Maine, a terror that has been part of the DNA of Derry since people
first dwelt there.

Throughout the story we are invited into childhood and the ability
of children to "see" in ways that adults are unable to. This seeing is not
simply something done with the eyes, but a seeing with the eyes of faith, a
belief in the way of the world that children are able to inhabit in ways that
adults either struggle with or simply leave behind: "When I was an infant,
I spoke like an infant, I thought like an infant, I reckoned like an infant
. . ." (1 Cor 13:11). The adults of Derry cannot or will not "see," although
completely aware of the deaths, aware of the violence and murder present
in their small town, aware of the horrific way children are targeted and
killed, aware of the violent history that has seeped into every pore of Derry's

13. King, *It*, 15.
14. King, *It*, 16–17.
15. King, *It*, 17.
16. King, *It*, 17.

existence—although aware, are somehow completely unaware, unable to begin to grasp that a malevolent force has gripped their town for centuries, lost in the faith of *maintaining the world around them*. Fear creates within us unconscious desire for the destruction of others, or more accurately, the protection of ourselves; this is Derry's problem. In our desire to grasp onto what we already have, any sense that it may be taken from us, or, indeed, any fear, however unfounded, that we might lose what we have, is met with our desire to sacrifice to save what we have. The children of Derry are sacrificed to the fear of It in order that what Derry has—sameness—can remain.

Ancient Sacrifice

We offer our children up in sacred violence all the time in order to protect what we have. Throughout human history we have sacrificed our children to the gods in order to bring blessing to our communities, sure of the gods' desire for blood, and that the innocent blood of our children is the greatest and highest-value offering we could possibly give. For those that believe we have become a more enlightened culture, you only need to look at abortion rates, eating disorders among young people, the age we send young people off to war, as well as the children murdered in war through drone bombings, children who the state ruthlessly and despicably call "collateral damage," to recognize that child sacrifice is alive and well. Fear is a powerful weapon and yet also a destroyer of creativity, and so we lose imagination and compassion, unable to work out how we can best support, for instance, those mothers who feel that abortion is the only option. We continue to push consumerism upon our children and then wonder why they have debilitating self-image problems. We continue to believe the scandalous lie that war will bring peace, and we march our young people off into wars that have more to do with money and political power than anything to do with trying to create a peaceful world. We continue to drop bombs in countries we have no right to be in, like we are in a simulated computer game, and then wonder why young boys are radicalized and hate Western powers.

In the ancient act of human sacrifice, as we have already noted, the victim—the one who is blamed and scapegoated for the instability, rivalry, and violence within the community—is murdered by the collective community, offered up to the gods that peace might be restored. The power of this act lay in the way the violence of the group is poured out upon the victim, an act of catharsis that gathers the community together, temporarily restoring a superficial peace. The victim, chosen at random, but probably because of their oddness, is killed, and in their death peace falls down, and the people believe that the gods have visited them, that this act of sacrifice has been acceptable to the gods, that this offering is life for the community, a pleasing aroma rising up to the nostrils of the divine pantheon. Why do you think burnt offerings have been part of our communities for thousands of years? How else will the gods know that we have offered them something unless we create smoke that will rise up to the heavens, a sweet smell to these temperamental deities that will finally bring peace and blessing to our fractured and volatile relationships. Because the scapegoat brings peace, their status changes from the cause of conflict to the one who brings peace, thus resulting in the belief that the gods have visited the community through this victim, belief that becomes embedded within the collective consciousness. In the act of sacrifice the human person is raised to the status of divinity, and when that sacrifice appears to bring peace, then we will continue to use this act to transform the instability around us and maintain the normality that we desire, doing all that we can to protect what we have for fear that what we have will be taken away.

It is simple to project our fear and conflict and lack of peace upon another, especially in societies consumed by consumerism. We love what we own—our possessions a continued source of temporary peace for us, a means through which we can suppress our fears and anxiety; with each purchase we get a rush of adrenaline, a momentary emotional boost that makes us feel better until the high wears off and we need another purchase to replicate the boost. Consumerism is a powerful tool in the sacrificial mechanism, disguising our violence through the power of advertising, the chosen ignorance of the consumer, and the hiddenness of those we are sacrificing. The poor become a divine source for the rich as we hold them up in idealized ways, imagining them, in their poverty, to have somehow attained a simplicity and depth of meaning to life that those of us in the West can only dream of. This kind of sentimental bullshit philosophizing helps us to maintain the status quo and does not demand us to ask too many questions as to our current way of life. We symbolically hold out a hand of help to the poor so long as they do not demand too much off us in return. We give small gestures of help toward them all the while ensuring that we can continue in our capitalistic, consumerist desires,

> Žižek highlights the modern trend with corporate big business like Starbucks to give a fraction of the cost of coffee you have just bought to help communities in the majority world trapped in poverty. Žižek makes the point that this has resulted in us being able to carry on with our consumerism while at the same

time feeling better about ourselves because some of our money has gone to help a starving child.[17]

This enables us to sacrifice them with ease, for we can be assured within our own consciousness that we have done just enough to help them, while continuing in our materialism, and in doing so we raise them to deified levels; the figure of the poor child starving in the majority world becomes a type of god whom we both loath and worship. The poor are not the only ones who are sacrificed today by Western powers in order to maintain our way of life, for in the act of war, the continued invasion of Iraq, Afghanistan, and Syria, we sacrifice, not only the poor on the altar of militarism, but also our young people as we encourage them to sign up for the armed forces, to build better lives for themselves. In the UK the Royal Navy promote themselves through television adverts telling us that you will be "made in the Royal Navy" and that you can, "Travel the world. Make friends for life. Develop skills you never knew you had. And go places you never imagined. Could you be made in the Royal Navy?" The army tells us that "this is belonging" when you join them; a community who you can be part of and so discover your purpose in life, and that elusive identity. Of course, the army does not want you to have an actual identity, as they seek to mold you into a clone killing machine who will obey orders and do whatever is required of you. The armed forces are, through their promise of discovery and identity, seeking to appeal directly to the lives of young people. Not only that, but the Western world is still embedded within Empire mentality, a belief in the ultimate good of war and its ability to change the world for the better and bring peace. With the defeat of Hitler in World War II our belief in the military complex was cemented here in the West for we truly believed we had defeated evil through our weapons of war, and we are still a people who believe in a glorification of war and the idea that we can literally change the world through might. Culturally, what has taken place is the deification of the armed forces, so much so that any criticism of the armed forces is swiftly shut down, with soldiers raised up to high levels of glory, both in life, and especially in death. A trend within the UK has been the virtual worship of those who have died in wars over the last one hundred years. Go to any Remembrance Day service in the United Kingdom today and the language is predominantly of "sacrifice," a language that demands that we, those who have survived or who benefit from their death, show our eternal gratitude to the fallen, and nothing short of overt gestures of gratitude will do. And this narrative enables us to maintain the status quo, to quench any dissent, block out any imagination, and ensure the narrative can continue without disruption. This is It's power, certain of

---

17. Haward, *Ghost of Perfection*, 60.

how adults will not perform any truly brave action in seeking to defeat It, or search for what is the actual truth, because there is a desire to maintain what is in existence for them at this particular moment. As It reflects,

> *The former power of their imaginations would be muted and weak. They would no longer believe that they were piranha in the Kenduskeag or that if you stepped on a crack you might really break your mother's back or that if you killed a ladybug which lit on your shirt your house would catch fire that night. Instead, they would believe in insurance . . . Instead they would believe in . . . television . . . running to prevent heart attacks . . . in Dr Ruth when it came to getting well fucked and Jerry Falwell when it came it getting well saved.*[18]

The monster known as It is confident of how adults are unable to use their imagination in the same way children can, that their belief system is now in the tangible and material, rather than the immense power of the imagination, the ability to believe beyond the realm of what can be touched, and seen, and this is a crucial issue in today's world.

Truth and Lies

The realm of scientific belief and understanding is of immense importance and, to my mind, crucial to humanity and our ability to progressively move forwards as a species. What we continue to discover through scientific enquiry is providing us with insight, not only into our past, but also how we might navigate our future. That is not to say, however, that scientific enquiry is the ultimate fount of knowledge and understanding, or that science is the source of all truth. There has been a danger in recent years, especially in light of writers and thinkers like Richard Dawkins, Daniel Dennett, and A. C. Grayling, that the materialist, naturalist philosophy—the doctrine that there is nothing apart from the physical order, and certainly nothing supernatural—and the reduction of all knowledge to a mechanistic world-view is the very best way to understand the world around us and our place within it. Coupled with this is the concept, espoused especially by Dawkins, that true knowledge flows from the past four hundred years, where a post-enlightenment rationality is the ultimate basis for truth and knowing. Such is the strength of this belief that ancient myth and religious stories are often fully dismissed, a belief that they are such primitive stories from an ancient past that reveal our ignorance about the world, and now look at how

18. King, *It*, 1232–33.

far we have advanced and progressed today as a species—talking snakes, lightning-throwing gods, and animals in an ark belong to the fairy-tales that we move on from once we become reasoned, thinking adults. Today, such is the dearth of thinkers who actually grasp what is truly meant theologically when we say "God," we find theist and atheists alike really only disagreeing,

> . . . between differing perspectives within a single post-Christian and effectively atheist understanding of the universe. Nature for most of us now is merely an immense machine, either produced by a demiurge (a cosmic magician) or somehow just existing of itself, an independent contingency (a magical cosmos). In place of classical philosophical problems that traditionally opened out upon the question of God—the mystery of being, higher forms of causality, the intelligibility of the world, the nature of conscious-ness, and so on—we now concern ourselves almost exclusively with the problems of the physical origin or structural complexity of nature, and are largely unaware of the difference.[19]

These ancient myth stories are rejected out of hand at our peril for they con-tinue to not only speak into our humanness today, a humanity that contin-ues to live in certain ways, but also open up incredible understanding into our past and our evolutionary journey. Jordan Peterson has highlighted how the story of Adam and Eve, a story that, at least in oral form, is thousands of years old, is highly instructive for us today; recent studies revealed how at one time in humanity's evolutionary journey one of our greatest predators were snakes, and the reason for that was because we dwelt in trees. Not only that, but our main diet was fruit, and that is why we have incredible vision, so that we could differentiate the many different colors of fruit; it's all there in the opening chapters of Genesis. Then there are the stories of the Egyptian gods, stories that reveal hierarchical systems built into our DNA. Or the founding of first culture in the Cain and Abel story, and how through mimetic desire, rivalry, and murder human societies emerge. Examine any ancient myth story and you will discover truth, that is to say, truth about who we are as human beings and why we are the way we are, even today. To call these stories true is not necessarily to say they happened, or at least it is not to say they happened in the way that we have them, but it is to say that events in our history, the unconscious lessons and thinking that emerged from these events and experiences, lead to the telling and re-telling of these stories, and with each one we encounter deep insights into our humanity. This is why truth matters, and the exclusion of some avenues that enable us to discover truth will always lead to misery for us as a species. The exclusion

19. Hart, *Experience of God*, 302.

and dismissal of ancient religious stories by those such as Dawkins reduces knowledge to a materialist philosophy whose only pathway is some version of Utopian ideology and, as we observed earlier, the belief in humanity's ability to use naturalist scientific enquiry and practice to create transformed societies that will be free from suffering. Even within certain streams of environmentalism there is the belief that if humanity gets its act together then we will tame Mother Nature, stop raping her, and bring peace to the global environment. Now there is little doubt that our addiction to fossil fuels, the amount of plastics we throw away into the sea, and our destruction of rainforests are all evident examples of the way we abuse the earth, cause immense environmental damage, and expose the need for humanity to change and repent.[20] There is no doubt that we need to change our ways, to stop killing animals and making them extinct, and to learn how to live in greater harmony with creation. And it is also a remarkable thing when through our knowledge, compassion, and technological advancement we can eradicate worms that burrow into the eyes of children, provide water in times of drought, and create sources of energy through sun, wind, and sea. But that is not the same thing as saying that by somehow living in total harmony with Mother Nature, living in some kind of mutual dance of cooperation, that the environment will somehow become a sort of peaceful, trouble-free paradise; Mother Nature is beautiful and terrifying all at the same time. I used to work on the water as an oyster fisherman, and there were times when the sun would rise above the horizon, bringing warmth and majesty in the clear blue sky, while my boat cut through the mirrored sea, and a seal swam next to me. There were other times when the rain and sleet would lash against me, the sea a murky, grey vicious rage, almost demanding that I went home and got out of its way. This is a trivial example of the double reality of nature and how beautiful and violent it can be, a beauty and violence that have been around for its entire existence. Ancients feared the sea for a reason, and the stories of mountains falling on heads, earthquakes, and floods that stretch back as long as humans have been able to share stories reveal, alongside archaeological discoveries, that the natural world is not "all sunshine and rainbows." This is why truth matters. The longer we tell one

---

20. Repentance is not simply a form of apology, it is much more than that; it is a change of heart, mind, and action, a recognition of forgiveness already given, and out of that place of forgiveness radical transformation can take place. This is an important point to be made. In traditional charismatic, evangelical versions of sin and repentance, forgiveness only results when someone has confessed to their sins. But if the cross of Christ is the full revelation of God into all eternity, whereby we see in the crucified Jesus the eternal character and nature of God, then forgiveness has already occurred across time and space, with repentance humanity's finite capacity to catch up with the infinite forgiveness.

another philosophies and ideologies that hide the scope of lived experience throughout history, then the worse these distorted visions will become.

It is a strange thing that the experiences of humanity are so roundly dismissed by scientific materialists as part of how we understand truth in the modern West. This is not to endorse some kind of relativism whereby we say that if something is true for you then it is true, but it is to say that what we directly experience within our lifetimes is true for us; the suffering and joy in your life cannot be reduced to a set of empirical experiments and evaluations, examined under a microscope. The lived reality of these moments in your life have a force and a meaning outside of scientific enquiry and hold a truth about them in that you have experienced them. Now the suffering and joy you experienced may have happened through a destructive means, such as the delight in another's pain, or the infliction of pain upon yourself for past guilt, but you have still actually lived it. And so our experiences do matter as we learn how to discern and uncover truth about our humanity and the way of the world. Truth is vital, and if we are going to navigate the transforming land-scape of our culture in light of technological advancement, and the sociologi-cal impact of the internet and social media, then truth telling is going to be perhaps our most vital and powerful tool. Stanley Hauerwas has said that we need to learn how to tell the truth, or at the very least, stop lying. Initially that might seem like an almost absurd thing to say, as perhaps our first thought is that we are not liars. But, as you examine yourself and seek to gain a greater self-awareness, it becomes obvious that lying, or not telling the truth, are fairly normal modes of behavior; this is not something new to our human species. Deceit, often linked with desire, is commonplace within the continued story of humanity, stretching back as far as oral history goes. Returning to the Gar-den of Eden for a moment, we see deceit and desire played out as truth telling is thrown out of paradise, closely followed by the first humans. However old that story is, what it shows us is that humanity struggles to be the speakers of truth, covering it up, distorting it, bending it, and outright lying so that we might maintain and pursue the desires that we have, however distorted those desires might be. This is one of many remarkable things as we scan through the literature of our collective human experience, whether written or painted or in film, we will notice our common capacity to lie and struggle with the truth. Our struggle with the truth is not simply our concealing of facts, although it can be that, but a failure to own the reality we are in and live in light of that. What I mean by that is facing up to who we honestly are, the people that we know ourselves to be, and seeking to deal with ourselves appropriately; and if that means getting serious help, then we have to get it. Or it might mean speaking truthfully to those that we love or are in relationship with, not simply agreeing with what is said to us because we do not want to cause any kind of disturbance to the way things are, even though you know that the way things are is not the best situation for anyone; tell the truth, be honest, do not lie.

The rise of deceit through social media is causing serious problems in mental health across many sections and ages within our communities. The media assault of the "perfect" person, glowing and radiant and beautiful, wearing or holding the latest product, creates within us a desire for that product so that we might be like that person, "people who are not disfigured in any way, whose faces and bodies are in perfect balance and proportion, and who shine with color and radiance."[21] The photoshopping of models has been highlighted for many years as a real problem as it creates a false image of what people look like, and creates impossible standards that many of us, consciously and unconsciously, strive to imitate. On top of this, however, we have the rise of platforms such as Instagram, an image-focused branch of social media that has exploded in popularity and is showing no sign of slowing down. Indeed, for young people Instagram is fast becoming the most popular platform for them to connect on social media. Yet Instagram is the worst social media platform for mental health among fourteen-to-twenty-five-year-olds, as they struggle with issues of self-identity, body image, loneliness, and a fear of missing out. Instagram creates a world of untruth. The images that are posted reflect our desire to show the best version of ourselves, and yet, with our modern phones, clever angles, a variety of filters, and a moment captured, we can create a version of ourselves that says nothing about the reality of our lives. Indeed, we can reject the desire to tell the truth in order that though this online version of ourselves we can, to the viewing world, create another us. With the amount of time we spend on our phones searching through social media, we are always being confronted with images of others whose lives and bodies can seem far better than ours. Even though we instinctively know that what we are looking at is not real, we cannot help but feel caught up in a system that makes us feel worse about our own lives. So we enter the games and create our own version of events, learning how to filter our faces and our lives to convince others that what we have is "good" and "very good." Of course not everyone is using Instagram or social media to actually create a false self, but what I am suggesting is how, although we are not lying, we use social media to manipulate our world to look a little bit less truthful than it actually is; my face/body/life is not really like this, but it looks enough like it to not raise any alarm bells. It is damaging us in ways beyond our comprehension. Throughout human history our capacity to lie and not tell the truth has hurt us and damaged our ability

21. Haward, *Ghost of Perfection*, 67.

to be in relationship with one another and build communities of love and peace. In the history of the Soviet Union we witness how the suppression of truth, the perpetration of falsity, creates terrible conditions for people to live in. Aleksandr Solzhenitsyn, writing his masterful *The Gulag Archipelago*, highlights how, for those living under Soviet regimes there could be no authentic speech, no way of owning your own suffering, for by doing so you would be admitting that society was not perfect, that the State had failed, and therefore your own suffering was an indictment upon the State and seen as an act of treason. So people learned not only how to lie about their own suffering, they learned how to deny the truth of their reality. And this is one of our greatest challenges with social media because it pushes us to *not* be truth-tellers, but truth telling is the means through which we will be a fruitful, holistic individuals within our communities. Every time a young person filters an image of themselves, taken at an angle that makes them look a certain way, they are unconsciously feeding their ability to hide the truth of who they are. It creates within them the unconscious attitude that we simply do not need to be honest with ourselves or with others. This then feeds the destruction of our mental health, because we instinctively know that the image of our lives that we have just posted is not who we really are, and so we feel a sense of loss, a growing awareness of our inability to tell the truth—and it hurts us. We are created for truth, for in the truth we are free, free to become more like the One who is Truth, the True Human that we are shaped in the image of. When we hide or suppress the truth, we lose something of our humanity. When we lie we murder our self-awareness and fail to live according to the divine life put within each of us.

Jesus closely relates the presence of God and being united with God with truth,

> . . . but now you are trying to kill me, a man who has told you the truth that I heard from God . . . Why do you not understand what I say? It is because you cannot accept my word. You are from your father the devil, and you choose to do your father's desires. He was a murderer from the beginning and does not stand in the truth, because there is no truth in him. When he lies, he speaks according to his own nature, for he is a liar and the father of lies. But because I tell the truth, you do not believe me. Which of you convicts me of sin? If I tell the truth, why do you not believe me? Whoever is from God hears the words of God. The reason you do not hear them is that you are not from God. (John 8:40–47 NRSV)

When we live in opposition to hearing the truth we lose something of who are created to become. The "father of lies" is the Accuser, the one who brings accusation, condemnation, and judgment, hiding the truth and lying in order to draw people away from the presence of God; lies and losing self-awareness and wandering away from the love of God are all closely linked; it is the murder of our human/divine calling. Because we are each, in varying degrees, a people who know how to lie, the truth can be a painful reality, and the level of pain can relate to the depth we have gone in seeking to conceal the truth of who we are and the lives we inhabit. Take the story of the Two Sons in Luke's gospel:

> Then Jesus said, "There was a man who had two sons. The younger of them said to his father, 'Father, give me the share of the property that will belong to me.' So he divided his property between them. A few days later the younger son gathered all he had and traveled to a distant country, and there he squandered his property in dissolute living. When he had spent everything, a severe famine took place throughout that country, and he began to be in need. So he went and hired himself out to one of the citizens of that country, who sent him to his fields to feed the pigs. He would gladly have filled himself with the pods that the pigs were eating; and no one gave him anything. But when he came to himself he said, 'How many of my father's hired hands have bread enough and to spare, but here I am dying of hunger! I will get up and go to my father, and I will say to him, "Father, I have sinned against heaven and before you; I am no longer worthy to be called your son; treat me like one of your hired hands."' So he set off and went to his father. But while he was still far off, his father saw him and was filled with compassion; he ran and put his arms around him and kissed him. Then the son said to him, 'Father, I have sinned against heaven and before you; I am no longer worthy to be called your son.' But the father said to his slaves, 'Quickly, bring out a robe—the best one—and put it on him; put a ring on his finger and sandals on his feet. And get the fatted calf and kill it, and let us eat and celebrate; for this son of mine was dead and is alive again; he was lost and is found!' And they began to celebrate.
>
> Now his elder son was in the field; and when he came and approached the house, he heard music and dancing. He called one of the slaves and asked what was going on. He replied, 'Your brother has come, and your father has killed the fatted calf, because he has got him back safe and sound.' Then he became angry and refused to go in. His father came out and began to

plead with him. But he answered his father, 'Listen! For all these years I have been working like a slave for you, and I have never disobeyed your command; yet you have never given me even a young goat so that I might celebrate with my friends. But when this son of yours came back, who has devoured your property with prostitutes, you killed the fatted calf for him!' Then the father said to him, 'Son, you are always with me, and all that is mine is yours. But we had to celebrate and rejoice, because this brother of yours was dead and has come to life; he was lost and has been found.'" (Luke 15:11–32 NRSV)

Both sons lack an awareness of who they are, creating a world in which neither of them know themselves and so engage in thought, speech, and action that fails to recognize the truth of who they are—loved. The younger son, in failing to know or care about his father, takes his inheritance and uses the money in a wild journey of self-discovery, and yet fails to discover anything. On the way home he still has no idea that he is loved, and so rehearses a groveling speech in order to at least get a roof over his head. He does not have the awareness of who he is, and who his father is, and so he lives beyond the place of authenticity, somewhere in the realm of unconscious deception. The older son is the same, yet so deep is he embedded in layers of untruth that even when he sees the reality of his father's love and forgiveness, he finds it offensive, excessive, and an attack on his own personhood. The truth, as I have already said, can be painful, especially when we encounter the lavishness of grace, the full extent of God's love for all. It makes no sense to us, leaves us reeling, and stirs within us questions over fairness, justice, and the ongoing belief in exchange, that those who do good should be rewarded and those who commit evil should be punished.

Authentic speech brings freedom from this deception,

"And you will know the truth, and the truth will make you free."
(John 8:32)

Social media has the very real danger of preventing us from telling the truth, of seeking to create a world of our own making, of believing that we are individuals able to construct a reality that suits us first, that we alone matter. This is the problem the Two Sons had, believing that they alone mattered. When we work out how to manipulate the world around us, and in what way we can make the world in our own image, then authentic speech is lost, for what we desire is not the truth, or even freedom, but the ability to make ourselves our own masters. When the truth is lost we get trapped within constructs of our own making, desiring to maintain a way of life that we know makes no sense and is painful, but we no longer have the imagination to pursue anything else.

This is Derry's problem.

The truth is that It is feeding off their children, devouring them, and yet the people of Derry are caught in the desire to maintain what they have, too frightened to confront the terror or change what they know. So It continues to murder their children, and Derry continues to live under this monstrous curse, and in doing so, in not confronting what is real, in not speaking truth to the reality of what is happening, the adults of Derry lose their imagination, unable to contemplate a different world or a more hopeful future. This is how the stripping away of authentic speech breaks communities, for in no longer having an imagination—the ability to create a world of beauty and deep relationships that imagination enables to happen—communities crumble, lost in the maintenance of the untruth that they now dwell in. Crumbling communities are those who no longer know how to relate truthfully to one another, who are unable to build lives of honesty, vulnerability, and trust, whereby all that is shared together is a show, a desire to not let anyone in, for anyone to get too close, all relationships to be kept at a distance.

Without authentic speech humanity loses its imagination. Now you might be thinking, "I have known some very imaginative liars!" Indeed, we could reflect on those Instagram images where, through creative angles and filters, we can make an image of ourselves or our lives that looks nothing like what is true. But this is not imagination. Lying is not imagination, but deceit, and there is a world of difference between them. Deceit "steals, kills, and destroys" whereas imagination creates life, beauty, and hope. What I mean by this is that when authentic speech disappears, with it goes the capacity for us to create words and actions of love and unconditionality; truth opens the doorway to love, to the discovery of who we really are. In the discovery of our true selves we enable the opportunity to love and be loved without pretense, in authenticity and vulnerability. This is why truth is so powerful, for it unmasks the principalities and powers, exposes the lies that hold us captive, rebukes the powers that seek to enslave us through deception, and creates the possibility of compassionate communities of grace.

I Believe!

The Losers Club understands the power of truth, of speaking the truth, and owning the reality of the curse upon Derry, and therefore how to defeat It: the Ritual of Chüd. The creature bringing terror to Derry is known by different names in other cultures, and in different times:

The Plains Indians called it a manitou, which sometimes took the shape of a mountain-lion or an elk or an eagle . . . The Himalayans called it a *tallus* or *taelus*, which meant an evil magic being that could read your mind and then assume the shape of the thing you were most afraid of. In Central Europe it had been called *eylak*, brother of the *vurderlak*, or vampire. In France it was *le loupgarou*, or skin-changer, a concept that had been crudely translated as the werewolf, but, Bill told them, *le loupgarou* . . . could be anything, anything at all . . .[22]

The way to defeat this ancient monster is through an ancient ritual, the Ritual of Chüd:

If you were a Himalayan holy-man, you tracked the *taelus*. The *taelus* stuck its tongue out. You stuck *yours* out. You and it overlapped tongues and then you both bit in all the way so you were sort of stapled together, eye to eye.[23]

Bill Denburgh discovers that this is the only way to defeat It. He enters the Ritual of Chüd with It, not physically, but in some kind of psychic connection, and they battle "outward into utter blackness, the blackness was everything, the blackness was the cosmos and the universe, and the floor of the blackness was hard, hard, it was like polished ebonite and he was skidding along on his chest and belly and thighs like a weight on a shuffleboard. He was on the ballroom floor of eternity, and eternity was black."[24] Here Bill becomes aware of It's power, "a thing of unshaped destroying light," a "homicidal endless hungry being."[25] Bill also becomes aware of how It speaks a lot, boasting in Itself and power,

"... *feel the power brat, and then speak again of how you come to kill the Eternal.*"[26]

"... *wait until you break through to where I am! wait for that! wait for the deadlights! you'll look and go mad . . .*"[27]

Throughout the story, It uses words and images to bring fear and terror, creating the illusion of supreme power, causing all who encounter It to shrink back in terror, unable to even begin to contemplate a way of defeating It,

22. King, *It*, 811–12.
23. King, *It*, 812.
24. King, *It*, 1275.
25. King, *It*, 1276–77.
26. King, *It*, 1274.
27. King, *It*, 1278.

such is the power It appears to possess. But Bill begins to realize that "so much of Its talk is nothing but a bluff,"[28] and so begins the fight back.

When authentic speech is lost, what it is replaced with is fear, for without authentic speech creative acts of love are lost, lost to illusionary acts that maintain a culture of deception. This is how It holds so much power over Derry, by creating fear through the illusion of words and forms, channeling the horror that lay deep within each of us. Illusion is a powerful thing, masking the true form of what lies beneath: "Our culture of illusion is, at its core, a culture of death."[29] This is how It works. But Bill finds a way to break the illusion through the Ritual of Chüd, and metaphorically bites down deep into It's tongue, and in doing so showed It that he no longer swallowed the lies and the deceit and the fear and the death, but that he believed in truth, in creativity, in imagination—in love,

> (Chüd, this Chüd, stand, be brave, be true, stand for your brother, your friends; believe in all the things you have believed in, believe that if you tell the policeman you're lost he'll see that you get home safely, that there is a Tooth Fairy who live in a huge enamel castle, and Santa Claus below the North Pole, making toys with his trove of elves . . . that our mother and father will love you again, that courage is possible and words will come smoothly every time; no more Losers, no more cowering in a hole in the gouda and calling it a clubhouse, no more crying in Georgie's room because you couldn't save him and didn't know, believe in yourself, believe in the heat of desire)

He suddenly began to laugh in the darkness, not in hysteria but in utter delighted amazement.

'OH SHIT, I BELIEVE IN ALL OF THOSE THINGS!'[30]

Now at this point you might be asking how believing in the Tooth Fairy and Santa Claus has any significance with truth. Why does Bill's belief in these things give him the power to defeat It, if defeating It is about truth? Because Bill is describing the belief in the power of love and creativity, in the power of imagination where truth and hope is made possible. When It kills Georgie, hope dies in Bill and his parents. Every time It kills a child, Derry loses even more hope, to the point where no one can imagine beyond its boundary, where life exists in this cursed place, but don't expect anything

28. King, *It*, 1279.
29. Hedges, *Empire of Illusion*, 192.
30. King, *It*, 1280.

more. In biting down on Its tongue, Bill is exposing the lies and conceal-
ment of truth; Bill is in effect saying, "Enough! The lies you feed us with,
the horror you terrify us with, the hope you drain from us, is over!"[31] It is
no wonder then that the form It reveals Itself to the Losers Club is of a giant
monstrous spider. Of course King is inviting us into J. R. R Tolkien's world
and the lair of Shelob, but in this form It is the life-sucking, fear-inducing
monster that represents what It is all about; if you do not die instantly from
fear of seeing It in this form, then you will be caught in Its web of fear,
trapped, and all life and hope will be sucked out of you, sustaining through
fear, Its existence. And in Tolkien's epic story we encounter the power of
fear through the monster Shelob in her lair at the end of *The Two Towers*.
Again, like It, Shelob dwells in spider-form (although, there is a suggestion
she has existed in other forms), a monster of "rage and hunger,"[32] a thing of
great evil and wickedness, whose desire is for blood and flesh, "for all living
things were her food, and her vomit darkness."[33] When we meet her fully,
she is a monstrous sight:

> A little way ahead, and to his left he saw suddenly, issuing from a
> black hole of shadow under the cliff, the most loathly shape that
> he had ever beheld, horrible beyond the horror of an evil dream.

31. This is what needs to be said to those who continue to promote versions of
heaven and hell that bear little resemblance to the gospel that Jesus and Paul preached.
Christian thought around the "end times" has led to a variety of understandings as to
the nature of the afterlife, and the way God will one day deal with the whole cosmos.
One of the unfortunate "theological" births resulting from thinking around eschatology
is "rapture" theology, the belief that God will literally zap believers up to heaven while
unbelievers remain on earth. Now there are a variety of ways this is understood and
taught, and I have no desire here to go into the various flavors of rapture theology, but
what is clear is the belief that the chosen ones will float up to heaven, meeting Jesus in
the air. This is in part based on a disastrous, literalist, faulty interpretation of various
biblical texts including early Pauline theology in 1 Thessalonians where Paul writes,
> "For the Lord himself, with a cry of command, with the archangel's call and
> with the sound of God's trumpet, will descend from heaven, and the dead in
> Christ will rise first. Then we who are alive, who are left, will be caught up in
> the clouds together with them to meet the Lord in the air; and so we will be
> with the Lord forever" (1 Thess 4:16-17 NRSV).

The dominant narrative of those who subscribe to rapture theology is fear. And so
we find preachers within these streams loudly declaring the violent fate of unbelievers,
the judgment and fire that is coming upon the wicked, and the apparent good news
of how those who have accepted Christ as Lord will be taken, lifted up to the heavens
like the smoke from a sacrificial offering. In this line of theology and thought, I think
Pennywise the Clown describes it best,
"You'll float too."

32. Tolkien, *Lord of the Rings*, 708.
33. Tolkien, *Lord of the Rings*, 707.

> Most like a spider she was, but huger than the great hunting
> beasts, and more terrible than they because of the evil purpose
> in her remorseless eyes . . . Great horns, she had, and behind her
> short stalk-like neck was her huge swollen body, a vast bloated
> bag, swaying a sagging between her legs; its great bulk was black,
> blotched with livid marks, but the belly underneath was pale and
> luminous and gave forth a terrible stench. Her legs were bent,
> with great knobbed joints high above her back, and hairs that
> stuck out like steel spines, and at each leg's end there was a claw.[34]

Shelob represents pure fear, that which paralyses us, a terror that horrifies us
into inactivity. In Tolkien's world, her history stretches far back, "before Sau-
ron, and before the first stone of Barad-dŭr . . ."[35] Her age, and ruthlessness,
history, and form are such to create a world of terror that few can compare
with. This is the kind of terror that exhausts our imagination and drains us
of hope. The only way to overcome such fear is through love,

> "In love there is no fear; rather, the love that is perfect casts out
> fear . . ." (1 John 4:18a).

Sam's love for Frodo is able to rescue Frodo from Shelob because it is white-
hot, pure love that is able to overcome the fear that he is initially confronted
with; Sam will not let his best friend be devoured by this monster,

"You've hurt my master, you brute, and you'll pay for it."[36]

Love is the most powerful force in the world. It is no wonder, then, that King
uses Tolkien's image of a monstrous spider to frame the finale of *It*. When
the children enter It's lair they cry out in stunned horror, confronted with
"a nightmare Spider from beyond time and space, a Spider from beyond
the fevered imaginings of whatever inmates may live in the deepest depths
of hell."[37] For fear to win, then we must be silenced, and truth must be suppressed. Here is the depth of what we encounter with It: a monster that
crushes us with fear, silencing us from speaking out in truth and love. But
Bill refuses to be silenced, refuses to back down in fear; indeed, the Losers
Club will win because they know, somewhere deep within, of the power they
possess together, the incredible strength of their friendship, the way that
love does overcome the darkest corners of our humanity. We must never

34. Tolkien, *Lord of the Rings*, 709.
35. Tolkien, *Lord of the Rings*, 707.
36. Tolkien, *Lord of the Rings*, 713.
37. King, *It*, 1269.

underestimate the power of the deepest relationships, the way that together we truly are stronger. Relationships matter because they are the foundation of what it means to be human, and it is in these relationships that we are able to overcome the power of fear, a fear that demands that we sacrifice others for the sake of our own survival. The Losers Club refused to offer It their fear any longer, and in the power of their relationships overcome It with the power of love, the power of truth, the power of unconditionality. The Losers Club, in truth-speech, represent Christ's ascent to the cross, the act of ultimate truth whereby, through his life of authentic speech and action, the cross is seen for what it really is, the murder of an innocent victim. As Jesus hangs in darkness we recognize not only that his death is totally unjust, that he should never have been killed, but that we have continually killed innocents to satisfy our own rage, fear, violence, and wrath. The resurrection of Jesus is God's vindication of his Son, and the vindication of all innocents murdered because of deceit, murdered because of the failure of us all to hear the truthful voice of the victim. As the Losers Club walk out of the darkness of the sewers of Derry, they symbolize the march of Jesus out of the empty tomb; the Losers Club leave behind them the power of It and the fear, terror, and suffering this monster ravaged upon them all; Christ walks away from the tomb, with sin, death, and hell exhausted on the cross, left behind in the darkness of the grave. This is the wonder of love, a power we must continually be dazzled by, a force so remarkable it should leave us breathless:

> The power of love is greater than the power of death. It cannot be controlled . . . love constantly rises up to remind a wayward society of what is real and what is illusion. Love will endure, even if it appears darkness has swallowed us, to triumph over the wreckage that remains.[38]

At the end of the story, Bill takes his wife, Audra, for a bike ride on Silver, the childhood bike he owned and used to escape the monster It many years earlier. Audra is in a catatonic state after being caught in It's "deadlights," and Bill hopes that this ride on Silver, a bike that represents freedom, will do something to revive her on this bike ride of love and hope. As they ride, Audra comes out of her catatonia and holds Bill close, finally released from her fear. At the end of this remarkable story we are left with the enduring hope that, in the face of our greatest fears, and through the challenges of our deepest terrors, ultimately, love wins.

---

38. Hedges, *Empire of Illusion*, 193.

6

Demons

The Horror of Trust

Promises matter. It's the currency of faith.[1]

—PREACHER

The Flood Story is a remarkable myth that reveals the depths of humanity's fear of chaos, a chaos that threatens to overwhelm us. Water, within ancient mythology, represents our greatest fears, an untamable force that is beyond our control. There are a variety of ancient Flood myths from around the world, represented in a variety of ways by different ancient cultures, yet each one says something remarkably similar: humanity can be overwhelmed by forces beyond itself. The version of the Flood that we have received within the Judaeo-Christian story sits in the early chapters of Genesis. We read of how God regrets creating human beings and so vows to destroy the earth with a global flood and thus cleanse the earth of all wickedness, creating the opportunity for a new beginning, a blank canvas through which God can effectively start again. Before the great deluge we are told of how "the sons of God" saw that the daughters of men were pleasing to the eye and so decided to take them as their wives. These "warriors of renown," heroes of old, are giants living in the land of men. The coming together in sexual activity of giants or gods from the heavens, and human woman, is the ancient fear that

---

1. Jesse Custer, *Preacher*, Season 1, Episode 1, "Pilot," 2016.

forces beyond our control will claim what we believe is rightfully ours (and how much does a patriarchal dominance hierarchy believe that woman are the ownership of men), that our ability to remain in control and that forces beyond us will not consume us into their own image; children born of these divine beings or giants from human woman will mean that children will no longer be "flesh of my flesh" and thus strip us of our male power. So before the flood occurs we have humanity battling with gods for the right to the woman of the earth, and thus the children of the earth are a mixture of human and divine, their fathers those of formidable status and force, violence, and dominance. Humanity is already being wiped out by the gods, all memory of them slowly being erased as these gods take our daughters to bear their children, a sign of our path to destruction as divine beings take our place. Not only that, but God declares that he will no longer "abide" within us, removing his spirit from us, a further sign that our lives will no longer be sustained by the Creator; the end is upon us. The Flood then symbolizes the onset of chaos, the fears of our own mortality and abandonment of God to our own destruction.[2] The "sons of God," these warriors of old, symbolize humanity's descent into chaos that overwhelms our children, our failure to provide for them the beauty of relationship with God and with one another. Humanity is created in the beginning to be in relationship with God, a relationship expressed through their relationship with one another, a relationship of mutual, self-giving love that reflects the Divine Life. Within the evolution of the God–Human story, humanity seeks power beyond its creaturely capacity, a power to forcefully take divine status upon itself and so become "sons of God" by force—ancient warriors who believe in their own violent power to climb to the heavens and take the place of God.

Within the early chapters of Genesis, humanity and God walk together in the Garden of the created order, a harmonious relationship of love where humanity fully recognizes the gift of life given to them, seeking to care for and tend to the world for their own flourishing and the betterment of the created reality. Not only this, but humanity is, by the natural[3] order of

2. There are passages in the Bible, such as the Flood story, that can be read as God committing mass genocide, or commanding others to commit such an act on his behalf. It is impossible to devise a morally good ethic that justifies genocide, it simply does not exist. Genocide is always pure evil. Therefore, any passages in the Bible where "God" commands genocide are morally evil within any interpretive lens, and so need to be named as such. You simply cannot say that the God revealed by Jesus of Nazareth is the same as the god who commands genocide. However, there is no need to throw those passages out of the Bible for it tells us something about what humanity is like (and the ways we make God in our own image), and there is a need to read these passages honestly, intelligently, and in light of who Jesus is.

3. By "natural" I mean that which is God's cosmic desire for all of creation, the way things are being called to become in and through the Son.

things, created to grow into divinity, created for the journey toward its goal in Christ, created to eventually become fully and truly human in and through the Eternal Son. The rupture in this journey of relationship happens through humanity's insistence that we can, within our own strength and capabilities, reach our divine potential. Chaos thus looms large as all that we think we are is fractured as we can no longer clearly see our true image, and so the descent into violence ensues as we forcefully seek to claim that which is not ours. The Flood story is our ongoing desire to violently become "sons of God"; it is the story of our never-ending quest for power. Whereas in relationship with God we are shown what it looks like to be truly human, and how power is actually defined, in that rupture of relationship we become overwhelmed with our desires for power and violence, believing that through our own strength we can be masters of all things. The Flood represents our descent into violent chaos, completely submerged within our own power struggles that defeat us as we implode in upon ourselves. All of this that I have said serves as an introduction to the fundamental theme and insight that demons represent to us within popular culture; the power of chaos and the fear of trust. Demons bring fear for they represent our inability to be in control; they represent a chaos of flood-like proportions, and it is this revelation, symbolism, and depth within demonic stories that we will explore together.

Argument for God

When *The Exorcist* was released in cinemas in December 1973, it caused a shockwave due to the subject matter and the intensity of the horror it was depicting. Critics argued that there had never been anything like this on the screen before, a film of pure terror that was sure to disturb and profoundly scare cinema audiences. And indeed it did according to the stories of people fainting, vomiting, and crying upon seeing the film for themselves. Arguably, *The Exorcist* was the birth of the modern horror movie, providing a shock factor that both wowed and repulsed movie-goers in equal measure, resulting in queues of people winding around the block in order that they might get to see this controversial phenomenon. Renowned critic Roger Ebert gave the film four stars out of four, but described the experience of seeing the film as a raw and painful experience, that through it we feel "shock, horror, nausea, fear, and some small measure of dogged hope" and wondered why people would actually want to go and see it,

Are people so numb they need movies of this intensity in order
to feel anything at all? It's hard to say.[4]

The book that the film was based on, by William Peter Blatty, had gained a
significant reputation with tales of people so frightened by it that they kept
it in separate parts of the house. For Blatty, the novel was a work of theology, an expression of his own Catholic faith and beliefs: "It's an argument
for God . . . I intended it to be an apostolic work, to help people in their
faith. Because I thoroughly believed in the authenticity and validity of that
particular event."[5]

The Exorcist tells the story of 12-year-old Regan MacNeil, who starts
displaying strange behavior after playing with a Ouija board and making
friends with "Captain Howdy." Regan's physical and psychological health
rapidly deteriorate and her mother, Chris, takes Regan to be examined
by doctors and psychologists in order to try and find the reasons behind
her daughter's disturbing behavior. Eventually Chris seeks the help of local troubled priest Father Damien Karras, a sceptic who resists the idea of
demonic possession:

What's the answer then? Genuine possession? A demon? He
looked down and shook his head. No way. No way. Paranormal
happenings? Sure. Why not? Too many competent observers
had reported them. Doctors. Psychiatrists . . . But the problem is
how do you interpret the phenomena?[6]

Karras, although shocked by the physical appearance and unexplainable
abilities and knowledge of Regan, refuses to believe that she is possessed by
a demonic force and continues to appeal to his own skepticism, scientific
faith, and psychiatric training. As Sara Gran's novel Come Closer highlights,
there is, at times, an intriguing balance between the psychological and supernatural, with the story's main protagonist, Amanda, seemingly accepting
of her spiral into the outrageous and destructive behavior she is engaged in,
unaware or perhaps embracing the demonic force that now grips her. This
theme of accepting the cause of demonic possession as opposed to rational, medical explanations is also explored in the 2005 film The Exorcism of
Emily Rose, where we encounter a priest on trial for the negligent death of
nineteen-year-old Emily Rose after performing an exorcism on her. And
while Karras is uncertain, he eventually concludes that the only hope to

4. http://www.rogerebert.com/reviews/the-exorcist-1973.

5. https://www.washingtonian.com/2015/10/19/think-the-exorcist-was-just-a-
horror-movie-author-william-peter-blatty-says-youre-wrong/.

6. Blatty, Exorcist, 214.

find a cure for Regan would be to perform an exorcism, even though he
continues to be racked with doubt,

> 'You're convinced it's genuine?' the Bishop asked finally.
> 'I've made a prudent judgment that it meets the conditions
> set forth in the Ritual,' answered Karras evasively. He still did
> not dare believe. Not his mind but his heart tugged him to this
> moment; pity and the hope for a cure though suggestion.[7]

Karras is not allowed to go and perform the exorcism on his own, and the
diocese enlist the help of Father Merrin. We encounter Merrin at the beginning of the book on a dig in Iraq where he becomes aware of an impending
battle where he would soon "face an ancient enemy."[8] Karras finds himself
in awe of the authority of the old Merrin, the way Merrin speaks with such
power to the demon and at the same time has a deep compassion and gentle-
ness toward those gathered, and to Regan herself, who has been completely
consumed by this demonic evil.

As the exorcism takes place, Karras becomes convinced of Regan's predicament, convinced in part by Merrin's certainty that what is taking place is
an ancient evil, a demon he has "met once before," a demon who is "powerful," a form of demonic chaos with no purpose other than destruction.

> I think the point is to make us despair; to reject our own human-
> ity . . . as ultimately vile and putrescent; without dignity; ugly;
> unworthy. And there lies the heart of it, perhaps; in unworthi-
> ness. For I think belief in God is not a matter of reason at all; I
> think it finally is a matter of love; of accepting the possibility
> that God could love us . . .[9]

Although receiving mixed reviews from critics and a poor performance in
the box office, this despair and rejection of humanity is key to the film *Fall-
en*, starring Denzel Washington. As a story it provides an interesting take on
the demonic genre, proposing that the demon Azazel can move from person
to person by "jumping" or through touch, but has to enter another person
within the space of a single breath or it will die. What this means is that the
usual acts of exorcism whereby human touch (a sign of the cross is placed
upon the forehead of the victim for instance) is excluded, so John (Washington's character) purposely allows himself to become possessed by Azazel,
and then, through the previous drinking of poison, kills himself while alone
in order to end the demon's existence. The story within *Fallen*, as a concept,

7. Blatty, *Exorcist*, 262.

8. Blatty, *Exorcist*, 17.

9. Blatty, *Exorcist*, 293.

is remarkable for it speaks directly into the heart of that which will destroy us: the lack of human contact. We are relational beings, and *Fallen* is the horror of the removal of human touch, the interaction we have face to face. John's death at the end symbolizes the evil of aloneness, the felt need to "separate people out" to end evil, and yet this is the very heart of evil; it is not good for us to be on our own. In the Gospel of Mark we encounter the man, chained to rocks, cut and scarred through self-harm, excluded from the community, possessed by Legion.[10] This demoniac lives alone, tormented night and day, screaming in agony through the mental, emotional, spiritual, and physical pain he endures. His condition is the condition of one who has been abandoned by the community, whose very humanity is taken from him because to be human is to be in relationship, to be in community, to be loved and known in that love. Demonic possession frightens us because that is what it does—it threatens our basic humanness, our capacity for love, and our inability to be in control, to live out of control.

When Father Merrin walks into the room of Regan MacNeil we, the reader and viewer, encounter a child who is enduring this very same agony as described in the gospels, a child tortured by an unseen malevolence, sub-jugated by degradation and humiliation on levels that shock us to the very depths of our soul. The scene in both the book and the film that left many reeling was when Regan's mother walks into her daughter's bedroom and is confronted with her daughter poised over a crucifix, the demon just about to force her to masturbate with it. Chris is unable to stop the demon from this act of total abuse and humiliation, screaming and crying and begging for the evil to stop while the demon laughs and jeers, causing suffering and pain on a level of untold consequences. This horrific scene should not be dismissed as an episode of pure "torture porn" or crass and unnecessary vileness. Rather, it is an insightful and almost prophetic understanding of childhood and the way our culture treats children, of the way they are sexualized within the media, of the abuse they have endured from priests and religious people in power, from authorities, both ecclesiastical and state, abuse that can only be described as demonic. The victims and survivors of abuse need to have their voices heard, their stories told. There needs to be an end to the continual covering up of the abuse that has happened behind the doors of government buildings and within church walls and children's homes. This horrific scene in *The Exorcist* is the uncovering, the exposing of the demonic abuse that has happened to our children and continues to happen, and we all have a duty to do all that we can to protect our children today, to do all that we can to expose the abusers and bring them to justice. Jesus' words to us all as to the severity of judgment

---

10. "My name is Legion, because we are many." Mark 5:9b.

against those who hurt children should sober us up to how God feels about abuse: "Better for him that a millstone be placed around his neck and he be thrown into the sea rather than that he should cause one of these little ones to falter" (Luke 17:2).

The innocence of children is something of immense importance for the health of our society. Our children reveal our need to trust, to learn how to trust again, to be assured of our relationships with others, to be vulnerable and *believe* in the people that we commit our lives to, that they do love us, and that their desire for us is good. This is a powerful message for adults, for in the lives of children, in their innocence, in their ability to trust, in their authentic speech, we enter the Kingdom of heaven, "Amen, I tell you, unless you turn back and become as children, you most certainly may not enter into the Kingdom of the heavens" (Matt 18:3). To trust God is ultimate vulnerability, for we commit ourselves to live out of control, the very thing that horrifies us by demonic possession! However, to live out of control with God, to be in that place of trust with God, is to be assured that God's ultimate desire for us is our good because God has ordained all things to one day reach their *telos*, namely God, the source and Ultimate Good. Demonic possession is to be out of control for the purpose of our destruction, shame, and humiliation. To live "out of control" runs very much against modern people in the West. Humanity has become the master of many things, able to adapt and change, reinvent, and solve the complexities of our survival throughout the centuries. Our technological advancement has created the illusion of our approach to immortality, so much so that trans-humanists believe that one day we will solve the decay of life through technological advancement. Now of course many people would not think of themselves as trans-humanists (although, as a system of belief, it is growing), but, certainly in the West, our belief in our capabilities to "overcome" knows no limit, hence why we are continually shocked by death. This becomes all too apparent when a celebrity dies, for in that moment we are confronted with the truth that, regardless of wealth and status, everyone dies. In many ways we seek to shield ourselves from this truth by using language that does not speak of death but merely a transference to another place: passing on, loss of loved ones, gone to heaven. It is painful for us to recognize our own frailty, inabilities, and woundedness. In the United Kingdom, in 2016, Frank Sinatra's "My Way" was the most popular song played at funerals, further embedding the idea that we are the ultimate masters of our destiny, and that no matter what, we did it our way. In honesty, however, we are buffeted around in life according to the people and circumstances we find ourselves in. True freedom is a myth in that every decision we make is determined and influenced by factors beyond our control. We are the people that we are because of the people in our lives, and the lives we have lived, and the lives they have lived, and the lives of all those that have lived before us. We discover that we are located in the time and space that we are in, and out of that time and space and circumstances we make decisions, and build relationships, and make mistakes, and share in joy, and laugh, and change, and discover. Our lives are enriched when we recognize the impact upon us that others have, and so are able to understand our own place within our communities as a response to what and who has gone before us. For any of us to say "I did it my way" is pure fantasy. There will always be situations beyond our control that leave us shocked and bemused, unable to think or act in any real way, but rather leave us simply falling.[11] To speak in such ways of doing things "my way," is the belief that we can be masters of our own destiny, masters of the seemingly uncontrollable, much like King Canute (Cnut). The important thing to recognize about Canute's story is not the misinterpreted belief of a king's ego, but that, in the recognition that he could not stop the tide, he never again wore his crown.

> And then he spoke to the rising sea saying "You are part of my dominion, and the ground that I am seated upon is mine, nor has anyone disobeyed my orders with impunity. Therefore, I order you not to rise onto my land, nor to wet the clothes or body of your Lord". But the sea carried on rising as usual without any reverence for his person, and soaked his feet and legs. Then he moving away said: "All the inhabitants of the world should know that the power of kings is vain and trivial, and that none is worthy the name of king but He by whose command the heaven, earth and sea obey by eternal laws". Therefore King Cnut never afterwards placed the crown on his head, but above a picture of

11. During 2017 there were natural disasters across the planet that wrought devastation and destruction on a massive scale, a destruction that killed and ruined lives of people in various places, with many of those people living in poverty, a poverty increased and furthered by these terrible events. The destruction of the lives of these people is on a level that no one knows how to deal with, that leaves us feeling like we are falling and failing, and so much more could be done in order to help them in their suffering. But equally, such disasters highlight how powerless we are in the face of such natural power, how utterly helpless we can be. Our approach to global warming in the West is lukewarm as we continue to bow our knee to the oil companies, allowing them to dictate the terms of our carbon footprint and the pursuit of alternative modes of energy in a world struggling to breathe through the cloud of emissions and the increase in global temperature. In a world that is so dependent upon oil, a dependence that spreads into every conceivable realm of our modern life, governments know that the oil companies hold the power and what they demand is bowed to. The United States and United Kingdom governments could do so much more to pursue sustainable and cheaper energy for their citizens, but the lobbying power of oil companies mean that this is always going to be unlikely.

the Lord nailed to the cross, turning it forever into a means to praise God, the great king.[12]

For Cnut the episode with the tide brought the revelation that he was not in control, that there existed a greater power beyond him that he was unable to tame or bring to his own will. As a result of this revelation, Cnut took off his crown and placed above his throne the Crucified Jesus, a sign of who Cnut believed to be King, Ruler, and the One where all power lay. To modern ears this may seem a strange, and naive story, an example of how backwards, uninformed, and superstitious earlier people were, but in actuality Cnut's story is remarkably perceptive, exposing a common thread throughout the human story, a thread that finds itself woven into our own modern lives and experiences. You see, for the modern we have become accustomed to our own crowns, the belief in our superior place within the universe, the certainty that we rule our own dominion, that where we stand we rule—or to put it slightly differently, that we have our own little kingdom, the space that we inhabit as a human being at any given time is our own ruled space, and the rights of our own ruled space is ours and no one else's. This hyper-individualism pervades our societies, whereby we have, as modern Western people, forgotten the interconnectedness of our humanity, making it very difficult to understand or interpret cultures and texts that speak in the plurality of "you" rather than the individuality of "you." We, in the sense of the individual "I," become convinced that we are the masters of our destiny, the rulers of our own dominion, the ones who are seated on the throne of our own lives, seeking subjects to rule over. But as we are all aware, the tide continues to come in, a force beyond our control, unable to be stopped or commanded by us. Circumstances and situations arise that highlight our inability to control everything, the recognition that we are not in control, and therefore it demands from us a response. Now we could stay on the throne of our own lives, continue to grasp the crown on our heads, and shout and command the tide to turn and to retreat, resulting, in all likelihood, finding ourselves out of our depth, consumed by the waves that are beyond our control.

My family trade is as an oyster fisherman, a trade that my own family has been working since 1732 in and around the creeks of Mersea Island in Essex, UK. When I began working for my father I became the eighth-generation oyster farmer in my family, and I became aware very quickly how little I knew about the trade that is part of what it means to be a Haward on Mersea Island. I remember my father telling me to never get complacent and believe that I have learned everything I need to know about the sea and

12. https://faculty.history.wisc.edu/sommerville/123/Canute%20Waves.htm.

working on the water. He told me that there will always be something new to learn, something that will surprise you, something that will frighten you, something that will remind you that you are never the one in control. Little did I know back then that my father was training me in theology, showing me through the grit, hard work, and wisdom he had accumulated, not only in his lifetime but a knowledge he had acquired through the passing on from one generation to the next, that to live out of control is a deeply theological task, indeed, it is a deeply gospel-oriented Way of living. When my father and I were out on the water we had to be fully aware of what the tide was doing, how it was "behaving" on any given day. We would go out on the water with our own expectations, and yet often our expectations would be confounded as the tide behaved in ways, sometimes subtle, that we were not expecting, perhaps because of the wind or the air pressure. Now that did not mean we were then in trouble, because my father had learned to "expect the unexpected," to be aware of the reality that the tide will do whatever it wants to do regardless of your own expectations. Now we always knew that the tide would rise and fall, that at some point it would reach its lowest point on that particular day, turn, and then rise again. And we knew roughly the time it would reach that low point and begin to turn and rise again, yet we also were aware that sometimes the tide would go lower than we thought it would, stay lower for longer than anticipated, or perhaps surge faster than we expected. The key thing in all of this was that we were never in control of the tide. We were consistently working with the tide to do our job, but always at the mercy of its ebb and flow. When we dredged for oysters we always had to have an eye on the horizon to make sure, when sailing against the tide, we were actually moving forwards, because the water can be deceptive on the eyes whereby you think you are going ahead, whereas you are actually static. The landscape gave you the vision to see if the boat was moving as you wanted it to, so whatever the tide was doing we sought to work with it to ensure we caught our oysters. This is the work of theology, the recognition that we are not the ones in control, that the tide, or rather the Spirit, "will blow where She pleases," our task is to be aware and respond in humility to the One who is in control.

And herein lies the power of *The Exorcist* as a story, as a work of theology, as a commentary on the human condition; at the end of the story Father Karras places his trust in God, not in his own power, to deliver Reagan from this power of evil that had overwhelmed her and is destroying her. This is a frightening thing to do, to believe that there is One beyond us far more capable and trustworthy than anything we could ever create with our own hands and minds, and to place our trust in this One, to live "out of control" and believe that whatever happens nothing will ever separate us from this great Love. This One who is in control, according to the gospel story, is One who dies on a cross, whose life is exemplified by trust in God, in acts of radical forgiveness, in serving others; God's control is to live in the risk of servant love, to place others before you and show them how God's love was manifest in the person of Jesus. This was Father Karras's great final act, the giving of his life, the willingness to be consumed by the evil that held that young child, to take that evil into his own self, and then die so that she could live. This is what Jesus did, an act of absorbing the fullness of evil, taking into himself the powers of sin, violence, and death, in order that we could live. Demonic stories are the horror of being out of control, the horror of being consumed by that which takes our lives and does whatever it wants with them *in order to destroy us*. Read through every encounter Jesus has with demons, or any modern text of demonic possession, and each time we find the human person being destroyed, their identity taken from them, the heart of their very humanness violated and crushed; it is to be out of control that in turn rips trust away from us, rips our ability to trust from us. In *The Devil's Advocate*, Mary Ann (played by Charlize Theron) spirals into despair and paranoia as trust is ripped from her through demonic forces. Her very humanity is taken from her as all control is taken from her, for the sake of her very destruction. Jesus, near the end of his life, tells his disciples to trust him, and in trusting him they will know the divine life that Jesus embodies, a life that is from God, a life that reveals our true humanity, a humanity that will result in our flourishing, a life that, although trouble will come, will know that God has not abandoned us, that we are loved. At its very heart *The Exorcist* is a story about redemptive love, a love that is "out of control" because it trusts, not in our own strength, but in the strength of the One who is Love.

7

Aliens

The Horror of Weakness

Mara: If we coexist, we shall dominate you. That is inevitable . . .

Dr. Alan Chaffee: That's a cruel sport.

Mara: Life is cruelty. We all feed on each other, exploit each other in some way to survive.

Dr. Alan Chaffee: I don't agree with you. I think that adaptation is the key to survival. Cooperation and symbiosis, and compassion.

Mara: Why do you think your own survival depends upon emotion from us? Should we pity you?[1]

—*VILLAGE OF THE DAMNED* (1995)

THE STORY OF PANDORA'S Box is said to begin with Prometheus, versions of which appear in various myths and legends. The detail that unites all the tales of Prometheus is that he is given the task (the gift, some versions call it) of populating the Earth with life. Prometheus, who is known as the god of foresight, is believed to have created the first humans, while his brother, Epimetheus, known as the god of hindsight, is said to have

1. *Village of the Damned*, John Carpenter, Universal Pictures, 1995.

88

made all the other creatures. Severely lacking his brother's gift for anticipation, Epimetheus is said to have hastily given away all the wondrous qualities available to populate the planet with—qualities like speed, flight, and
beastly strength—to his creatures, leaving none for the humanity created
by his brother. Prometheus, then, is said to have stolen fire from Zeus—the
god who had assigned the brothers the task of populating the planet—by
lighting a torch from the sun, and offered, with his torch, the wonder of fire
to the humans he so loved. This he did to the rage of Zeus, who had wished
and warned Prometheus to keep fire a secret of the gods. An enraged Zeus
then chained Prometheus in unbreakable fetters and had an eagle devour
his liver each day, leaving him in eternal pain as his liver grew back each
night. Zeus declares,

> But I will give men as the price for fire an evil thing in which
> they may all be glad of heart while they embrace their own
> destruction.[2]

Seeking to punish the humans for accepting the stolen offering of fire, Zeus
then had the first woman created, called her Pandora, and sent her off with
gifts from the various gods (gifts of beauty, health, cunning, dexterity, and
musical talent) to Earth so that she could entice and marry Epimetheus,

> So he ordered. And they obeyed the lord Zeus the son of Cronos.
> Forthwith the famous Lame God moulded clay in the likeness
> of a modest maid, as the son of Cronos purposed. And the god-
> dess bright-eyed Athene girded and clothed her, and the divine
> Graces and queenly Persuasion put necklaces of gold upon her,
> and the rich-haired Hours crowned her head with spring flow-
> ers. And Pallas Athene bedecked her form with all manners of
> finery. Also the Guide, the Slayer of Argus, contrived within her
> lies and crafty words and a deceitful nature at the will of loud
> thundering Zeus, and the Herald of the gods put speech in her.
> And he called this woman Pandora . . .[3]

Despite his suspicion of Zeus's creation and gift, Epimetheus fell immedi-
ately in love with Pandora, and asked to marry her. It was then that Zeus
gifted Pandora a box, or more accurately, a large jar, as a wedding present,
but instructed her never to open it. Epimetheus would ensure this, by keeping the key to the box with him at all times. But one day, while Epimetheus
was asleep, Pandora is believed to have given in to her curiosity[4] and stole

2. http://www.theoi.com/Text/HesiodWorksDays.html#Pandora.

3. http://www.theoi.com/Text/HesiodWorksDays.html#Pandora, lines 69–82.

4. Has not humanity always been curious? Is this not part of the way we have

the key from her husband, to finally open the box. As she did, out came the terrifying evils of greed, envy, hatred, pain, disease, hunger, poverty, war, and death. Before she could quickly shut them back in, the evil spirits went off and about to plague mankind, leaving her with regret far deeper than her curiosity had been,

> For ere this the tribes of men lived on earth remote and free from ills and hard toil and heavy sickness which bring the Fates upon men; for in misery men grow old quickly. But the woman took off the great lid of the jar with her hands and scattered all these and her thought caused sorrow and mischief to men.[5]

Desire is a powerful thing, and in our desires we can unleash upon ourselves and others great good, but also great suffering. Alien films often revolve around desire, the belief that what has been unopened, what has, as yet, been unexplored, needs the lid taken off so that we might discover the unknown that we have been missing. This is why the story of Pandora resonates with us so deeply, and why films and stories of uncharted planets, of newly discovered life forms intrigue and fascinate us, for we hope that in the discovery of the new we will discover something new about ourselves. The *Alien* films are a particularly powerful example of this, of our desire to lift the lid off Pandora's box, but even more significantly, to find in the hidden corners of the universe the secrets of our own humanity.

Brutal Awareness

Alien has endured as a film for its remarkable themes, genuine tension, and powerful female lead. The story, for those unaware, follows the crew of *Nostromo*, a commercial spaceship returning to Earth. The ship's computer, Mother, wakes the crew of seven out of stasis when an unusual signal is detected on a nearby planet. They go to the planet to investigate and discover a crashed spacecraft with the remains of a dead alien whose rib cage has exploded from the inside. One of the crew members, Kane, discovers a room filled with what appear to be eggs. Upon touching one of the eggs it opens and a creature jumps out of the egg and attaches itself to his face. When they get Kane back on board they discover that this "facehugger" has covered his entire face, wrapping a tail around his neck, and filling his throat with another long member:

---

discovered new stars, built Empires, pursued love?

5. http://www.theoi.com/Text/HesiodWorksDays.html#Pandora, lines 67–69.

The Facehugger secures its eight finger-like appendages tightly
around the head of its victim and wraps its tail tightly around
the host's neck, eliciting a gasping response and allowing the
insertion of an ovipositor into the host's esophagus.[6]

Later in the film we discover that "the company," that is, Weyland-Yutani
Corporation, knew of the existence of the alien creature and sought to
bring it to earth in order to study it because it is believed to be the "perfect
organism." According to the company, the capture of, what they call the
Xenomorph XX121, is in order to dissect it, understand it, and use that
knowledge to create weapons that would enable humanity to continue to be
the dominant species in the universe.

It makes sense to interpret *Alien* in light of Pandora's story; the egg is
Pandora's box and the opening of desire. We could interpret this mythological story sexually and understand Pandora's box as her virginity, the key as
Epimetheus's penis, and therefore the opening of the box as the beginning
of human sexuality, the conscious awareness of sex and lust, the awakening
that the human species went through whereby sex was no longer simply an
act of reproduction, and dominance hierarchy, but an act that engaged our
consciousness—a means through which we discovered our humanity, our
self-awareness, and the fear and anxiety that self-awareness brings with it.
Notice in Genesis how the first humans, in eating the fruit of the tree, have
their eyes opened and see their own and each other's nakedness. This sexual
self-awareness is something that differentiates us from all other animals,
for in the act of sex we find pleasure and enjoyment, but also the ability to
cause harm, to exert power, and to discover ourselves. Now that is not to
say that sex is the goal of our humanity, or that, as Freud believed, it is all
about sex, but it is to say that sex can be something beautiful that enables
us to encounter not only something remarkable about ourselves, not only
something remarkable about the person that we love, but also something
remarkable about God,

> . . . sexual desire and the desire for God is a "messy entangle-
> ment." All desire, no matter how godless or wayward, springs
> forth from a desire for God, a longing for relationship and
> friendship with the Trinitarian Life. Our desires are always a
> search, a reaching out to become truly human, to know we are
> loved and have been discovered by our Creator.[7]

---

6. http://aliens.wikia.com/wiki/Facehugger, lines 9–13.

7. Haward, *Ghost of Perfection*, 100.

In our sexual desire we are awakened to the other, and in that desire we can be overwhelmed by them, and by our desire for them. Herein lies the challenge with all desire within creation, in that our longing for someone or something can become a means of idolatry, that which consumes us until we are satisfied, and yet, in the initial satisfaction of that longing we encounter the return of that desire; overwhelming desire can never be satisfied, and this is one of the great challenges to our humanity. Pornography, consumerism, adrenaline rushes, and drugs are but an example of how powerful desire is upon us, both physically, but also psychologically, spiritually, and emotionally. Such is the power of desire upon us, chemicals in our brains are released in order that we respond to those desires, something in of itself that is no bad thing, for these desires have enabled us to survive and thrive as a species since our emergence upon this planet.

Our brains have what is called a reward system, made up of three different regions, connected to what is called the *mesolimbic dopamine pathway*. These three areas, called the *amygdala* (for positive and negative emotions, emotional memory), the *hippocampus* (for processing and retrieval of long-term memories), and the *frontal cortex* (coordinates and determines behavior), make up the reward system pathway along with the other connecting regions and control many things including memory, pleasure, and motivation. Sex and eating activate the reward center, and this is a good thing for it has enabled the behaviors we need in order to survive. Addiction, then, moves from those impulsive actions that enable us to survive and are based on positive reinforcement (i.e., eating properly makes us feel better physically and emotionally, and provides us with the energy we need to function well), to compulsive behavior that is learned through negative reinforcement (i.e., the gambling addict who cannot control winning or losing money, and no longer feels able to function unless placing bets). There are three stages to addiction:

1. Binge/intoxication

2. Withdrawal/negative affect

3. Preoccupation/anticipation

Depending on the drug, the reward system is activated differently, but the universal result is a flood of dopamine into the reward center of our brain. As a result, we desire to reinforce the behavior that initiated the flood of dopamine, a chemical in our brains that provides us with feelings of pleasure and reward. What then follows is something called the *acute positive reinforcement of the behavior* that initiated the flood that leads into the impulsive stage, resulting in addictive-related learning associations as the continued release of dopamine into the reward center leads to an increase in dynorphin levels, leading to a decrease in the function of the reward system, resulting in a decrease of the reward threshold and an increase in tolerance.

In stage two, the "withdrawal/negative affect," the dopamine flood is over, the area of our brain associated with fear and pain management is activated, and we are thrown into a negative emotional state that our bodies need to deal with—and so kicks in our brain's anti-stress function, but our sensitivity to the reward has been compromised. So, we increase the behaviors associated with the initial reward hit to avoid the negative effects of withdrawal, and thus find ourselves engaged in the cycle of addictive behavior, a shift from impulsive to compulsive. This impact is universal regardless of the specific addiction. While different drugs will physiologically affect the person in different ways when in the state of withdrawal, the "withdrawal/ negative affect" is to do with how addiction to anything impacts the brain; withdrawal and detoxification are not one and the same thing. Aversive emotions such as anxiety, depression, dysphoria, and irritability are indicators of withdrawal in this model of addiction.

This then leads to stage three of craving or "preoccupation/anticipation." The area of our brains responsible for motivation, self-control, delayed reward discounting, and other cognitive functions are impaired and damaged, resulting in the increase of learned drug-related cues, and the deficiency of our top-down inhibitory control; in other words, our brains and our bodies become obsessed by the addiction, and we become entirely motivated by the stress of not satisfying the addiction and the satisfaction of that addiction. Recent studies have found that there is consistent overlap between drug-related addictions and internet addiction, such as gaming, pornography, and shopping. Studies carried out with those who are addicted to heroin found that there is poor functional connectivity between the right caudate and left dorsolateral prefrontal cortex area of the brain, the area most associated with memory and attention. Recent research suggests that the same poor functional connectivity exists with those addicted to internet pornography. These studies also indicate that when someone is addicted to internet gaming certain pathways in their brains are triggered in the same intensity and directness as when someone is addicted to drugs.[8] And this pursuit of relief and reward seen within addictive behavior crosses over into many areas of modern life. Our desires are a powerful thing, so powerful that once pursued we can change the very way our brains operate and function. This is why Pandora's story is a remarkable ancient tale, highlighting the power desire has upon us.

8. For more on addiction and the brain, see https://www.ncbi.nlm.nih.gov/pmc/articles/PMC2238694/.

Desire

In Clive Barker's 1987 film *Hellraiser*, we are introduced to characters for whom pleasure and pain have become indistinguishable. The film follows the story of Frank Cotton, who buys a puzzle box from a dealer in Morocco. Returning home, he discovers how to solve the puzzle and open the box, unwittingly opening a portal to a hell-like dimension, resulting in his death. Sometime later the house becomes inhabited again by Frank's brother Larry and his second wife, Julia. As the film unfolds Frank partially returns from the other realm in need of resurrection through the blood of others. We discover, through Frank, that his pursuit and opening of the puzzle box was the pursuit for unrealized desires, desires he felt only another dimension could offer what he was after. Monsters from the other realm enter earth through the portal of the puzzle box, monsters who have lost all ability to differentiate between pleasure and pain, resulting in demonic creatures of terror. Now all of this sounds horrific, but it does enable us to interpret modern life to some degree, in that if we pursue, at all costs, our desires—desires sought regardless of the consequences, sought for the reward, relief and satisfaction they bring—then we open the door to destruction and will lose all perspective of own humanity and the humanity of others. Indeed, the horrific pursuit of our compulsive desires will tear us apart. It is another version of Pandora's Box, a mythic story that reveals the danger of a humanity that pursues its desires at all costs. *Alien*, although told differently, follows the same premise, in that for "the company" the alien creature is Pandora's box, something of desire that must be obtained and opened regardless of the cost to life.

> *Ripley*: Ash, can you hear me?
>
> [slams her hands down on the table]
>
> *Ripley*: Ash?
>
> *Ash*: [awakens and starts speaking in an electronic and distorted voice] Yes, I can hear you.
>
> *Ripley*: What was your special order?
>
> *Ash*: You read it. I thought it was clear.
>
> *Ripley*: What was it?
>
> *Ash*: Bring back life form. Priority One. All other priorities rescinded.
>
> *Parker*: The damn company. What about our lives, you son of a bitch?
>
> *Ash*: I repeat, all other priorities are rescinded.
>
> *Ripley*: How do we kill it, Ash? There's gotta be a way of killing it. How? How do we do it?
>
> *Ash*: You can't.

Parker: That's bullshit.

Ash: You still don't understand what you're dealing with, do you? The perfect organism. Its structural perfection is matched only by its hostility.

Lambert: You admire it.

Ash: I admire its purity. A survivor . . . unclouded by conscience, remorse, or delusions of morality.

Parker: Look, I am . . . I've heard enough of this, and I'm asking you to pull the plug.

[Ripley goes to disconnect Ash, who interrupts]

Ash: Last word.

Ripley: What?

Ash: I can't lie to you about your chances, but . . . you have my sympathies.[9]

The arrival of the Xenomorph on *Nostromo* is the unleashing of the contents of Pandora's box. Humanity is confronted with its frailty, and the arrival of something far greater and more powerful than itself, something that cannot be stopped, controlled, or reasoned with. After the Facehugger has detached itself from Kane, all appears to be well, until the baby Xenomorph explodes out of Kane's chest, a sign and symbol of hope disappearing, of humanity's inability to stop destruction, of the very core of who we think we are—in control, death deniers, the most powerful—destroyed from the inside out. Within the *Alien* universe we are confronted with a monster that seeks to ravage and destroy our identity, taking from us that which makes us human and utterly annihilating it from existence. The Facehugger removes our reflection, our face consumed by a monster that is slowly growing and incubating an identity within us that will kill us. The chest-burster that emerges from within us symbolizes the horror of our identity ripped from us, the ability for compassion removed, our capacity for evil released out from within us into the world around us. The Communist Soviet Union exposed the depth of humanity's capacity for evil bursting out from within us, unshackled from human identity; as the Facehugger masks the face of the victim, so Utopianism like that pursued within the communist Soviet State removes all human identity and replaces it with ideology, a way of being that requires total allegiance and complete sacrifice of identity in order to ensure its success. What emerges is a monster out from the hearts of all who follow its siren's call, a monster that simply needs to feed in order to survive, no compassion or empathy, entirely devoted to its desire. The contents of

Pandora's box have burst out of our chest and reach out across the globe. We are a people in the West whose hearts have exploded to the appeal of the box, whose desire for what is in the box is so powerful that we will do all that we can to ensure its survival. And in many ways, we call out to a god who will rescue us, who is powerful enough to save us from the crisis that looms; we seek a *deus ex machina*, much like a Schwarzenegger character who appears just in time to save us from certain death.

Messiah in an Exosuit

Ellen Ripley is a classic *deus ex machina* character. She consistently appears throughout the *Alien* franchise as the hero who rescues just at the last moment when all hope seems to be lost, perhaps most iconically with the "get away from her, you bitch" line, rescuing the young girl Newt from the Queen Alien who is sure to kill her. Ripley appears, clothed in an exosuit, and battles the Queen, eventually casting it out into space through an open airlock. Ripley's power is her character, her loyalty, her strength, and her determination to defeat the powers of evil, an evil epitomized by the alien creature and Weyland-Yutani Corporation. When Ripley walks through the hangar doors to rescue Newt, it is a classic Gnostic–Messianic scene: the human Ripley clothed in an outer suit, taking on the power of divinity, the power to defeat evil previously unavailable to her in her purely human form. The exosuit gives her the divine power, the power of the great Other that she needs to rescue the young girl who is certainly going to die at the hands of evil without Ripley's help, who is the model *deus ex machina* in this scene. Within church history the belief of *Adoptionism* and its variants was condemned as heresy at various points in her history, a belief that held Jesus to be born merely and only as a man (although in remarkable circumstances) and then to subsequently become divine at a later point in his life, either at his baptism or at his resurrection. Hippolytus of Rome (c. 170–c. 235) contended,

> . . . there was a certain Theodotus, a native of Byzantium, who introduced a novel heresy. He announces tenets concerning the originating cause of the universe, which are partly in keeping with the doctrines of the true Church, in so far as he acknowledges that all things were created by God. Forcibly appropriating, however, (his notions of) Christ from the school of the Gnostics, and of Cerinthus and Ebion, he alleges that (our Lord) appeared in some such manner as I shall now describe. (According to this, Theodotus maintains) that Jesus was a (mere) man, born of a virgin, according to the counsel of the Father,

and that after he had lived promiscuously with all men, and had
become pre-eminently religious, he subsequently at his baptism
in Jordan received Christ, who came from above and descended
(upon him) in form of a dove. And this was the reason, (according to Theodotus,) why (miraculous) powers did not operate within him prior to the manifestation in him of that Spirit
which descended, (and) which proclaims him to be the Christ.
But (among the followers of Theodotus) some are disposed (to
think) that never was this man made God, (even) at the descent
of the Spirit; whereas others (maintain that he was made God)
after the resurrection from the dead.[10]

All that we have of Theodotus and his theological beliefs is what Hippolytus
tells us of him, and so we need to tread carefully (how many of our oppo-
nents accurately and fairly frame our belief system?), but in terms of a theological position, we can confidently explore it, even if we cannot confidently
understand the person who allegedly gave us this position!

Jesus, according to Adoptionism, *became divine* through radical obedience to the will of God, someone of such character and a life of sinless
devotion to God, earned the status Son of God, adopted by God into this
supreme divine Life. Jesus receives the Holy Spirit and is clothed in the
Christ, becoming someone of miraculous power, able to cast out demons,
heal the sick, raise the dead, and thwart the powers of evil. We should say
then that *the human Jesus thus takes upon himself the Christ exosuit.* Ripley
portrays this early belief system of the hero who, through obedience to
the great Other (and in Ripley's case, the great Other is the human spirit
and the belief in loyalty at all costs), is clothed in power to defeat the
forces of evil and rescue humanity. Ripley represents the messianic *deus
ex machina,* the god who rescues humanity when all hope is lost, when it
would appear that evil has conquered and that there is no way out. When
Ripley walks through the doors dressed in the exosuit, it is a powerfully
symbolic representation of the divine figure who enters our world and
confronts the powers of evil that seek to consume and destroy, that part of
us which continues to pursue all that is good, pure, and worth rescuing.
The young girl Newt is a symbolic representation, a figure of innocence,
survival, and purity who is for us what *we* hope we can be. Yet we are also
acutely aware of our ability to give in to the forces of evil, the darkness
within that is displayed so violently throughout human history, and we
can often be all too aware of those moments when we each consider the
reality of our capacity for great harm against one another.

10. Hippolytus, *Refutation of All Heresies,* 7.23.

Ripley steps into the chamber of existence, as all messianic saviors do, and confronts the evil head on, yet she now confronts it clothed in power not usually given to human beings, a power able to overcome the forces of darkness that seek to destroy us. This is a *theology of glory*, a god who is known to us as the One who comes in power to rescue us and cast into outer darkness the monster that will defeat us unless a savior comes. The *deus ex machina* hero is certainly not uncommon within modern Hollywood representations. Although not a horror film, *Taken* has the archetypical Hollywood male hero who rescues the archetypical Hollywood female—innocent, virgin, adventuress—and in that process of rescue thus delivers us from our greatest fears: that our mistakes can be overcome through the wonder and innocence of childhood, that the hope they represent can lead to a brighter tomorrow, but that there are powerful forces that seek to turn that hope into despair, and we might lose what signifies our greatest hopes for a brighter future. Brian is the dad who rescues the daughter from that which represents and symbolizes total depravity and evil: men who have kidnapped the innocent virgin daughter, drugged her, and sold her into sexual slavery. Brian symbolizes the true divine Father figure: noble, brave, ruthless; Brian is the divine Father who executes justice against forces of total evil that seek to destroy that which is good within our humanity. At the end of *Taken* Brian saves his daughter just in time before her virginity is taken from her, before she is consumed by drugs, before she becomes a shadow of herself. It is interesting to note that Brian's daughter is kidnapped alongside another girl who is not the innocent virgin but is clearly sexually active and open to experiment with drugs and take risks with strangers. Part way through the film Brian discovers her dead, handcuffed to a bed in a place of prostitution, her body wracked with signs of drug abuse and misery; this woman is not worth saving within Hollywood ideology. In *Taken*, Brian fills the *deus ex machina* figure, the Father who rescues the Daughter, the god who rescues humanity from certain destruction. At the end of *Taken* Brian bursts through the door and shoots dead the Muslim[11] protagonist, an impossible rescue that the divine Father has managed to accomplish. And in the same way Ripley represents for us that same figure, the divine One who enters into the chamber of our human terror, our fear of certain destruction, or at very least, our fear of that which represents total innocence, and hope, in the jaws of an evil that could consume us unless

11. It should be of no surprise that in a climate of fear-induced relating, Hollywood will seize upon that figure that represents the West's anxiety, and that which is also the scapegoat of our political establishment, and media forces. The film seems to grade the levels of corruption and evil, and it is always the foreign "other" who is the figure of absolute cruelty.

something rescues us. Ripley, in her exosuit, represents One who is clothed with power from on high, and after a great struggle casts the monster into outer darkness, symbolizing the defeat of evil by the messianic figure. Ripley is clothed in that which has come to her from the great Other—in this case it is humanity's technological advancement and development, the scientific genius of Weyland-Yutani Corporation; with seemingly limitless resources, Weyland represent the ideological belief in our unending capacity to master our own mortality. Ripley stands in her exosuit as the one who can rescue us, fully suited in Weyland's divine power; she has, in the *Alien* world, become the Son of God through the gift of the Weyland spirit, through her own humanity, through our scientific power, able to "boldly go where no one has gone before."[12] Peter Weyland, the father of the technology that

12. *Star Trek* epitomizes the humanist, materialist, scientific worldview that all that we do not yet know can and will be discovered through scientific progression and technological advancement. Gene Roddenberry was deeply critical and suspicious of all organized religion, a man who believed in the capacity of humanity to reach new heights in our desire for betterment once released from the shackles of religious superstition. Roddenberry believed in a form of Utopianism, a belief that the human spirit and capacity for advancement would enable us to eventually discover that which is beyond us right now, that through science we will one day know all that we currently do not know. It is interesting how Roddenberry failed to see how faulty Utopianistic ideology is when examined through the lens of twentieth-century history. Certainly, Nazism and Stalinism have revealed that the capacity for human evil for the ideology of Utopianism knows no limit. Of course, the argument goes that when Utopianism is applied through the correct moral and political philosophy, then the evils of those committed under Stalin, for instance, can be avoided, yet it is difficult for this writer to see how that is possible; each person holds to a version of events, informed according to their own circumstances, upbringing, traditions, and morality. While some Utopian ideals might pursue "the common good," it is difficult to maintain what that common good might look like without naturally imposing on some a version of society that is oppressive and potentially destructive to some. While the argument that scientific discovery and knowledge will ultimately lead to an understanding of all things that will enable us to live according to the best of humanity might sound wonderfully appealing, but ultimately it is fanciful and magical thinking; science has its limits, not because we have not yet discovered the our scientific potential, but because science cannot give us knowledge and understanding to all things—the reality of consciousness, the wonder of beauty, the mystery of love. Notice how different in ideology the *Star Trek* universe is to the *Star Wars* universe; both have impacted our modern consciousness in remarkable ways yet are radically different in their approach to the cosmos. In *Star Wars* we encounter a universe of remarkable technological progression (light sabers!) and yet it is a universe that does not regard technology, science, and the capacity to create through these advancements as the answer and solution to all things. In one scene in *A New Hope* there is an encounter between Darth Vader and Admiral Motti,

> **Admiral Motti:** Any attack made by the Rebels against this station would be a useless gesture, no matter what technical data they have obtained. This station is now the ultimate power in the universe! I suggest we use it!

permeates the *Alien* universe, declares, "At this moment of our civilization, we can create cybernetic individuals, who in just a few short years will be completely indistinguishable from us. Which leads to an obvious conclusion: We are the gods now."[13] The desire that we have to be clothed in power from on high—a power that Ripley possesses in her exosuit, a power displayed within Adoptionist versions of Christ—stems from the belief in the human capacity to overcome through our own development *and* obedience to the great Other, whether that is God, science, Utopianism, or any Other number of possibilities that we attach meaning to. To believe that it is possible to be masters of our own destiny, that somehow, and in some way, we can ensure not only our own survival but soar to new heights previously unimagined within the human endeavor, is not unusual today, and has never been unusual. The Tower of Babel in Genesis 6 highlights our never-ending quest to reach the heavens and becomes the gods:

> The Titan Prometheus wanted to give mankind equal footing with the gods and for that, he was cast from Olympus. Well, my friends, the time has finally come for his return.[14]

Again and again humanity feels inferior to the gods, unable to reach the heights of power that they have at their disposal, punished by our own mortality. Weyland believes, however, that the time is soon approaching where we will overcome, where the gods will no longer have the power to stop us from reaching our potential. Within certain charismatic streams of Christian thought there is the belief that we can reach those heights that Weyland desires

---

Darth Vader: Don't be too proud of this technological terror you've constructed. The ability to destroy a planet is insignificant next to the power of the Force.

Admiral Motti: Don't try to frighten us with your sorcerer's ways, Lord Vader. Your sad devotion to that ancient religion has not helped you conjure up the stolen data tapes, or given you clairvoyance enough to find the rebels' hidden fort . . .

[Vader makes a pinching motion and Motti starts choking]

Darth Vader: I find your lack of faith disturbing.

The Force is of supreme importance within the *Star Wars* universe. Unlike *Star Trek*, where all things can ultimately be explained through a scientific, materialist understanding, *Star Wars* offers a version of events that recognizes that there is far more beyond what can be seen and known through our own understanding and scientific discovery. The Jedi and Sith, each in their own way, devote themselves to a greater commitment to the Force, convinced of its necessity in all things, and its power to unlock potential, fully aware that despite all technological development, the Force is of supreme importance.

13. Peter Weyland, TED Talk 2023. See https://youtu.be/dQpGwnN3dfc.

14. Peter Weyland, *Prometheus* (2012).

in the *Alien* universe, and that, through our own faith and obedience, we can possess power and previously unknown possibilities. The Adoptionist Christ enters into this realm of possibility through his own obedience. Consider this quote from the second-century work *The Shepherd of Hermas*:[15]

> The holy, preexistent Spirit, that created every creature, God made to dwell in flesh, which he chose. This flesh, accordingly, in which the Holy Spirit dwelt, was nobly subject to that Spirit, walking religiously and chastely, in no respect defiling he Spirit; and accordingly, after living excellently and purely, and after labouring and co-operating with the Spirit, and having in everything acted vigorously and courageously along with the Holy Spirit, He assumed it as a partner with it. For this conduct of the flesh pleased Him, because it was not defiled on the earth while having the Holy Spirit. He took, therefore, as fellow-councillors His Son and the glorious angels, in order that this flesh, which had been subject to the body without a fault, might have some place of tabernacle, and that it might not appear that the reward [of its servitude had been lost], for the flesh that has been found without spot or defilement, in which the Holy Spirit dwelt, [will receive a reward].[16]

Jesus is regarded here as one who walks "nobly" with the Spirit, someone who lives in the way of excellence and obedience, pleasing to God and thus exalted in his flesh to a higher status, becoming more than he was, transcending the limitations of the flesh, but in no way casting off the flesh, rather exalting the flesh to a higher level than previously assumed. This is an important point. Within Gnostic thought the flesh was a prison that needed to be escaped from, a limitation to our potential, a hindrance to that which can be attained with the right knowledge. Unhelpful interpretations and poorly exegeted parts of Scripture has led, at times, for some to view the flesh as a hindrance to true spiritual perfection, regarding Jesus' sayings on the flesh[17] and Paul's teaching on the Kingdom of God[18] as an indication

15. *The Shepherd of Hermas* is a remarkable and visionary book regarded by many to be Scripture up until the late fourth century. Irenaeus of Lyons (c.130–c. 202) considered it Scripture stating, "Truly, then, *the Scripture declared*, which says, 'First of all believe that there is one God, who has established all things, and completed them, and having caused that from what had no being, all things should come into existence . . .'" *Against Heresies*, 4.20.2, [Emphasis mine].

16. *Shepherd of Hermas*, 3.5.6.

17. "It is the spirit that gives life; the flesh is of no worth." John 6:63a.

18. "What I am saying, brothers and sisters, is this: flesh and blood cannot inherit the kingdom of God, nor does the perishable inherit the imperishable." 1 Cor 15:50 NRSV.

that true life with God is an entirely spiritual encounter, and the flesh is something to be rejected, tamed, and freed from.

Now, within a secular materialist perspective, the flesh is once again a hindrance to humanity's pursuit of a brave new world. John Paul Sartre, from his own atheistic interpretive lens, believed that the narrative of the human species was one of fall and redemption, saying, "There is an original fall and striving for redemption—and that fall with that striving constitutes human reality."[19] Our lives then, according to a strictly materialist ideology, could be seen, if we take Sartre seriously, as the pursuit of redemption from our fallen state, not in terms of the overcoming of our sinfulness, but in the redemption of our mortality, the defeat of death, the journey toward immortality, the overcoming of our flesh, a flesh that is a hindrance. Stephen Hawking, speaking at the Cambridge Film Festival in 2013 said,

> I think the brain is like a program in the mind, which is like a computer, so it's theoretically possible to copy the brain onto a computer and so provide a form of life after death . . . However, this is way beyond our present capabilities. I think the conventional afterlife is a fairy tale for people afraid of the dark.[20]

This is a vision that far surpasses the concept of "being remembered" or our existence simply being passed on through our children, our genes continuing through our ability to multiply; rather, it is the desire for who we are—at least, a materialist definition of who we are—to be continued beyond the decay of our body. Our flesh hinders us from immortality, and so a new vision of humanity emerges whereby we are unshackled from our decaying bodies and plugged into a computer, thus enabling our existence to continue. Certainly, if our brain was simply "like a program in the mind" and our humanity simply an outworking of that program, then Hawking's theory might provide a possible future of a totally renewed and transformed humanity, yet this is utterly unlike anything conceivable of what it means ·to be human. Our lives are determined by more than simply the functions of our brains; watch the unfolding relationships of people in all their complexities and you will soon discover how remarkable humanity is, and the depth our humanity takes—a depth that cannot be measured by scientific enquiry. Within each person lay their own consciousness, something that is utterly beyond the realms of all human understanding, yet integral to what makes us who we are. Our own consciousness informs our memory, a memory that we consistently live in with each passing moment; every single

---

19. Sartre, *The War Diaries*, 110.

20. http://pioneer.chula.ac.th/~pukrit/bba/hawking.pdf.

moment is lived in memory as the present instantly becomes the past, and
so we live as a people who remember. This shapes every relationship we
have, for in our relationships we are relating to one another as memory, our
lives lived with others through what has already gone before us. The only
way we do not remember falsely within our relationships is through the
lived correction of that person within our lives, their ability to remind us of
what is our authentic lived experience, the *truth of who they are* not *who we
remember them to be* according to our own consciousness and bias interpretation. Of course, twenty years into a relationship can bring a hazy recollection of how things were; indeed, it can be a challenge for us to even know if
our memory of a past event resembles what actually happened—yet within
relationships of authentic speech, any memory that is not true of who we
know one another to be will be challenged and exposed as inconsistent with
the lived reality of that relationship. In death that corrective can be lost, our
identity shaped no longer by the authenticity of our mutual relationship but
by the recollections of another. As Sartre rightly points out, to exist simply
as someone else's memory can radically transform who we ever were:

> "The terrible thing about Death," said Malraux, "is that it
> transforms like into Destiny." By this we must understand that
> death reduces the for-itself-for-others to the simple state for-
> others . . . Those dead who have not been able to be saved and
> transported to the boundaries of the concrete past of a survivor
> are not *past*; they along with their pasts are annihilated.[21]

Here Sartre recognizes that after our death we are thus defined by those
who come after us, and those who outlive us; their gaze, so to speak, is that
which brings the meaning to our own identity now that in death "we are
no longer able to resist the meanings others give us."[22] In other words, the
memory others have of us, and the way they seek to remember us after our
death, is that which defines our continuing existence. This is why authentic
speech remains imperative in life and death. It is entirely possible to be at
a funeral service and wonder who the eulogy is actually about when what
is said seems to say nothing that resembles the person who has died and
who *you* remember them to be. And this is Sartre's contention: we shape the
identity of others through our own memory of them, a shaping that may
indeed transform them into something wholly other than they were in their
lives. Authentic speech refuses to allow such deception to take place, not
only in your own memory of others, but also in the process of remembrance
that you are witness to from the reflections of others. What does that mean

21. Sartre, *Being and Nothingness*, 165–66.
22. Kirkpatrick, *Sartre and Theology*, 37.

in reality? It means that sentimental nostalgic remembrance of a loved one does not define or determine the actuality of their existence, rather, we accept who they were in life in all its honesty, enabling us to remember them well. We cannot mourn someone who we misremember, for our grief will not be for them but for someone who does not exist, thus vanquishing the possibility of our mourning and healing; authentic speech reminds us that we are all flawed, and that our death can be a source of healing to others, so we need to be remembered authentically.

As we saw in *The Shepherd of Hermas*, the coming in the flesh of Jesus is not in any way denied or negated, that who he is in the flesh is imperative to understanding humanity and divinity. To remember Jesus well and authentically is to recognize that he is fully human, calling humanity to be human, and in doing so, to enter into divinity. In this act of remembrance, encapsulated within the sacrament of Bread and Wine, we are invited into the Life of Jesus, to share in His Story and, by the Spirit, to discover within His Story our own story. The broken body of Christ, enacted through this Meal, reminds us, calls us to remember authentically the God who suffers and dies in the flesh and so define once and for all how God is present to us in the world. The Incarnation is the act of God whereby God is, as Bonhoeffer says, pushed out in to the world, weak, and in that place of weakness, is present to us. Here we remember Jesus authentically, an authenticity that chastises us when we define God apart from the cross, rebuked with Peter when we would rather a *deus ex machina* god, a god like Zeus or Superman, rather than a God shaped like the Crucified Jesus. Unlike Ripley or the Son of God portrayed within texts like *The Shepherd of Hermas*, Jesus does not take upon himself the exosuit of divinity later on in his life due to some obedience to the great Other, clothed in violent, glory power because of this life perfectly devoted to this Other; rather, at his birth he is already fully divine, "In the beginning was the Logos . . . and the Logos became flesh and tabernacled amongst us." In his weakness and vulnerability God is fully revealed, the baby of the manger who cries out in hunger is the Creator of the cosmos who spoke and brought all things into existence, the splintered wood of his temporary bed at birth an echo of the cross that would be on his back, a cross that has left scars into eternity.[23] The flesh is not something

23. "Then I saw between the throne and the four living creatures and among the elders a Lamb standing as if it had been slaughtered . . ." Rev 5:6a.

"But Thomas (who was called the Twin), one of the twelve, was not with them when Jesus came. So the other disciples told him, 'We have seen the Lord.' But he said to them, 'Unless I see the mark of the nails in his hands, and put my finger in the mark of the nails and my hand in his side, I will not believe.' A week later his disciples were again in the house, and Thomas was with them. Although the doors were shut, Jesus came and stood among them and said, 'Peace be with you.' Then he said to Thomas, 'Put your

to be escaped, rather it is that which will be redeemed, taken up into the Divine Life and transformed from the perishable into the imperishable,[24] the Son becoming flesh in order to bring humanity into the Eternal One[25] and thus enable us to reach our *telos*, the goal for which we have been created for, namely Christ,

> "There can be neither Judaean nor Greek, there can be neither slave nor freeman, there cannot be male and female, for you are all one in the Anointed One Jesus." (Gal 3:28)

> ". . . for in him all things in heaven and on earth were created, things visible and invisible, whether thrones or dominions or rulers or powers—all things have been created through him and for him. He himself is before all things, and in him all things hold together. He is the head of the body, the church; he is the beginning, the firstborn from the dead, so that he might come to have first place in everything." (Col 1:16–18 NRSV)

Peter Weyland and the company he created desired to locate the alien species because it represented to them the perfect organism, a creature of total power, hostility, lacking the weaknesses of guilt, regret, or fear, and lacking all capacity to love—a weapon of untold power. Yet this is precisely why Jesus, in his humanity, is everything we need God to be, because God is *not* like the Xenomorph, and *is exactly like Jesus*. When God is likened to total power then God quite easily becomes like the very monsters of our nightmares, but when known through the truly crucified and risen human, then humanity has a model to live by that is utterly compelling, beautiful, and potentially remarkable for every community that values unconditionality over power.

---

finger here and see my hands. Reach out your hand and put it in my side. Do not doubt but believe." John 20:24–26 NRSV.

24. "What is sown is perishable, what is raised is imperishable . . ." 1 Cor 15:42b.

25. "Thus he has given us, through these things, his precious and very great promises, so that through them you may escape from the corruption that is in the world because of lust, and may become participants of the divine nature." 2 Pet 1:4. ". . . the Word of God, our Lord Jesus Christ, who did, through His transcendent love, become what we are, that He might bring us to be even what He is Himself." Irenaeus, *Against Heresies*, 5, Preface.

8

Ghosts

The Horror of Time

Don't go chasing shadows, Arthur.[1]

—*THE WOMAN IN BLACK*

IN EDGAR ALLAN POE'S *The Masque of the Red Death*, Prince Prospero holds an elaborate party at his secluded, lavish, and magnificent castle for a thousand guests of nobility and status, a party held while the land is ravished by the "Red Death," a brutal disease that produces "profuse bleeding from the pores," dizziness, and sharp pains; it is a disease marked by "the redness and horror of blood." The prince's party is one of wine, music, and dancing; outside is the "Red Death" while inside is revelry and defiance to the disease, a place of security within where the "external world could take care of itself." And so they dance and enjoy a masked ball of "unusual magnificence," one that contained "delirious fancies" where "the music swells, and the dreams live" so that those who are present can forget the terror that dwells beyond the gates of the castle.

The castle is filled with delights and treasures "of the beautiful, much of the wanton, much of the bizarre, something of the terrible, and not a little of that which might have excited disgust." Within the castle there are seven

---

1. Daily, *The Woman in Black*, James Watkins, Cross Creek Pictures, 2012.

chambers, one of which is the grand chamber where the masquerade is taking place, and within this chamber stands a gigantic clock of ebony that,

> . . . when the minute-hand made the circuit of the face, and the hour was to be stricken, there came from the brazen lungs of the clock a sound which was clear and loud and deep and exceedingly musical, but of so peculiar a note and emphasis that, at each lapse of an hour, the musicians of the orchestra were constrained to pause, momentarily, in their performance, to hearken to the sound; and thus the waltzers perforce ceased their evolutions; and there was a brief disconcert of the whole gay company; and, while the chimes of the clock yet rang, it was observed that the giddiest grew pale, and the more aged and sedate passed their hands over their brows as if in confused reverie or meditation. But when the echoes had fully ceased, a light laughter at once pervaded the assembly; the musicians looked at each other and smiled as if at their own nervousness and folly, and made whispering vows, each to the other, that the next chiming of the clock should produce in them no similar emotion; and then, after the lapse of sixty minutes, (which embrace three thousand and six hundred seconds of the Time that flies,) there came yet another chiming of the clock, and then were the same disconcert and tremulousness and meditation as before.[2]

Then into the midst of the revelry stands a masked figure of such presence, whose appearance goes beyond the boundaries of the etiquette of masked balls, whose presence brings with it terror, shock, and disgust, a stranger who drains from the whole company all wit and humor, a figure of abject misery and horror. Prince Prospero becomes aware of this new guest, a guest who is able to walk slowly and freely through the different chambers evoking fear into the heart of every guest with each step. The prince is filled with rage at the presence of this intruder, one who has come into the security and fantasy of the ball and brought panic, shattering the illusion of the gathering, all that are present shaken once again, as with the chiming of the clock, from the "gay and magnificent revel."

Prospero draws a dagger and approaches the back of the walking unwanted guest ready to kill him in a moment, at which moment the guest unmasks and faces the furious prince. With a cry of fear the prince drops dead. Guests at once pounce upon the "tall figure" who stands "motionless within the shadow of the ebony clock" only to find themselves grasping in their hands a "corpse-like mask." It is at this moment that the guests become

2. http://xroads.virginia.edu/~hyper/poe/masque.html, lines 27–35.

aware that the "Red Death" has come among them "like a thief in the night," ready to consume each of them "one by one" until such time "Darkness and Decay and the Red Death held illimitable dominion over all."[3]

Poe's story is a powerful parable of humanity's fear of time, the horror that overwhelms us and strikes us down when we face, unmasked, the reality of our condition, that time and the present cannot be avoided or hidden from, that our humanity is subject to the "slow and solemn movement" of time throughout the vestiges of our lives. The masquerade is a wonderful analogy of the ways we seek to pretend that we are not subject to power of now, that we can hide behind the walls of our nostalgic castles and dance ourselves away from the "Red Death" that ravages the lives of others, that somehow, if we wear the masks of our certainty that life was better once before, then we will stay hidden and protected and secure from the inevitability of time's decay upon human existence. Nostalgia is what Poe's parable is all about, and no wonder Stephen King uses a portion of this parable in the opening pages of his book, *The Shining*. We will return to Poe's story shortly, but for the moment let us walk the corridors of the Overlook Hotel, the place where the Torrance family find themselves one winter, a winter that will tear their family apart.

Let it Shine

In the 1970's, Jack Torrance is hired to be the caretaker of the Overlook Hotel, a place of significant reputation, now falling into disrepair, located up a road that is impassable during the winter months and so cutting the hotel off to all visitors. A caretaker and his family are hired for these times in order to maintain the building, ensure the heating continues to work, and deal with any repairs that need to be carried out as the winters are so harsh that the fabric of the hotel suffers greatly. The book charts the slow descent into madness of Jack, a madness that his five-year-old son Danny is all too aware of because of his special gift called "the shining," a psychic ability that becomes unbearable for Danny the further into madness his father descends. Danny knows that the hotel has an evil force, a force catapulting his father into pure, murderous lunacy that will destroy them all. Danny, through his gift of the shining, sees beyond the fabric of the hotel to what lurks beneath, a murderous and terrifying force that brings violent insanity upon those susceptible enough to its powers. Danny has a deep awareness of what is happening to his father and the horror of the evil within the walls of the place,

The hotel caught Daddy.[4]

3. http://xroads.virginia.edu/~hyper/poe/masque.html, lines 82–83.
4. King, *The Shining*, 412.

Jack's wife, Wendy, encounters the brutality of the evil within the hotel when Jack tries to kill her, and barely escaping with her life, she realizes what the hotel wants from them as a family: "The hotel has gotten into him, Danny. *The Overlook has gotten into your daddy* . . . It wants to hurt us all."[5] Because of Danny's shine, the Overlook gains a power and a strength and is somehow woken up and released into its terror, seeking to actively consume those who inhabit it, feeding off them in order to maintain its existence. By taking Danny, through Jack, the hotel could absorb Danny's shine and grow in power, becoming something as yet unknown but truly terrifying. Once Wendy and Danny are aware of this they try to escape, but by this time Jack is utterly possessed by an inescapable journey toward total madness and evil.

In one scene, Jack walks into the bar of the hotel and finds himself surrounded by the hum of laughter and conversation, people filling the booths, drinking and smoking, dressed in cocktail dresses and fine suits from the 1920's and 1940's, discussing "profit and loss, life and death."[6] In this deserted hotel in the middle of winter, a place cut off from all human civilization, Jack could hear all of them, these "beautiful strangers."[7] As Jack sits at the bar, he is surrounded by the ghosts of the Overlook, ghosts that look like guests and encapsulate the desire of the hotel; the preservation of a time long since vanished; "Hello boys," Jack said softly, "I've been away but now I'm back." The nostalgic dream, the desire to reclaim something that has long since gone, the belief that in some way we can return to a better time when life was simpler, when everything worked, when people knew who they were, when society had a sense of its own identity and we could be part of that identity, safe in the knowledge that this identity was for our own flourishing. And so Jack drinks his gin amongst these beautiful strangers, these ghosts that remind him of a time once past that he could have flourished in, a time once past where life would have been different for Jack Torrance. All the hotel requires is his wife and son, the total commitment of Jack to the desire of the hotel by giving, in blood, to the Overlook, his very family through brutal chastisement,

> You must show them the error of their ways, Mr Torrance . . . A man who cannot control his own family holds very little interest for our manager. A man who cannot guide the courses of his own wife and son can hardly be expected to guide himself,

5. King, *The Shining*, 411–12.
6. King, *The Shining*, 378.
7. King, *The Shining*, 378.

let alone assume a position of responsibility in an operation of this magnitude.[8]

The hotel is the manager, and the manger requires total subservience to its cause, a subservience that is written in blood, the blood of your own flesh and blood, and so Jack pursues the lives of his wife and son, seeking to kill them and sacrifice them to the will of the hotel. This is a phenomenal insight from King in regard to how our family lives can be determined by *the lack of time* and the ongoing sense that who we are is in constant threat, our very identity at risk from erosion through the forces that we sense want to lay claim over and above us.

Identity Crisis

Men within Western society are overwhelmed with an identity crisis. In the United Kingdom, suicide is the biggest killer of men under the age of forty-five years, meaning that if you are in this age bracket you are more likely to die of suicide than any other cause of death.[9] The research into this crisis from central government is minimal, a shocking indictment upon those who have been appointed by the public for the welfare of the whole society. These suicide rates among men within the United Kingdom are alarming, and much more research is needed in order to begin to address some of the reasons why this might be happening. Speaking personally, my identical twin brother tried to take his own life on October 23, 2015, aged thirty-four.[10] His mental health had reached breaking point, a point where he felt the only way out was suicide. Friedrich Wilhelm Nietzsche once said, "The thought of suicide is a great consolation: by means of it one gets through many a dark night." My brother, writing at *Huffington Post*, said,

> When you're suffering from depression the difficulty of the speed and pressure of the world can seem gargantuan. Sometimes the pressure breaks your brain and makes you wonder if you really belong to this world. Instead of trying to control the whirlwind of without, you are desperately attempting to quiet the storm within. I believe suicide isn't an act of cowardice but

8. King, *The Shining*, 388–90.

9. https://www.ons.gov.uk/peoplepopulationandcommunity/birthsdeath sandmarriages/deaths/bulletins/suicidesintheunitedkingdom/2016registration.

10. http://www.huffingtonpost.co.uk/tom-haward/mental-health-suicide-men_b_8450420.html.

part of an ongoing battle to quiet the storm. The way the storm
ends is different for different people.[11]

Suicide is an extremely emotive and difficult topic to think and talk about,
but talk about it we must. Recently it was highlighted that one hundred
men a week take their own lives in the UK while suicide rates in the USA
continue to rise, particularly amongst men. In 2016 in the UK, 75 percent
of those who died by suicide were male. The reasons behind this continue
to be unclear and perhaps will never be clear, but what we need are far
greater levels of robust, honest, and authentic conversation about suicide,
hearing the stories, like my brother's, as to why people seek to kill themselves. It does not help that we are a society of death deniers, constantly
seeking ways to avoid death, not only in our conversations but also how
we understand it, and our human desires to overcome it. We need to embrace the reality of death, its inevitability for all that exists,[12] and, despite
our greatest future technological advances, our inability to do anything
about it. So, it is good that people are talking about suicide and that people
are beginning to feel able to write and share so openly about their own
lived experiences and realities. Without open and honest dialogue and unconditional, loving, vulnerable relationships we will not easily find ways

11. http://www.huffingtonpost.co.uk/tom-haward/is-suicide-a-cowardly-
act_b_6562258.html, lines 11–15.

12. God, quite simply, is not like created "stuff." You will not find God by looking
through a telescope or under a microscope because God is not part of created reality. Certainly, God is deeply and passionately involved with all things, but God is not like
created things. God does not exist the way you and I exist. In the resurrection of Jesus,
we see that death has no part in God. Death stands against all that God is. In the death
of Jesus, we see and recognize our own violence and sin and how human reality is one of
death. The death of Jesus exposes our mimetic, rivalistic violent desires, and the way we
scapegoat and expel the innocent victim to satisfy our vampiric violence in order to try
and overcome death on our own terms in our own violent ways. In the resurrection we
see God nonviolently overthrow our violence, expose our scapegoating, trample down
death and declare its toxicity, as well as revealing how it has no place in who God is.
Created reality decays and dies; plants, animals, stars, humans—everything dies. God,
however, is not like created reality. Death and decay have no place in God's own Self
because God is beyond and completely Other. God cannot be empirically tested or
examined because God is Ultimate Reality, wholly Other to creation. If materialists and
strident atheists, as well as religious fundamentalists involved in apologetics, could at
least begin to grapple with this point then at least the debate could start from a place
of validity. The resurrection of Jesus reveals this God who is not like us yet invites us
to become like God, to share in the Divine dance and know Life. God is present with
us, loving us, beckoning us to know this love for ourselves, inviting us into this eternal,
everlasting, all-encompassing embrace. When the early Christians declared "Jesus is
alive!" they were declaring that God is Life, in God there is no death. So God is not
MAN said in a loud voice as Karl Barth highlighted. God is not like creation. God is
wholly Other. In other words, God does not exist.

to help people when suicide appears the best and only consolation when living in those dark nights.

There are, I suspect, many different reasons why the suicidal storm rages; we are all unique, but in our uniqueness we also live in time and space that is shared, and that shared space impacts us all uniquely. There is also the commonality to our unique experiences, the shared reality of how it feels to live in time and space, not only at this moment, but in the universality of the human experience. So today in the West while we are all wonderfully different and our perception of the world in relationship with others will be unique to us, we also recognize that shared perception of reality, trends within our society that spark in many of us. Take, for instance, the civil rights movement. There were people that collectively knew that things needed to change (and of course those that wanted no change), that oppression and persecution and discrimination needed to stop and so joined together to bring about radical transformation. While each person's experience of racism and oppression was unique to them, there was a collective "crying out" that sparked revolution. That revolution was inspired through a prophetic act, an act of refusing to give up her seat on a bus, an act of defiance by Rosa Parks: "I was not tired physically, or no more tired than I usually was at the end of a working day. I was not old, although some people have an image of me as being old then. I was forty-two. No, the only tired I was, was tired of giving in."[13] The seeds of transformation had been scattered and tended to for hundreds of years, as a people who had been abused, dehumanized and deprived of their equality, sang songs of freedom,[14] nonviolently and subversively creating the fertile soil for freedom to ring out and awaken

13. Parks, *Rosa Parks*, 116.

14. "Songs were used in everyday life by African slaves. Singing was tradition brought from Africa by the first slaves; sometimes their songs are called spirituals. Singing served many purposes such as providing repetitive rhythm for repetitive manual work, inspiration and motivation. Singing was also use [sic] to express their values and solidarity with each other and during celebrations. Songs were used as tools to remember and communicate since the majority of slaves could not read. Harriet Tubman and other slaves used songs as a strategy to communicate with slaves in their struggle for freedom. Coded songs contained words giving directions on how to escape also known as signal songs or where to meet known as map songs." http://www.harriet-tubman.org/songs-of-the-underground-railroad/, lines 1–6.

Harriet Tubman (c. 1820–1913) helped bring over 300 slaves to freedom, thus earning her the nickname "Moses." Born a slave, she dedicated her life to the cause of freedom, devoting her life and work and money to rescuing people from slavery, opening schools for African Americans, and campaigning for woman's rights. She conducted many slave songs that were a means of hope and inspiration, following in the tradition of Africanized Christian spirituality where slave songs, such as those written by Wallis Willis (c. 1820–c. 1880), expressed the community's new faith, sorrows, and hopes, such as "Steal Away to Jesus" or "Swing Low, Sweet Chariot."

within the unconsciousness of generations of slave owners and oppressors the monumental sin of their actions, the need for repentance, the reality of the pain inflicted and horror realized. Of course, we still live in a time where racism and oppression exists on a global scale, where the horrors of the past continue to be a reality of the present, where people not only do not want to, but cannot see that they are perpetrators of horrendous evils that murder their fellow humanity.

When Rosa Parks refused to give up her seat it sparked into existence the Montgomery Bus Boycott, "a thirteen month struggle to desegregate the city's buses."[15] It was movement that thrust Martin Luther King Jr. and Rosa Parks into the national spotlight, a movement led by King seeking to bring equality and freedom to the black community. King, when writing near the end of his life, reflecting on all that had happened since Parks's prophetic act of civil disobedience, remarked,

> Humanity is waiting for something other than blind imitation of the past. If we want truly to advance a step further, if we want to turn over a new leaf and really set a new man afoot, we must begin to turn mankind away from the long and desolate night of violence. May it not be that the new man the world needs is the nonviolent man?[16]

Within the spark ignited by Parks, King led a movement that saw how transformation needs to be realized, a transformation that can only happen within a nonviolent ethic, a pursuit of peace that is only possible when violence is relinquished and a new reality is imagined.

So for us, here in the West, there are things happening around us that might collectively spark. Many are disillusioned by the political system, are tired of the blatant stealing, greed, and deception of big business, banks, the rich, and the powerful. We are told of our greatness, a greatness that can be reached if we work a little harder, sacrifice a little more, give of ourselves beyond what we are already giving, but that greatness is almost always out of reach. There is a sense of disconnectedness among us, of people "connected" through the wonder of our technological progression, but not really in relationship and ultimately actually disconnected. People are concerned about many things, about money, about jobs, about family; life. So we look and search and pursue for a way to change things, buying things we don't need, picking up and rejecting relationships to make ourselves feel better. Sometimes it may be that all of this feels too much for some and then the feeling

---

15. http://kingencyclopedia.stanford.edu/encyclopedia/encyclopedia/enc_parks_rosa_1913_2005/index.html, lines 3–4.

16. King, *Where Do We Go From Here?* 68.

that the only way out is death. Issues surrounding mental health are consistently handled poorly within the media and amongst the political elite. Money is consistently being withdrawn from mental health research, help, and support. Without resources it is no wonder suicide rates are increasing in the West. We need money invested into research and collaborative care to enable understanding, methods of holistic care, and cultural research that seeks to understand the nature and character of why people, particularly males, see suicide as the only option. This has to be a community effort, a coming together of people within their own communities seeking ways to tell a different story, bring hope, and collectively walk alongside those who are suffering the dark night of the soul. Girard's mimetic theory could be important within this whole area. Could it be that men are sacrificing themselves, believing themselves to be the cause and problem within our society? Could it be that through myth and prohibition, a religion of consumerist sacrifice has been created in the West creating the myth of success, the prohibition of failure, the scapegoat of males who believe through their death society will be better off? There are many unanswered questions, many studies that need to be done, and many communities of hope that need to come together. Only when we start talking, sharing, and opening up, naming the reality of suicide in our midst and giving the space to talk and express the reality of it, will we even begin to stem the tide that breaks in waves of pain across our society. Jack Torrance, as a character, is a symbol of the pain of identity crisis, and the resulting pain, a pain we see within our culture, a pain exemplified by suicide rates.

Time Waiteth for No One

Jack Torrance opens up for us the authentic speech that is required if we are to speak with truthfulness into the midst of our collective anguish. As he finds himself surrounded by ghosts in the bar, drinking, dancing, and listening to the voice of the hotel calling him to murder his wife and son, he notices a clock on the mantlepiece,

> The clock began to chime delicately. Along the steel runner below the clock face, from the left and right, two figures advanced. Jack watched, fascinated . . . One of the figures was a man standing on tiptoe, with what looked like a tiny club clasped in his hands. The other was a small boy wearing a dunce cap. The clockwork figures glittered, fantastically precise. Across the front of the boy's dunce cap he could read the engraved word FOOLE . . . The steel mallet in the clockwork daddy's hands came down on the boys head. The clockwork son crumbled

forward. The mallet rose and fell. The boy's up stretched, pro-
testing hands began to falter. The boy sagged from his crouch to
a prone position. And still the hammer rose and fell to the light,
tinkling air of the Strauss melody, and it seemed he could see the
man's face, working and knotting and contracting, could see the
clockwork daddy's mouth opening and closing as he berated the
unconscious, bludgeoned figure of the son.

A spot of red flew up against the inside of the glass dome.
Another followed. Two more splattered beside it.

Now the red liquid was spraying up like an obscene rain
shower, striking the glass sides of the dome and running, ob-
scuring what was going on inside, and flecked through the scarlet were tiny ribbons of tissue, fragments of bone and brain. And
still he could see the hammer rising and falling as the clockwork
continued to turn and the cogs continued to mesh the gears and
teeth of this cunningly made machine.[17]

In stark and brutal terms King recognizes how fearful of time we are, the
way we are deeply afraid of the confutation of time, something we can do
nothing about, our inability, like King Cnut, to do anything about the in-
coming time. The figurine son within this scene represents all of our youth,
each of us, once upon a time, embraced by the possibilities that our youth
presented us with. Yet time is no one's friend, and the figurine father represents the brutality of time, and the sense within Jack's own world of total
loss, that all he hoped and wished to be, all that he hoped and wished to
achieve, has been taken from him through the mallet of time, through his
own failures and poor decisions, and it all comes crashing down upon him,
a sea of scarlet disappointment. The hotel offers Jack redemption, a chance
to become that which he has yet to become, a second chance in the midst of
his crushing failure; all he needs to do is sacrifice his son. In this act of sacrifice he will attain a version of events he thought forever lost by the power
and inevitability of time; he can live his life through his son. In some versions of atonement theology this is, at its crudest level, what God does with
Jesus: kills his son on a cross to deal with his crushing failure. The death of
Jesus is far more profound, complex, and remarkable than that, though—a
death that is cosmic in scope, redemptive for all things. And the mallet that
comes down on Jesus is swung by our own hands, not God's, swung by the
strength of our own wrath and violence, our faces contorted in rage.

King's insight through Jack's vision of the clock is an important narrative into our own stories, for it asks what we could have been in a time
before, it presents us with our own disappointments, disappointments that

17. King, *Shining*, 391–92.

we desire to overcome through our own children. Today, within the Western celebrity narrative, our children are told "you can be anything you want to be." The rise in the so-called reality television celebrity, the opportunity to become famous without having to be exceptional at anything in particular, has become common place. Therefore, we have a generation of people who believe that they can become a global sensation, rich and famous, by being a reality star. Social media has perpetuated this belief through the ability to film yourself and post videos of you doing anything, from dancing to commentating on toys—you can become a global star; some of the most famous people on the internet simply talk about makeup or toys and generate millions of followers. As a result, certainly among men in their forties, they witness a generation of people growing up who have recognition, financial security, and lifestyles they could only dream of and were unable to achieve. So perhaps, through their own flesh and blood, they might be able to make something of their lives, sacrificing them to the whims and will of a culture that seeks to make us a resource that will generate further resources that sustain its continued desire for growth. Nostalgia, as so is often the case today as we saw with the chapter on Apocalypse, plays an important and pivotal role within this whole narrative.

The 1998 Japanese film *Ring* is a modern parable on the power of nostalgia and our fear of time. The film tells of a videotape that, once watched, brings about the death of the viewer seven days after watching it. The curse can only be avoided if the tape is copied and passed on to someone else, a never-ending cycle of survival. The curse is discovered to be a result of the murder of Sadako, a young girl with psychic capabilities who was murdered by her father. It is the spirit of Sadako that crawls out of the television screen seven days after watching the tape and kills the viewer through fear. This, like King's clock in *The Shining*, is our fear of the advancement of time, a failure to become that which our hopes and dreams believed we would become. Society faces a real *Ring* dilemma in that we continue to tell our children that something amazing is waiting for them around the corner, only for time to advance and nothing seeming to happen of any significance, *according to the narrative of celebrity and success*. I have often heard within religious settings the belief that God desires for us all something remarkable, the belief that "God has plans to prosper us" and do something remarkable things through us that will change the world. I remember in around 2009 there was a competition in the United Kingdom to find the next great music worship leader, a chance to win a recording contract and lead big Christian festivals. I believe this is a prime example of how unlike the Way of Jesus we can be. In many more subtle ways the turning away from the Way of Jesus happens through the embrace of the dreams and the desire to resist the power of the ticking clock. With every sermon and song of your own personal greatness, that through you singularly God will bring his divine power and transform the world, then the cruciform path of Christ is wandered from.

The Shining of the Cross

To be shaped by the cross is to see in the now the power of God's presence, the promise of his enduring love in the midst of often painful lived experience. As Paul declared, "I decided when among you to know nothing except Jesus the Anointed, and him crucified" (1 Cor 2:2). Dietrich Bonhoeffer declared in no uncertain terms that, "In a world where success is the measure and justification of all things, the figure of him who was sentenced and crucified remains a stranger."[18] It is the path of a cruciform discipleship that Bonhoeffer preached, a cruciform humanity that needs to be reclaimed in order to know what it looks like to live truly human. Five hundred years ago Martin Luther called the church to a theology shaped by the cross, a theology that recognized that it is through the Crucified Lord that we encounter the One True God, and thus, through this insight we will encounter what it looks like to be truly human. In the Heidelberg Disputation that took place on April 26, 1518, Luther was invited by the Augustinian Order, of which Luther belonged, to expand upon and defend his views, first expressed through his ninety-five theses that he sent to his superiors along with a letter setting out his dispute, and then developed in Heidelberg in ways that his first letter did not. Three of the these, 19–21 from the Heidelberg Disputation, were as follows:

> 19. That person does not deserve to be called a theologian who looks upon the invisible things of God as though they were clearly perceptible in those things which have actually happened (Rom 1:20; cf. 1 Cor 1:21–25). This is apparent in the example of those who were »theologians« and still were called fools by the Apostle in Rom 1:22. Furthermore, the invisible things of God are virtue, godliness, wisdom, justice, goodness, and so forth. The recognition of all these things does not make one worthy or wise.

> 20. He deserves to be called a theologian, however, who comprehends the visible and manifest things of God seen through suffering and the cross . . .

18. Bonhoeffer, *Ethics*, 77.

21. A theology of glory calls evil good and good evil. A theology of the cross calls the thing what it actually is. This is clear: He who does not know Christ does not know God hidden in suffering. Therefore he prefers, works to suffering, glory to the cross, strength to weakness, wisdom to folly, and, in general, good to evil . . .[19]

Luther is unequivocal of what a theology of the cross as opposed to a theology of glory looks like; one knows the God who is "hidden in suffering." To recognize God is to see him in the "humility and shame of the cross," and this is the path to which Jesus followers are called toward, one that does not imagine a world transformed by your own glory but a world transformed through the suffering God, the One who dies outside the walls of the city, crucified in obscurity, surrounded by drunks and gamblers, dying and crying out in darkness, counted as the Criminal among criminals. Yet this is the One we are called to follow, to imitate,

> . . . if you also desire [to possess] this faith, you likewise shall receive first of all the knowledge of the Father. For God has loved mankind, on whose account He made the world, to whom He rendered subject all things that are in it, to whom He gave reason and understanding, to whom alone He imparted the privilege of looking upwards to Himself, whom He formed after His own image, to whom He sent His only-begotten Son, to whom He has promised a kingdom in heaven, and will give it to those who have loved Him. And when you have attained this knowledge, with what joy do you think you will be filled? Or, how will you love Him who has first so loved you? And if you love Him, you will be an imitator of His kindness. And do not wonder that a man may become an imitator of God. He can, if he is willing. For it is not by ruling over his neighbor, or by seeking to hold supremacy over those that are weaker, or by being rich, and showing violence toward those that are inferior, that happiness can be found; nor can any one by these things become an imitator of God . . . On the contrary, He who takes on the burden of his neighbor; he who, in whatsoever respect he may be superior, is ready to benefit another who is deficient; he who, whatsoever things he has received from God, by distributing to the needy, becomes a god to those who receive [his benefits]; he is an imitator of God.[20]

---

19. http://bookofconcord.org/heidelberg.php, lines 243–267.
20. Mathetes, *The Epistle to Diognetus*, X.

The cross, then, is the power of now, the power of staying in the moment, of refusing to wish this moment to be past, but embracing that which we are in at this very time; this is the shining. Danny Torrance is able to see beyond what is seen, able to understand the presence of now, able to perceive things for what they really are, recognize where evil lurks, and lock it away so that it was "never getting out."[21] Danny Torrance, as he grows, is able to confront the ghosts that destroyed his father and sought to kill him and his mother, confront them and destroy them. His shining gives him the ability to "see" evil, to know of its existence, and face it. That facing leaves him wounded though, a woundedness that leads to imitation of his father's alcoholism when he becomes an adult, but a woundedness that also enables him to overcome his demons and find healing. His shining gives him the ability to help people to embrace their death, to find comfort in those last moments and not to be afraid, to recognize that, "You only need to sleep."[22] Death as the great enemy to be feared is symbolized with stark brutality in Clive Barker's *The Great and Secret Show* when Tommy-Ray calls the ghosts of those who were not buried nor blessed, the dead who are cursed, to follow him. What he quickly becomes aware of, however, is how out of control these phantoms are, creatures of fury and hunger, destroying all in their path, consumed by their desire to consume. These ghosts represent the fear of death and time, humanity's final enemies that destroy all things without prejudice. Time is not to be feared in Danny's world though, for it is a gift that he has been given after the horror he witnessed, a horror that saw his father consumed by the fear of time, a horror that he will not repeat.

To live in the shining of the cross is to live in the knowledge of God's continuing presence in the now, that in this moment there is all and everything, that whatever this moment is, it is a moment where God has not given up on us. The ghosts of the past lurk in every shadow, reminding us, like Jack Torrance, that what we had is gone, and the clock keeps ticking by leading us further away from what we used to be. To live like that will destroy us for we will never be satisfied in anything that we do, nor in any relationship that we have, for we will always be looking back with no intention of it helping us know the way ahead. When the disciples cry out, "It's a ghost!" when they see Jesus walking on the water, we could understand this through the lens of the horror of time; the disciples are on the water, their boat symbolic of what they have always done and known, and they see a vision of what they first believe is their past, a belief in how things have always been, and it frightens them for they may never be able to move beyond that.

21. King, *Doctor Sleep*, 18.
22. King, *Doctor Sleep*, 482.

Yet Jesus comes to them in their boat and declares, "Don't be afraid, it is I." Jesus shows them that their past matters, but he is leading them on in the now, to be a people of Today, and this is no ghost,

> . . . again he sets a certain day—"today"—saying through David . . . "Today, if you hear his voice, do not harden your hearts." (Heb 4:7 NRSV)

The cross is the place where God is revealed through suffering, where Jesus "shines" and recognizes the power of evil but confronts it full on in order that it might be locked away and destroyed once and for all. Whereas Jack Torrance heard voices demanding the blood of his son, God's voice never demands blood, but speaks love, a love that is always found in today, and so beckons us to never fear the past, to never long for what has been through the nostalgic fear of time, but to walk boldly and bravely in the now, a today where God is always present, a presence of total, unending relationship.

9

frankenstein

The Horror of Loneliness

The Monster: Alone: bad. Friend: good![1]

—THE BRIDE OF FRANKENSTEIN (1935)

WHAT DOES IT MEAN to be human? I asked this question in *The Ghost of Perfection*, exploring some of the ways we can experience dehumanization and directly strip others of their humanity through our own actions, attitudes, and behaviors.[2] Part of my conclusion to this question is that our humanity is defined through relationship, that who we are is determined by the people we are in relationship with:

> We are who we are because of those who we are in relationship with, because of others we have shared our lives with, for good or for ill.[3]

It is this sense of loss of relationship that leads humanity to seek satisfaction elsewhere, to reconstruct the whole meaning of human relationships via creations of our own hands, resulting in, ultimately, a loss of our own humanity. For instance, the rise of "digisexuality" now means that there

1. *The Bride of Frankenstein*, James Whale, Universal Pictures, 1935.
2. See Haward, *Ghost of Perfection*, xvii—xxi.
3. Haward, *Ghost of Perfection*, xviii.

will be a growing number of people whose sexual identity comes primarily through technology.[4] While the rise in a sexuality informed through technology is nothing new, the way human sexuality is expressed through technology is changing: "Digisexuality is far from new. The growth of digital technology and its use for sexual purposes have been intimately interconnected throughout its history. We believe, however, that we are entering a new, distinct phase of this process."[5] Pornography has been available online for many years, and with the rise of webcams people are able to interact online with someone else for their sexual gratification. The development of technology and artificial intelligence though is changing even this, whereby people are able to use virtual reality and "sexbots" so that no human partner is present or needed in order for the experience to take place. Sex robots are gaining considerable attention from media outlets and creating significant conversation within popular culture as we seek to understand, as societies, the implications of this new wave of technological desire. The recent television series *Westworld* raises some important questions surrounding human desire and how we understand the basic questions of what makes us human. Augustine once said that all sin is misplaced desire. There is a deep question surrounding whether the use of sexbots is an example of misplaced desire, or if it is an example of humanity's capacity to create new things that enable us to express ourselves in better and healthier ways. There is a scene in the Channel 4 series *Humans* where Joe tells his wife, Laura, that he had sex with their Synth that they named Anita, a robot of supreme artificial intelligence that is indistinguishable from humans that they bought to help them as a family. Laura is distraught, exclaiming that she knew their marriage was in difficulty but that she never believed Joe would cheat on her. At this Joe is utterly confused as he believes Anita is "just a machine, a sex toy," nothing more. This argument between Laura and Joe highlights exactly some of the challenges faced with the rise of these new technologies, challenges that are changing the way humans engage with technology. Not only that, but it also reveals the difference in understandings as to the nature of relationships

---

4. http://www.telegraph.co.uk/science/2017/11/26/rise-digisexual-virtual-reality-bypasses-need-human-intimacy/.

"VR represents the latest, and certainly not the last, development in what we are calling digisexuality: sexual experiences that are enabled or facilitated by digital technology (McArthur & Twist, 2016). In the coming years, sexual technology will become more sophisticated, immersive, and appealing. Many people will find that their experiences with this technology become integral to their sexual identity, and some will come to prefer them to direct sexual interactions with humans. We propose to label those people who consider such experiences essential to their sexual identity as "digisexuals." McArthur and Twist, *The Rise of Digisexuality*, 1–2.

5. McArthur and Twist, *Rise of Digisexuality*, 1–2.

and the way we each understand what it means to be in relationship, the way we connect, for at the heart of the issue is a question about humanness and what it means to be human beings in relationship. It also asks deep questions about how we become more human through our relationships, and what might indeed actually damage and dehumanize us.

Deep Loneliness

There is no doubt that an increasing number of people in the West have a sense of loneliness, a feeling of disconnect from others. There could be multiple reasons for this sense of loneliness and separation, with no one single answer able to fully reveal the depth to this societal problem. Human beings are social beings, created for relationship; we thrive because of the people we are in relationship with. Yet we live in a time of increased competition in every sphere of society, a competition that eclipses relationships whereby young people feel a conscious pressure to be who they believe others expect them to be, and to look the way they believe others expect them to look. Social media is a powerful tool in the modern world, able to connect us to people from virtually every part of the planet, giving us the ability to stay close to family who live on the other side of the world, and develop friendships with others who live in other countries that can indeed lead to face-to-face meetings and new deep relationships forming in a way that was never possible before. Yet we also live in the reality of how social media is disconnecting us from one another, creating a pressure and competition on our lives that leaves us isolated and lonely. When value is placed on body image, when your worth is determined by the particular body archetype of the moment and how you compare to it, whether it is Kim Kardashian's bottom, super model size zero, or any other body shape that happens to be popular among your social grouping at any particular time, it is tough to develop any meaningful relationship. Certainly, teenage girls feel this pressure in monumental ways. Isabelle Whiteley is a photographer and researcher who has travelled up and down the UK interviewing girls between the ages of 13 and 18 for her project called *That's What She Said*, seeking to understand how young people feel in this world of digital and media overload.[6] Her research confirmed the prevalence of photo editing and doctoring among teenage girls, a task made easy and quick with the technological capabilities of today's smartphones. These teenage girls and women express the pain of the endless competition they feel, not only with models and actresses, but with their peers and with themselves, always feeling a sense of inadequacy,

6. www.thatswhatss.com.

of never quite being good enough in comparison. While this is no doubt a problem among females, it is increasingly becoming an issue among males, with studies revealing the growth in body dysmorphia among teenage boys. Research suggests that "most men feel a lean and muscular shape represents the ideal male body type."[7] The biggest-selling men's lifestyle magazine in the UK is *Men's Health*, which has a monthly reach of over 900,000.[8] The significance of this magazine is its emphasis on getting the "perfect" body through diets, weight training, and supplements. Unrealistic expectations of our body shape and size leads to direct competition with ourselves and those around us, which in turn creates a sense of isolation and loneliness.

What has any of this to do with Mary Shelley's classic story? Well, Jordan Peterson has suggested that the story of Frankenstein is a representation of our fear of technology, yet I would suggest that it is actually a story about our fear of loneliness and loss of control. Victor Frankenstein creates the "monster" because of his great grief in losing his mother, a death that he describes as an "irreparable evil"[9] and something he never truly recovers from. Frankenstein's desire is to "renew life where death had apparently devoted the body to corruption."[10] This desire leads to his creation, two years of hard work "for the sole purpose of infusing life into an inanimate body."[11] Victor Frankenstein's creation is a desire to combat the great sense of grief and loss he feels, a desire to solve the mystery and pain of death, to be a master over life and death itself, something that "appeared to me ideal bounds, which I should first break through, and pour a torrent of light into our dark world."[12] Yet upon succeeding in bringing to life the "wretch," the "dream vanished, and breathless horror and disgust filled my heart."[13] That night, after bringing life to the dead, Frankenstein dreams of his dead mother, embracing her with great joy as he sees her alive, well, and walking the streets. Yet upon his embrace her body shrivels and decays, grave worms crawling out of her face, life replaced by the stench of death, a horror that wakes Frankenstein up in a cold sweat and panic, a nightmare that confirms to him that his creation is a monster that even Dante could not conceive of.

---

7. http://www.rcpsych.ac.uk/pdf/BDD_Poster_Presentation.pdf.

8. https://www.statista.com/statistics/246096/reach-of-selected-mens-magazines-in-the-uk/.

9. Shelley, *Frankenstein*, 35.

10. Shelley, *Frankenstein*, 43.

11. Shelley, *Frankenstein*, 45.

12. Shelley, *Frankenstein*, 43.

13. Shelley, *Frankenstein*, 45.

To reverse death is surely deeply rooted within the consciousness of humanity, a desire born from the time we became aware of our mortality, a desire to not only make sense of the horror of death but to heal the wounds that death brings upon our hearts and souls. While stories circulate of those who have died and returned to life, stories of visits to heaven and hell, stories used to warn others of what happens when we die,[14] in reality these stories are quite possibly the reaction of the brain under extreme circumstances, perhaps the result of electrical synapses firing information in a certain way due to the trauma the brain is under. What these stories highlight, however, is that deep desire within many to know what happens when we die, to have a sense of what waits beyond the veil of death. For others, though, this is of no consolation or desire, for what happens when we die is of little help to our lives today; at the death of loved ones we feel the bitterness of death *today*, the loneliness of *now*. What is needed, therefore, is the ability to overcome death in our present, to reverse the power of death through the power of our own hands, the knowledge and skill of our own minds, to no longer wait upon the vagaries of what *might* be, of a God who *might* exist, of an afterlife that *might* be waiting, for such dreams can do little to ease the pain of now for Frankenstein or others like him. As we have already noted, those who call themselves transhumanists are a people who believe that through the advancement of technology and the sciences we can become "better than well," one day "overcoming aging, cognitive shortcomings, involuntary suffering, and our confinement to planet Earth."[15] While such a desire is of course understandable, such a belief fails to recognize the depth of the problem that death brings, for to overcome death is not simply the ability to reduce risks, or even to stop the body from aging, for death permeates the whole cosmos, impacting all things, things beyond the realm of our knowing, our reach, and beyond the material. More than that, the development of technology that may enable us to live longer cannot overcome the complexities of relationships, relationships that have been impacted by the consciousness of death for hundreds of thousands of years, an impact that directly brings deathlike behaviors and attitudes toward the way we relate to one another. What do I mean by this? Unforgiveness cannot be overcome through the development of technology but by the pursuit and hard work of in-depth relating, the pure will to be more than our bitterness, a bitterness that is directly toxic to our well-being and wholeness. We have to be more than our material desires, and rather be those who value the power of that

14. Is it not interesting that in all the accounts of the dead being raised to life in the Gospels and the New Testament, not one documents what the person witnessed or experienced when they died?

15. Bailey et al., "Transhumanist Declaration," lines 1–2.

which is beyond scientific endeavor, the wonder of beauty, the mystery of love, the remarkableness of imagination.

We are, perhaps, a people who desire to be in control of our own lives and destiny, a people who believe in our own abilities to achieve, and who have become fiercely independent and capable. The horror of in-depth relationships stems from our inability to be in control of how those relationships manifest themselves and develop. In relationship we are bound together with another, our identity formed through our mutuality, the need to be vulnerable and authentic, willing to be formed through their lives as well as our own. This loss of control can be deeply unsettling, more so in times when we are encouraged to take back control of our diets, professional lives, where we live, health, and so many other areas of who we are. To live in the beauty of in-depth relationship is to live out of control, to be aware that who we are in our beautiful selves is to live in unconditional, non-coercive relationship whereby what we seek is not to rule over others but to serve, to model servanthood relating. Solidarity is, as Noam Chomsky mentions, "quite dangerous."[16] When people are driven by selfishness, when sympathy is driven out of people, then it becomes far easier for the powerful and the political elites to destroy those public services that require a sense of solidarity within society. So, welfare and the need to care for the most vulnerable becomes demonized and eroded by creating lies around where taxes are spent and to whom the money goes to. Free public education, as Chomsky points out, is attacked on every side and made out to be a terrible public burden that hinders economic growth. Eventually people ask why their taxes are being used to pay for people to go through school, and so privatization creeps in, resulting in young people leaving school with huge debts that they are never able to pay, vastly restricting their opportunities and enabling wealthy corporations and the banks to continue to thrive off the backs of the burden and debt of others. Solidarity, however, declares there is another way, that our lives are not to be lived in isolation and selfishness, but in the power of our togetherness. And we instinctively know that we are created for relationship, that we are not meant to be on our own, that loneliness is "unhuman," indeed, unnatural, something that does not belong to us, nor have any place within creation.[17] We are created for one another,

16. Chomsky, *Requiem for the American Dream*, 65.

17. The creation myth story highlights that humanity is created for relationship, "It is not good for man to be alone . . ." The picture of God "walking in the garden in the cool of the day . . ." reminds us of how connected God is to his creation, never removed from it, intrinsically involved with it but never consumed by it. The myth story of The Great Flood is interesting on a variety of levels in regard to relationship, and far more interesting than any literalist reading could provide. One of the insights the story could

and to be in relationship with God. Loneliness is an evil, something that is unbeing itself, which does not enable humanity nor creation to thrive nor flourish but is an active force against all that is good about relationality. Loneliness creates within us a sense of loss, of moving away from our place and purpose as human beings toward a mode of unbeing, an existence that does not create within us life, nor enable us to fully live. Loneliness is a monster that we can create out of the parts that pain and the fear of death leave in our lives, and such a monster can grow beyond our control or capabilities to contain; this is Frankenstein's monster. We instinctively know that we are not to be on our own, and it takes forceful and unnatural processes to purposely live in isolation, to pursue the way of ourselves without reference to those around us. It is impossible to be truly free and autonomous; there has never been "me" in isolation, for from the moment we begin our existence we are connected to another in the initial compassion of our mother's womb.[18] So before we are aware, we are in relationship. That relationship in the womb of course can be abused, and so from even before we are born, our lives, character, and personality can be shaped negatively; who we are, as already highlighted above, is shaped by those we are in relationship with, both good and bad. And it is because we relational beings that we fear death and the loss it brings.

Death is not simply an interruption into our existence, but a devastation upon our being, an evil that has no place within God's good world. Relationship is bound up in to our very existence, and death is the great enemy that steals those relationships away from us.[19] The fear of loss and loneliness has perversely opened up a culture blighted by fear and loneliness. Social media has created a culture of fear of separation, a fear that our lives will be insignificant, eventually lost in abyss of death, and so we can create a virtual life beyond our lives, enabling us to imagine who we might be, posting images of ourselves or a persona that is in our own control, an image of who we are that shields us from the reality of how we feel about ourselves, and

---

give us is how relational creation is. The Flood symbolizes chaos, social unrest, and overwhelming violence, with the ark a symbol for the saving power of relationships, the survival of humanity found in our solidarity. The animals enter the ark in pairs, a sign not only of fertility and reproduction, but also companionship and how creation is relational. This is no small matter. If God is primarily understood as triune, then all things find their place and their purpose within triunity, flourishing through relationship.

18. "The primary attribute of God, especially whenever the four-letter name Hashem is used, is compassion, the Hebrew word for which, rachamim, comes from the word *rechem*, meaning "a womb." "To Bless the Space Between Us (Vayera 5776)"; http://rabbisacks.org/to-bless-the-space-between-us-vayera-5776/, lines 33–34.

19. "The thief does not come except so that he may steal and slaughter and destroy . . ." John 10:10a. "Where death is your sting?" 1 Cor 15:55b.

controls the way others see us. But to live in such a way divorces us from right-relating, distorts the way we engage with one another, and leaves us grasping for meaning, a meaning that can only be found in depth of relationship. Now of course this is not a problem that every person recognizes for not all are bound up in the social media world, yet in a culture that is so infused with relating through social media, it directly impacts each one of us in some way, whether we realize it or not. It is too soon to know the true scale and depth of how social media is changing the landscape of relationships, and it may be that in fifty years from now we will have navigated these treacherous waters in remarkable ways, but it also might be that we are in ever greater need to change course. What is clear today is that we are struggling to know how to cope with the impact social media is having upon us, upon the way we see ourselves, and the relationships we are in.

Stay With Me

A strange dynamic to social media relationships is the way in which we can, with the click of a button, "unfriend" someone—a swift and silent way of removing someone from your life and ensuring that they know, without you actually speaking to them, that you know longer want to be part of their lives. These might be people who are simply acquaintances, people that you have met a few times in passing, and so the action of removing them from your friends list on Facebook may not be of any real significance to them or to you and will probably make little difference to the occasional face-to-face contact that you may still have. However, those relationships that are much deeper, where the history has greater meaning, such an action of "unfriending" could have a powerfully negative effect that leaves people utterly confused and anxious. Relationships are complex because *we are complex*, our emotions and stories, and desires, our pain, our joy, and so many other things mean that who we are today has been formed and shaped in ways beyond our comprehension or understanding. This complexity is managed through the importance of our physical proximity to one another. It is integral to our health and well-being to meet with others, to recognize that the physical contacts and interactions that we have directly transform us in multiple ways. Those who suffer with anxiety need the interaction of other human beings in a way that social media is unable to provide us with. In conversation and physically being together we pick up the subtle changes in facial expressions, the variant in our tone of voice, the touch of another, the energy of being together, all of which are vital to our ongoing health. This ongoing power of relationship takes a time that social media is often unable or unwilling to give us. The speed at which information is given and passed on moves at such a pace that even within an hour the news that grabbed the headlines has been relegated to an almost nonevent. Twitter is a good example of how what is *trending*[20] determines what is interesting and newsworthy, and that can change at such a pace that you might never be aware of certain stories that piqued the interest of the Twitterverse, and be wholly unaware of stories that had grabbed the attention of various online communities. So it can be easy to be sucked into this frenetic activity of information passed on from one to another, and find ourselves consumed by the speed of things, the ideology of things never happening quick enough, the belief that what is needed is economy of time in order to maximize productivity. Speed becomes then the means through which we judge the quality of an action and the worth of a service or task. Think for a moment the way we feel when an internet page takes longer than five seconds to open up, or if someone takes a few seconds longer than we would like to pull away from a traffic light, or how distracting we now find television adverts that disrupt our program. More worrying than these examples, however, is the speed at which our relationships are lived, a consequence that must directly be influenced by the transformation of our society toward fast-paced and speed-induced relating. As a result, we too easily give ourselves away without allowing the time, space, and patience for who we are to emerge in stages and at a slower pace to those whom we meet. What do I mean by this? Our own stories are fascinating, and it is always wonderful to hear about the lives of others. Take, for instance, the rise in autobiographical sales of books, television shows, or interviews that allow us into the lives of others. Personal testimonies within church services are another example of the power of the personal story, of how when we hear another's story it can have a powerful and profound impact upon our own lives. The sharing of our own stories is no new thing, for the Apostle Paul himself used his own story when speaking to crowds, and court, and rulers; what is new, however, is the way we divulge the tiniest and deepest parts of ourselves to strangers—how easily we disclose ourselves to others, the sometimes delicate and intimate parts of ourselves to people we hardly know. This is not simply about "casual sex," as humanity has always used sex in a variety of ways within various cultures; rather, it is about the seeming need, especially through social media, to divulge intimate details about our lives to strangers, with very little left about ourselves for people to discover as they build relationships with us.

20. *Trending* is a term that describes what news stories, major events, and subjects are being most talked about at any given time. YouTube will push those videos that are trending, with Facebook, Pinterest, and Google+ all promoting those events and stories that are most read and searched for on any given hour of the day.

An example of this is through your "#instastory," a way through which you can share photos and videos of yourself that enable people to watch your daily life unfold. There are, for want of a better word, "regular" people who have thousands of Instagram followers because they share their "regular" life experiences with others, videoing every argument with their children, every conversation with their partner, every bedtime, or trip to the shops. These stories stay visible for only twenty-four hours, meaning that once again speed is of vital importance as these stories that we become captivated by disappear so quickly. There is no need for strangers to know so much about our lives; indeed, there is no need for the vast majority of people in our lives to know so much about us, for who we truly are is surely that which we are to those whom we love the most, those people where no masks are needed, no show is required, where the giving away of vast information about us is unnecessary, for in just a look or a single word so much can be said, so much is understood by those who love us unconditionally and know us beyond the stories we share with the world around us. But these lines are becoming blurred as we share ubiquitously with all who would listen, watch, and share, where who we believe care about us becomes a painful journey as our story only matters when it is shared in the way that appeals to a culture of the instantaneous, a culture who delights in marvelously mundane, kept interested by the occasional shock or scandal. All of this relates to our fear of death, our fear of loneliness, our fear of being forgotten.

Augustine noted that Roman culture and the elites of the Empire indulged in various questionable practices to blunt the fear of death, using war to make a memory of themselves that would last beyond their death. The fear of death can pursue us to indulge in various things in order to be remembered, and in societies where what is spoken of today can be forgotten by tomorrow, we can lose the practice of waiting, of patience, of time, of prayer and meditation, of emerging as a person within our relationships, scared that we will be lost in the speed and plethora of information. Waiting is a profound practice, a challenge to the culture we live in, an act of defiance to a capitalist, materialist, consumerist society that demands our time and money, the sacrifice of our lives on the altar on Mammon. The act of prayer and meditation is a powerfully defiant act, for in that moment of silence and stillness we are rooting ourselves not in the frenetic activity of everything that demands some from us, but in the being of who we are, our identity as children of God. As Dietrich Bonhoeffer puts it,

> Waiting is an art that our impatient age has forgotten. It wants to break open the ripe fruit when it has hardly finished planting the shoot. But all too often the greedy eyes are only deceived;

the fruit that seemed so precious is still green on the inside, and disrespected hands ungratefully toss aside what has so disappointed them. Whoever does not know the austere blessedness of waiting—that is, of hopefully doing without—will never experience the full blessing of fulfillment. Those who do not know how it feels to struggle anxiously with the deepest question of life, of their life and patiently look forward with anticipation until the truth is revealed, cannot even dream of the splendor of the moment in which clarity is illuminated for them. And for those who do not want to win the friendship and love of another person—who do not expectantly open up their soul to the soul of the other person, until friendship and love come, until they make their entrance—for such people the deepest blessing of the one like of two intertwined souls will remain forever hidden. For the greatest, most profound, tenderest things in the world, we must wait. It happens not here in a storm, but according to the divine laws of sprouting, growing and becoming.[21]

The act of waiting and becoming is an act of patient growth, a confidence in who we are becoming in God, a patient hope that God has not given up on us, nor abandoned us to our own devices and desires; it is an act of relationship that directly combats loneliness. Our identity is as beloved children of God, created in the image of our Creator, never forgotten nor demanded to speed through life out of fear that our lives will be nothing but a distant memory, caught up in the wind of time, evaporated like a whisper in the echoes of eternity; no, who we are matters, and the words of our mouths and the meditations of our hearts last within the purposes of God, a part of the way through which the Spirit is creating and redeeming the cosmos toward its goal in Christ. That is not to say that God *needs* our words and actions as such; rather, it is to say that God chooses to take all that is uttered and actioned that is a reflection and sign of God's grace and kingdom and uses them for his eternal purposes. This is what the Creator does. Creation did not end on the day of "very good," but has rather been an ongoing process as all things require the eternal sustaining power of the Spirit to continue and then ultimately find their identity in Christ who is all in all, the One in Whom all things find their place, purpose, and goal. The Creator does not seek to abandon creation to a fire of destruction, nor see anyone perish into the abyss of unknowingness; rather, the heart of God is to see all things redeemed and welcomed into the Divine Life, partakers in the fullness of God's grace, eternally sharers of relationship, rescued forever from any sense of isolation, abandonment, or loneliness. And this glorious hope reveals the true horror of Frankenstein's creation and our own speed and fear-induced relating.

21. Bonhoeffer, *God Is in the Manger*, 4.

Monstrous Other

The terror that Frankenstein's monster unleashes upon his creator is due to the misery of loneliness, the pain of abandonment, knowing that he is a wretch and a monster in the eyes of all who see him. Yet his pain comes from his creator, a creator unwilling to provide a companion, a creator who would rather flee from his creation and avoid the reality of what he has unleashed upon the world, "I desired love and fellowship, and I was still spurned."[22] The monster has an inconsolable sense of grief, pain, and hatred—emotions that he can scarcely believe exist within,

> I cannot believe that I am the same creature whose thoughts were once filled with sublime and transcendent visions of the beauty and majesty of goodness. But it is even so; the fallen angel becomes a malignant devil. Yet even that enemy of God and man had friends and associates in his desolation; I am alone.[23]

This is the true horror. It is not the creation of the monster that should terrify us, but the creation of such loneliness and sense of abandonment that Victor Frankenstein inflicts upon his creation.

It is loneliness that lay at the heart of the werewolf genre. Of course, as we have seen with the chapter on demons, werewolves are also a powerful example of our fear of being out of control—there is little doubt about that. Not only that, but werewolves symbolize our desire to be fully released into our animal instincts, "We should never try to deny the beast, the animal within us."[24] In *The Howling*, Dr. George Waggner has a theory, "Repression. Repression is the father of neurosis, of self-hatred. Now, stress results when we fight against our impulses. We've all heard people talk about animal magnetism, the natural man, the noble savage, as if we'd lost something valuable in our long evolution into civilized human beings." Ginger, in John Fawcett's *Ginger Snaps*, sums it up perfectly: "I'm a goddamn force of nature. I feel like I could do just about anything."[25]

So, werewolves are a projection of the desire to live in pure instinct, released into our pure animal, base desires. Common to the genre is the victim of the curse locking themselves away on the night of a full moon out of pure fear, for once they have transformed into a werewolf they are no longer able to have any say over their actions, creatures of pure, violent, bloodthirsty instinct. But more than this I believe is the horror of loneliness

---

22. Shelley, *Frankenstein*, 169.
23. Shelley, *Frankenstein*, 168–69.
24. *The Howling*, Joe Dante, Embassy Pictures, 1981.
25. *Ginger Snaps*, John Fawcett, Copperheart Entertainment, 2000.

that those with the curse must endure, unable to form deep bonds of relationship because of the curse that they live with. In the 2010 film *The Wolfman*, John Talbot (played by Anthony Hopkins) has lost his humanity, not
only because of his cursed existence, but because of the loneliness it has left
him with, a loneliness caused by his own hands as a werewolf:

> I loved your mother with a passion like the burning of the sun.
> Her death finished me, I was devastated. But I still prowl the
> house at night, searching for her. But I'm dead all the same.
> Look into my eyes Lawrence, you see that I am quite dead.[26]

Remus Lupin from the Harry Potter universe is bitten by a werewolf as a
child and endures a childhood of loneliness and fear that others will discover who he is, the power of deep relationships removed from him because of
the curse upon his life. Ironically, in Victor Frankenstein's desire to reverse
death because of the loss of his mother, he misses that which werewolves
long for and what Shelley's story reveals to us: the power of relationship
and the horror of loneliness. Frankenstein dreamed of reversing the power
of death, of creating life, and yet he failed to recognize that what makes life
is not the ability to animate a body but to bring people together in relationship, to enable the flourishing of being joined together in our lives, to
dispel the darkness of abandonment and pursue lives of relationality. Victor Frankenstein, for all his genius and brilliance, misses the very core and
foundation of what it means to be human, of why existence even matters,
and how existence is even made possible; relationship. And so the monster
rightfully laments, "I, the miserable and the abandoned, am an abortion, to
be spurned at, and kicked, and trampled on. Even now my blood boils at
the recollection of this injustice."[27] This monster of loneliness bids farewell
at the end of the story, no longer able to sustain his existence or endure the
pain he feels, and so vows to build himself a funeral pile "and exult in the
agony of the torturing flames."[28] And this is the destiny of all loneliness, an
extinction that "will be swept into the sea"[29] no longer able to disrupt nor
damage any part of God's good creation. Not only that, but all versions of
a god who abandons any of his children, a god who loves some but hates
others, a god who is repulsed by the work of his hands, this god will die and
be burned up in the fire of Trinitarian Love.

26. *The Wolfman*, Joe Johnston, Universal Pictures, 2010.

27. Shelley, *Frankenstein*, 169.

28. Shelley, *Frankenstein*, 170.

29. Shelley, *Frankenstein*, 170. In the Revelation of John, the sea, a sign of chaos, is
no more, symbolic of God's overcoming of all that brings fear and despair to humanity
and creation, a despair that loneliness is integral to.

Victor Frankenstein dies through the horror and pain of his creation, unable to love the work of his hands, consumed by the fear of what his genius has brought to life. Frankenstein sees all that he loves die by the hands of his monster, and upon seeing the death of his creator, the monster pursues his own death and destruction; both creator and created are so bound together in Shelley's story that loneliness and death are their shared destinies. Yet the gospel is not bound up in such mutuality of death, for its power destroys all economies of exchange, all conditionality of a god who is only willing to love those that have performed the right sacrifice. And so the gospel brings about the true death of god; the god that, like Frankenstein toward his monster, is unwilling to love humanity due to lack of "election," dies; the god that, like Frankenstein, requires blood to bring life, dies; the god that, like Frankenstein, is repulsed by his creation, dies; the god that, like Frankenstein, abandons his creation, dies. God is dead, but the God of Jesus of Nazareth lives, and the gospel breaks out into all possibilities of the cosmos, bringing life to all things,

> ". . . for as all die in Adam, so all will be made alive in Christ."
> (1 Cor 15:22)

The scope of Christ's work on the cross and through the resurrection reaches beyond any and every barrier to God's love, transcends all modes of exclusivity, and vanquishes any trace of death that entered the cosmos through sin. God's redemptive power is wholly relational, a trinitarian affair, the final victory cry of oneness between God and his creation. This is the beauty of the gospel, a beauty that exposes the horror of all loneliness, separation, and abandonment, and breathes the life of relationship into every sphere of the cosmos.

10

Zombies

The Horror of Community

Columbus: Oh, America. I wish I could tell you that this was still America, but I've come to realize that you can't have a country without people. And there are no people here. No. my friends. This is now the United States of Zombieland.[1]

—ZOMBIELAND

The problems we encounter are not due to our differences but to our sameness. This is the great insight of the zombie genre, and one of the reasons why zombies fascinate and horrify us in equal measure. George A. Romero's cult classic *Night of the Living Dead* was released in 1968 and continues to be regarded as a remarkable piece of filmmaking, spawning sequels and spinoffs, a film that in many ways transformed the horror genre forever. Upon its initial release it was heavily criticized by film critics and commentators for its extreme violence, a film where some questioned the moral health of those who went to see this "orgy of sadism."[2] However, as time went on many have remarked on its depth of insight—the way the film, for instance, could be interpreted as calling to account the political ideology of the day, foreign policy, and the Vietnam war.[3] Then there is the way, as Elliot Stein

1. *Zombieland*, Ruben Fleischer, Columbia Pictures, 2009.
2. Russell, *Book of the Dead*, 65.
3. Sumiko, "Night of the Living Dead: A Horror Film about the Horrors of the

believes, that *Night of the Living Dead* directly challenges domestic racism, with Duane Jones, the only African American actor in the film, the sole heroic figure fighting against the army of zombies that seem to march on without fear, feeling, thought, or regard. In many ways, the true horror of the film is not the zombies but in its nihilistic ending as Duane Jones's character, Ben, the last survivor of the zombie attack on the farmhouse where he is holed up, is shot in the head by white rednecks who have come to hunt and kill the walking dead,

> *Vince:* "There's something in there, I heard a noise."

> *Sheriff McClelland:* "All right, Vince, hit him in the head, right between the eyes . . . Good shot! Ok, he's dead, let's go get him. That's another one for the fire."[4]

This scene would surely have evoked strong emotions and reactions within many audience members, especially the African American community, in light of the assassination of Dr. Martin Luther King Jr. earlier that year, as well as the assassination of Malcolm X in 1965. The not-so-subtle and powerful insight to this final scene is how Ben, as a black man, is regarded by the white police and zombie hunters as nothing, just "another one for the fire." Zombie or black, it makes no difference to a society steeped in racism, the goal being simply to get rid of and subdue anyone that is not white, that is different from us. The nihilism of the film would have been a shock to audiences, a work of desperation that was unusual for a film of the time, but at the same time it would have echoed a harsh reality for persons of color and been an emotionally charged experience for those watching because of the racist culture that existed, and continues to exist within America.[5] This nihilism is an important aspect of the film, for it highlights the ongoing struggle of persons of color against racism, a struggle that cannot be whitewashed by Hollywood's happy ending nor mocked by Hollywood's racist casting; racism is an evil that must continually be spoken of with deep honesty and spoken out against with flaming passion. This is why films like

---

Vietnam Era," 181.

4. *Night of the Living Dead*, George A. Romero, Image Ten, 1968.

5. There is still no doubt that racism is and continues to be a huge problem in America, a problem that is not going away any time soon. There is need for radical change within every sphere of society, of authentic speech, and direct political action to address the overt, institutionalized, and systemic racism within society. Watching *Night of the Living Dead* is like a punch to the stomach as the obviousness of the societal racism is presented in full force through the power of cinema.

Get Out and *Black Panther*[6] are of such significance to the cinematic and cultural world, for they refuse to cast black people within the racist ideology and framework that Hollywood consistently works within and offers a potentially new era to the cinematic universe, and, more importantly, the black community. Speaking of *Black Panther*, Carvell Wallace, writing for *The New York Times Magazine*, comments,

> Beyond the question of what the movie will bring to African-Americans sits what might be a more important question: What will black people bring to "Black Panther"? The film arrives as a corporate product, but we are using it for our own purposes, posting with unbridled ardor about what we're going to wear to the opening night, announcing the depths of the squads we'll be rolling with, declaring that Feb. 16, 2018, will be "the Blackest Day in History."
>
> This is all part of a tradition of unrestrained celebration and joy that we have come to rely on for our spiritual survival. We know that there is no end to the reminders that our lives, our hearts, our personhoods are expendable. Yes, many non-black people will say differently; they will declare their love for us, they will post Martin Luther King Jr. and Nelson Mandela quotes one or two days a year. But the actions of our country and its collective society, and our experiences within it, speak unquestionably to the opposite.[7]

African Americans are often typecast within film and television roles, their function simply to provide help, support, a comedic element, or rescue

6. "Black Panther is a historic opportunity to be a part of something important and special, particularly at a time when African Americans are affirming their identities while dealing with vilification and dehumanization. The image of a black hero on this scale is just really exciting," https://www.motherjones.com/media/2016/02/diversity-oscars-so-white-black-panther-film-joe-robert-cole/.
"If you are reading this and you are white, seeing people who look like you in mass media probably isn't something you think about often. Every day, the culture reflects not only you but nearly infinite versions of you—executives, poets, garbage collectors, soldiers, nurses and so on. The world shows you that your possibilities are boundless. Now, after a brief respite, you again have a President.
Those of us who are not white have considerably more trouble not only finding representation of ourselves in mass media and other arenas of public life, but also finding representation that indicates that our humanity is multifaceted. Relating to characters onscreen is necessary not merely for us to feel seen and understood, but also for others who need to see and understand us. When it doesn't happen, we are all the poorer for it . . . Black Panther matters . . . because he is our best chance for people of every color to see a black hero. That is its own kind of power," http://time.com/black-panther/.

7. https://www.nytimes.com/2018/02/12/magazine/why-black-panther-is-a-defining-moment-for-black-america.html.

to the main white character—getting them out of trouble, providing support for the white character to achieve their dreams, or being their moral consciousness. *Black Panther* offers something uniquely different, a film that celebrates the power, genius, strength, and possibilities that African Americans bring, not just to America, but to the world, possibilities that do not require anything from white imperialism. *Black Panther* offers us something different, a celebration of how the world is a place of diversity, that we bring our differences and our cultures to one another, and that is something to rejoice over, something that we should actively pursue within our communities together. This then also emphasizes the true genius and horror of Jordan Peele's masterful 2017 film *Get Out*. At one point in the film, the main character Chris, while visiting his white girlfriend's parents, is subjected to a form of hypnotism by the mother, Missy. Chris slides down the chair into a dark abyss, suspended into nothingness: "Now you're in the Sunken Place." Peele describes the Sunken Place as America's long and dark history with racism, a place that continues to silence and abuse black people. In a tweet he says, "The Sunken Place means we're marginalized. No matter how hard we scream, the system silences us."[8] *Get Out* refuses to allow us to ignore white privilege, refuses to allow us to be comfortable in our racism, the way black people are nothing but a commodity, a means through which white people can exert power and grow in power through the dominance over black people. It is a film that refuses to allow us to justify our violence toward persons of color. Not only that, but the film powerfully demonstrates the way white privilege has sought to take hold of other cultures and consume them, change them, and "whitewash" them, refusing to hear the voices of people from different races and cultures. *Get Out* gives that voice back with unflinching power, a film that calls us to difference, and not to the sameness that the white characters desire within the film, a sameness that zombies symbolize in violent starkness.

We are not called to be the same, to be a people who blend together in commonality, whose uniqueness as "I" is lost to the collective "us." And yet, as we have already discussed, there is no "I" without "us," and so we find ourselves in the predicament of how we relate together, how we exist within community, not a collectivized clone, but equally not in an imaginary lone. We are who we are because of others, in relationship with others, in our identity shaped by the relationships we are in, not a calling to become a homogenous group of undifferentiated people, committed to collectivizing beyond all racial, social, and gender boundaries; our humanity is one of

8. https://twitter.com/JordanPeele/status/842589407521595393?ref_
src=twsrc%5Etfw&ref_url=https%3A%2F%2Fwww.thewrap.com%2
Fget-out-director-jordan-peele-explains-the-sunken-place%2F.

beautiful diversity, and so we must celebrate our uniqueness as "I" within the wonder of "us." Among white working-class Americans, well over 60 percent are worried that America is losing its identity due to outside influence, a feeling of "strangeness" within the country that they live. One of the main reasons that people voted Leave in the British EU referendum was because of fears of migration. Of course not everyone who voted Leave shared those fears as we have already noted, but it has become clear that immigration became the single-most important factor that drove the Leave vote.[9] This fear of "other" is paradoxical as those areas within Britain that have the fewest recent new immigration were the highest percentage of Leave voters. Now this might well be due to the way immigration is framed both within media and political discourse, with a fear of what *could be* because of immigration rather than a fear of what *actually is* the driving force behind voting intention.[10] Whatever the reasons, there is a sense in both America and Britain that some kind of identity has been lost, that who we are is being eroded by influences beyond us, by those who are different to us. Yet the real cause of our fear, the rise of our conflict, results not from our differences but from our *sameness*.

We are each created unique, a wonderful individual within the collective of our human species. Every person has a unique fingerprint, quite literally, and we leave a symbolic fingerprint upon the world around us, shaping others and being shaped by others in wonderfully idiosyncratic ways. The flourishing of communities is a direct result of how well people can be uniquely themselves within the context of unconditional relating, where people are encouraged to be themselves within the beauty of relationships. Theologically, this is directly because of a triune God who lives in mutual, indwelling, relational love, a God who is known in tri-unity, who is One and Three, Father, Son, and Spirit. Created in the image of God, we are relational beings, our identity bound up in the "other" yet uniquely ourselves. The challenges we face flow from our assimilation into the "other" whereby who we are in our uniqueness is morphed and molded into the identity of others, where distinctions collapse and we, albeit often unconsciously, become no different to anyone else.

---

9. www.theguardian.com/politics/2016/jun/24/voting-details-show-immigration-fears-were-paradoxical-but-decisive.

10. There was an utterly ludicrous interview on Fox News where the "terror expert" said that there were places within the UK that were "no-go zones" because of Sharia Law, where he even went on to say that the city of Birmingham was completely off limits to non-Muslims, something which, as someone who regularly goes to Birmingham, can safely say is total nonsense! See https://www.youtube.com/watch?v=EmoeXxW3Gw4.

René Girard comments how he believes early humans became violent toward one another and descended into chaos because of "undifferentiation,"
people becoming just like one another within early human groups because
of their common desire; we desire the same thing as each other and become
rivals as we both seek to acquire this desire for ourselves, resulting in violence and a crisis in the community. This "crisis of distinctions" leads the
community to search out a cause and blame for the outbreak of violence and
lack of peace, with, as Girard believes, the birth of the "scapegoat," someone
on whom we can lay all blame and release our violence on to. So zombies
symbolize the horror of sameness, the way that in our sameness we become
rivals, infected by our collectivized desire for the same thing—a desire that
breaks out in total destruction and violence. And zombies represent the
power of the outbreak of that violence, the collectivized power that violence
brings, and the way violence is able to unite us in a common goal.

Zom-Me

Zombies are a wild and untamable beast, their sole purpose to kill and eat,
to consume human flesh, without thought or feeling. Major Henry West in
the film 28 Days Later has a theory about zombie infection: "This is what
I've seen in the four weeks since infection. People killing people, which is
much what I saw in the four weeks before infection, and the four weeks
before that, and before that, and as far back as I care to remember. People
killing people, which to my mind, puts us in a state of normality right
now."[11] Violence is a thoroughly human affair. From our earliest history
we have been killing each other, and nothing appears to be changing the
landscape of our capacity for violence. Zombies terrorize us because they
actually reveal how easy we find it to murder one another, how apparently
limitless our capacity is to inflict violence upon one another in inventive
and shocking ways. Zombies merely reflect back to us our own violence, the
way we can kill without prejudice on a monumental scale. Noam Chomsky
makes the point that when Bill Clinton ordered the bombing on the major
pharmaceutical factory in al-Shifa, Sudan, he did so without any regard for
the loss of human life that would entail. Chomsky notes that Clinton simply
did not care because he did not view the casualties as human in any way,
". . . it just didn't matter if lots of people are killed in a poor African country,
just as we don't care if we kill ants when we walk down the street."[12] This is
the power that violence has over us, and the difficulty we have in recogniz-

11. *28 Days Later,* Danny Boyle, DNA Films, 2002.
12. https://samharris.org/the-limits-of-discourse/, lines 596–7.

ing it for what it is. The zombie genre has the ability to "open our eyes"[13] to the reality of the violence that is constantly all around us, a violence we are consistently engaged with at all times in some form or another. Some might suggest hyperbole at this, but so imbedded within violence have we become, it is difficult to fully untangle and recognize the very depth and complex layers of violence we are engaged in each day, from our consumerist consumption through to our physical violence toward one another. Our global consumption of goods has demanded the driving down of prices, the ability to get what we want at ever cheaper prices; from chocolate, to clothes, to technology, we want to be able to get more for our money. And with a greater financial squeeze on the working and middle class, a squeeze that is the direct result of the gambling of investments by the rich and powerful, then being able to make your money go further matters. However, it comes at a cost as the poorest and most vulnerable in the majority world are the ones whose working conditions and wages are driven down in order to maximize the profits for shareholders and the owners of big business. It is a frankly horrendous situation with no quick or easy answers.

The web of violence extends across our planet, consuming all in its path. This infection of violence affects each and every one of us, so that those who seek to resist it, who seek a "cure" and develop a different mode of being to operate out of are usually regarded with suspicion and contempt, for we have come to believe that violence is the only way we can manage the world. We believe in "good" violence and "bad" violence, and that as long as we are supporters of, or administers of "good" violence then we will be on the right side of history. Yet if history is anything to go by—and it usually is—then there is actually no such thing as "good" violence, merely "regrettable" violence. Every act of violence creates a counter desire for vengeance, a belief in the need for the scales of justice to be balanced. Every human being is involved in a complex web of relationships, and so the impact of violence on one person, whether it be from the state or elsewhere, will always ripple out beyond, leaving a bitter and terrible trail that is not easily healed. What is often forgotten is how damaging and transformative it is to the human soul, to their entire being, when you take another person's life; there is a harrowing scene in *Saving Private Ryan* when an Allied and Nazi soldier are fighting one another and the Nazi soldier pins the Allied soldier down and begins to slowly drive a knife into his heart while the Allied soldier pleads

13. "Ghouls don't blink. I don't know why. Maybe because they don't have as much bodily fluid they can't keep using it to coat the eyes. Who knows, but they don't blink . . ." Brooks, *World War Z*, 158. Zombies operate out of pure violent instinct. There is no holding back for their desire to kill and consume, no moment when they close their eyes to their deepest desire, they simply pursue what they are, without regret.

with him to stop; their faces are inches apart from one another, eyes in full contact with each other while murder and death happen between them. It is a scene that not only highlights the horror of war, it emphasizes the brutality of violence and the dehumanizing effects it has on each one of us. For this is true scale of violence and the true horror of it, the level to which it strips us of our humanity and dehumanizes our fellow human beings in every way imaginable. Zombies are a significant and powerful symbolic representation of the power of violence to empty us of our humanity, its power to turn us into the walking dead and forget that our true collectiveness, our true path to human meaning and togetherness, is found in relationship and unconditional love, expressed through forgiveness and the forsaking of all violence. This is in part why Jesus is a model of all human relationships, and why his life and teaching are vital to all human flourishing. His rejection of all violence is the direct result of his commitment to the way of forgiveness and the path of peace, and flows from his understanding that violence can never resolve the challenges that humanity face, nor will it ever heal what is broken; "all who take up a sword will be destroyed by a sword. Or do you imagine that that I cannot ask my Father, and he will at this very moment place more than twelve legions of angels beside me?" (Matt 26:52b–3). Jesus is fully aware that every act of violence breeds an escalation of violence, and that an act of violence will do nothing to bring the gospel of peace that he has committed himself to. Swords must be put away, beaten into ploughshares in order that true peace can come, a peace that can unite humanity in nonrivalrous ways, because, right now, our similarities, our sameness is a result of our rivalry, and it is this rivalry that is tearing us apart.

What is striking about the zombie genre is how like us the walking dead actually are, similar enough to us, yet different enough to fear; this is requirement, Girard argues, of the scapegoat—enough like us so they can be blamed, yet different enough for us to fear them and not to care about their death. Zombies symbolize our fear of sameness, the violence that comes through undifferentiation. The unrest felt within communities in the West has nothing to do with immigration (although it is sometimes expressed in this way) and everything to do with our collective sameness, the way we have all become so similar and can no longer handle the rivalry that has broken out as a result. We are bombarded by selfish capitalism every day of our lives, the belief in unregulated and uncontrolled competition to succeed at all costs, to make the most money, and achieve the dream of buying a bigger and better life for ourselves. Now of course not everyone wants this, yet the dominant narrative we are faced with is an economic one, where the most important things are the banks, the markets, and the deficit. Television producers know that the viewing public love to watch the lives of the rich and famous, and countless shows allow us to peek inside their world, to get a glimpse of how the superrich live and imagine what it would be like to be in a position where money was truly no object. Not only this, but social media proves to be a highly lucrative and popular medium to display your money, showing people your everyday experiences as someone with extreme wealth. The competition is fierce to work out how you might join the ranks of elites and super wealthy. Of course, humanity has always struggled with the desire of what others have, a recognition of the ancients with the command not to covet your neighbor's possessions. The worry for us today in the twenty-first century is the vastness and accessibility into our neighbor's lives, the ability to "see over" a million different neighbor's fences through the power of the internet and covet what they have. Certain sections of society are getting richer and richer, levels of wealth that are unheard of, allowing people to buy things never before imagined or dreamed of, made to order by people who know the lust and desires of those with access to untold resources.

Distract Me

The pressure on the middle class in the West is being felt in greater degrees, and the burden of debt caused by unregulated banking and the gambling of public money is being ever more placed upon those who are unable to carry the immense weight of this debt. Distraction is a vital tool used by those in power and the elites who pull the strings of governments, and so the language of spending and deficit is repeated over and over again, encouraging us to be firstly consumers who are so caught up by the stuff we buy that they hope we will pay little or no attention to the role of lobbyists, or government bills, or anything else that we think has no direct impact on our lives. This weight is being felt in communities across the West, and it has been easier for us to place the blame, not on the ridiculously wealthy whose interests are protected by government, but upon the poorest and most vulnerable, to believe that the problems come through overcrowding or benefit cheats, or any other such narrative. Any degree of research would quickly expose this to be nonsense, and that it is quite clear how it is the vested interests of the most powerful and wealthy that has caused the extreme damage to economies across the world while protecting their vast empires, yet we live in a time when it would seem that people no longer want or care to do such research, where they feel their time would be better spent in other ways, protecting themselves, looking after their own. This is an understandable reaction in times of what feels like information overload, where we are constantly bombarded with stories, and yet is nothing more than mundane distraction that has nothing to do with anything in particular apart from keeping us distracted.

As consumers we are constantly distracted, and it is as consumers within a capitalist system that we have become undifferentiated and propelled into rivalry. We seek and strive and struggle for a better standard of living, the advice to work hard and then be rewarded, with families no longer encouraged to spend quality time together as both parents are encouraged to work full time. In the UK the Conservative government has introduced thirty hours of free childcare for three-year-olds, meaning that both parents can go out to work and leave their children in full-time care. Some children will not see either of their parents all week, save for an hour before bed. Now, for some, both parents have to work to cover the cost of the mortgage and rising living expenses, which are directly impacting the middle class, but governments could not care less about this dilemma, nor work out how to ease the pressure on families so that there is no need for children to be in childcare all week; their interests are determined, as we have already said, by the interests of the superrich. Zombies symbolize the majority of our society who have been overtaken by the need to work endlessly, who are trapped by a system that demands every hour of their day in subservience. People in the West are tired because our lives are a constant hive of activity, a sense that we never truly rest, where we are always working, never fully switched off. One of the single most destructive things to family time is the accessibility of work emails on our smartphones, an accessibility that means many of us never fully switch off and become fully aware of the moment we are in with those who we love the most. Zombies represent our predicament, how we have become rivals seeking to attain a better standard of life, but in doing so have lost something of our humanness in the process. We march on incessantly and without rest, each seeking to acquire something that will satisfy, and yet it is never enough, and we look around and we are all the same—all after something to feed our desires with.

In Max Brook's book *World War Z*, one of those interviewed remarks, "Confidence, it's the only fuel that drives the capitalist machine. Our economy can only run if people believe in it."[14] We have to continue to believe in the way the world is, to have confidence in it in order to continue to play by its rules, to believe that we could someday have more than we have now. If we were honest though, for many it is simply that we get up and do what we have to do because that is simply the way the world is. We are in conflict because we have become the same, so many of us feel bound up in this seemingly relentless charge of work and money, feeling the pressure, feeling

14. Brooks, *World War Z*, 337.

the sense of failure, feeling unable to do anything about it. So it is easier to blame the "others," whomever they are, in order to try and relieve that burden, to seek a way to deal with our emotional strain. Zombies represent our fear and our violence that flows from our disappointment and rivalistic desires and the subsequent violence that often breaks out of us. It is like a contagion that is difficult to resist as it sweeps over us, without thought or feeling. It has a profoundly numbing affect upon us as, through our distraction and sameness, alongside our desire to simply "get on" without adding to the stress and complexities of our lives. Notice the simplicity of zombies, the way they seem constantly distracted, how they are of total uniformity, and driven by an insatiable desire to "get on" and feed. This simplicity symbolized through the zombie genre is perfectly apt for the way discourse has evolved in recent years through social media.

We have become conditioned to be unable to talk reasonably and sensibly about politics in an age of immediate action and social media conversation. So much of social media and mainstream media is soundbites and memes, the outpouring of sentimentality and one liners that does nothing to further the conversation nor deal with the complexity of any given subject. The result is the inability to hear one another over the noise of our own arguments, a shouting match of opinions trying to make our opponent look stupid, trying to shame them, or seeking to silence them in some way. And once again we imitate one another in our approach, both sides of any given debate merely mirroring each other in the way they argue and approach discourse—undifferentiation.

Imitate Me

Zombies represent our fear of sameness that comes through rivalry. This is an important point that must not be missed: sameness through rivalry. It is not simply a fear of sameness, for we are by nature imitative, learning through imitation of those around us, growing, and discovering who we are through the lives of those around us. And as human beings we often find security, comfort, and belonging through those we share a commonality with, those with whom our lives are bound together in a shared understanding. There is nothing wrong with this. It is when we find ourselves identical in our rivalry, conflict and crisis arising from our shared desires to take hold of something that is not yet ours, to lay hold of something that we perceive to belong to another yet overwhelmingly feel compelled to make it our own. Sameness through rivalry is the zombie epidemic, a crisis that sweeps across nations, consuming all that fall in its path, a *crisis of distinctions.*

This is the power of capitalism, an ideology and global force that transcends creeds, race, economic status, and all distinguishing features and is able to adapt and evolve according to its surroundings; in many ways, it is a remarkable system. The crisis of distinctions occurs, however, not directly through a capitalist system, although this is the seedbed into which the crisis occurs; rather, it happens through a *market system*. In a truly capitalist economy the major financial institutions would have been left to fail; investors who took such monumental risks would have seen their investments wiped out, the institution allowed to follow its inevitable collapse, "But the rich and powerful, they don't want a capitalist system. They want to be able to turn to the 'nanny state' as soon as they're in trouble, and get bailed out by the taxpayer. They're given a government insurance policy, which means that no matter how often you risk everything, if you get in trouble, the public will bail you out because you're too big to fail—and it's just repeating over and over again."[15] The market system enables the rich and powerful to feed off every opportunity to increase their wealth and raise their level of power and influence, with no regard for anyone but themselves. This market system puts the majority of society into conflict as we strive and struggle toward the object and goal of a "better life." It is in this way that our sameness through rivalry occurs. The "plutonomy"—those who have extraordinary amounts of wealth—have managed to shift the perception of the narrative away from the financial decisions they make, the risks they take, and the level of inequality that they have created, away from themselves and onto the mass of the population, creating competition between working people around the world while all the while protecting their own interests. The continued maligning and destruction of labor unions, alongside the media narrative of aggressive protest movements, as well as the shifting of perception so that previously fairly centrist policies are regarded as "leftist, communist," has closed down so many opportunities for serious and well-reasoned debate and has created an aggressiveness to all economic and political discussion. The plutonomy have masterfully designed the narrative so that they may continue to control the outcomes. What we have witnessed is that wealth of such monumental scale is never enough and can never be satisfied. I was recently watching a program that interviewed the super-wealthy and observed some of the ways they spend their money. One person whose job was to fulfill the desires of his rich clients stated, "You give them one thing and their appetite increases. The rich always desire more, nothing is ever good enough."[16] This insatiable need for more represents the true horror of the

15. Chomsky, *Requiem for the American Dream*, 84–85.

16. http://www.channel4.com/programmes/the-worlds-most-luxurious-airline/
on-demand/67119-001.

zombie genre, and our crisis of sameness through rivalry is that we wonder why we cannot have what they have and work out how we might join them.

Max Brooks's *World War Z* is a masterful work of fiction, written and documented in such a way that you truly believe you are reading actual fact, an oral history that reads like reality. The zombie plague in *World War Z* transforms every continent, impacting every part of society, leaving no person unaffected by the sheer level of destruction that the plague brings. The book is a collection of interviews taken across the world, hearing the stories of all kinds of different people, from politicians, to army generals, to hospitalized patients, to people simply trying to rebuild their lives. In one interview with Joe, the owner of the town's bicycle repair shop in a small part of Washington, we hear that during the height of the zombie epidemic he was recruited to be part of a newly formed Neighborhood Security, a quasi-military outfit that patrolled the local area and exterminated any zombies. Joe, however, believed something else was a bigger problem.

> The biggest problem were quislings.

Quislings?

> Yeah, you know, the people that went nutballs and started act-
> ing like zombies . . . there's a type of person who just can't deal
> with a fight-or-die situation. They're always drawn to what
> they're afraid of. Instead of resisting it, they want to please it,
> join it, try to be like it . . . But you couldn't do it in this war.
> You couldn't just throw up your hands and say, "Hey don't kill
> me, I'm on your side." There was no gray area in this fight, no
> in-between . . . They started moving like zombies, sounding like
> them, even attacking and trying to eat other people . . . Quis-
> lings don't scream. They just lie there, not even trying to fight,
> writhing in that slow, robotic way, eaten alive by the very crea-
> tures they're trying to be.[17]

This is the struggle we are in: the struggle of simply becoming "quis-lings"—becoming like the very thing that is destroying us, and in the process being "eaten alive" by it. For the plutonomy the goal is not the overall welfare of the country but for their own concentrated wealth, the goal to make as much money in the next quarter as possible, with no perception or care for how this maximizing of personal wealth impacts wider society. Indeed, the levels of inequality that are now being seen matter little to the masters who control the flow of wealth. As Joe remarks, "Remember early

17. Brooks, *World War Z*, 155–59.

in the war, when everybody was trying to work on a way to turn the living dead against one another? . . . Stupid."[18] Everyone knows that those with the greatest concentration of wealth will ensure that those who enable that great wealth will look after each other, will ensure the wealth continues to grow; you won't turn them against each other as a way of breaking up that power and mastery of wealth. Zombies are symbolic of this power of inequality, a living dead force that cannot be stopped by simply trying to join it, for by joining it you become overwhelmed by it. The only way to defeat it, or at the very least, to subdue it, is by collectivity, the coming together in community.

Bind Us Together

The Walking Dead has proven to be one of the most popular television series of recent years, a post-apocalyptic tale that explores a world devastated by Walkers (zombies) and the plight of the remaining human survivors seeking to rebuild their lives and eradicate the zombie epidemic. The show follows Rick Grimes, a sheriff's deputy who wakes from a coma and discovers the world is overrun by zombies. Now in its ninth season, *The Walking Dead* has followed the fate of Rick and the various groups of people that have been involved in his life, and the ongoing fight to survive the plague of Walkers. Part of the series' ongoing appeal has been its ability to surprise and shock in equal measure, with no character in the show seemingly safe, not only from the zombies, but also from one another. Now, so far our analysis of zombies has led to recognize that they symbolize a number of different things:

- Sameness that comes through rivalry
- The power of collective violence
- Symbolic of inequality
- Insatiable need for more

The Walking Dead, however, gives us a different perspective that is perhaps the most striking and important, for it offers us a way ahead, an insight that can counter the bleak and apocalyptic landscape that I have offered so far!

Within *The Walking Dead* universe, the main struggle is actually not with the Walkers but with humanity seeking to build community together because of the devastation the epidemic has wrought on the world. Within each season the Walkers are often simply a background horror, albeit a real and terrifying part of the landscape, but it is actually the struggle between human beings to build community, to find a sense of *belonging and worth*

18. Brooks, *World War Z*, 159.

within the dynamics of human groupings, human collectiveness that has been radically transformed by the zombie plague, but also highlighting those things that seem to never change. The world can be eradicated of zombies, or any threat to our existence, but the real struggle of finding our place will continue, for this goes to the very heart of our desire, to the very core of our being, to know that we belong and have a purpose within this place of belonging. But *The Walking Dead* does not simply explore the complexities and philosophical intricacies of human belonging; rather, it challenges us in what it looks like for human beings to flourish within community, of how our lives are bettered and how we might positively grow as the best version of ourselves in a world that has been torn apart by violence, suffering, and pain. It is not enough to simply join a community in *The Walking Dead*, for that in and of itself does not always lead the characters to grow more human; indeed, in many cases there is little difference between the zombie's and human's unquenchable thirst for blood. As we have already noted, the pursuit of violence does nothing to bring out our humanness and does everything to mar the image of God within us and strip us of our humanity.

In the season 7 premiere we are witnesses to a brutal display of power and demand for loyalty by Negan, the leader the Saviors. Using a baseball bat covered in barbed wire, Negan kills two of Rick Grimes's friends, a horrific display of sadism that he uses in order to control those around him, a means through which Negan will ensure none dare cross or betray him. While some viewers were appalled at the sheer level of violence (and make no mistake, the scene in question is monumentally violent), the violence depicted powerfully highlights the descent into darkness and dehumanizing power that violence brings, as well as exposing the purposeless of being part of communities that strip away our humanity for the sake of belonging. To truly belong, to be part of true community, is to be enabled to flourish and thrive as human beings in the pursuit and practice of unconditional love. With each passing season, the characters in *The Walking Dead* find their humanity pushed to the limits and stripped from them as they wrestle with their own demons and act in ways that strip their humanity from them. Rick comments how "everyone who made it this far, we've all done worse kinds of things just to stay alive. But we can still come back. We're not too far gone."[19] The goal for all who have journeyed with Rick is to find somewhere they can call home, a place where they can settle in community, where all are cared for and nurtured; the goal is to settle and rediscover their humanity, to enter into the best version of themselves, with the hope of that version not becoming totally lost through the

19. *The Walking Dead*, Season 4, Episode 8, "Too Far Gone," Ernest R. Dickerson, AMC, 2013.

suffering and violence they have endured and inflicted upon others. The sheer level of violence that has walked with them has taken their humanity away from each person, but they believe redemption is possible. This is a wonderful insight that *The Walking Dead* provides to a Western society that is worn out through conflict. Jesus prayed that we might be one as he and his Abba are One, a prayer that is not simply about those that might believe a certain way, or pray a particular prayer; rather, it is a prayer from the Son, to the Father, a prayer that humanity might find its Way home to God in the beauty of our reconciliation, one to the other. We cannot continue down the wide road of destruction that we are so often keen to tread, for to tread that way can only lead to our misery. We must be willing to take the painful and difficult path toward peace, a peace that is won through our willingness to accept others as we have been accepted by God. We must seek to nonviolently fight for community, for the coming together of our common humanity for the common goal of our human flourishing, that is epitomized in hope, a hope that breaks out into the despair, and breathes the life of love into those places where hate has reigned. There have been those throughout history who have shown us, who have enabled us to glimpse at how powerful nonviolence is at bringing our humanity out, in showing us our true humanity when freed from our violent desires. For the first three hundred years of their existence, Christians were subjugated to extreme violence and persecution at times for their refusal to worship the emperor, engage in violence, or participate in war. This commitment to this peculiar way of life following the nonviolent way of Jesus only strengthened them as a community, causing them, despite their suffering, to be an attractive and growing body of people. From Russian peasants to South American workers, nonviolence has worked in overthrowing regimes and transforming the rights of the common person. Whenever nonviolence was used against the Nazis, it worked, with thousands of Bulgarian, Danish, Dutch, and Norwegian Jews saved from going to death camps directly as a result of nonviolent resistance. The terrible insight from history is that nonviolence is used with such infrequency when its power to change the world is so apparent. Nonviolent resistance is not the simple acceptance of your lot, the belief that you should simply roll over and die; rather, it is the active pursuit of liberation, the belief that transformation is truly possible *without violence*.[20] The teachings of Jesus on nonviolence, as well as his practice of it, revealed a model, not only for humanity in our individuality, but also for community, a way of life together that is exemplified by the power of forgiveness and unconditionality. It is no longer enough to believe that the repetition

---

20. For examples of how nonviolence has worked in resisting violent governments and bringing about real change, see Wink, *Engaging the Powers*, 243–57.

of our violent ways will eventually solve our global challenges, challenges that the zombie genre illustrates with brilliant clarity. The pursuit of nonviolence does not naively believe that human and global violence will be eradicated through human endeavor, for that is simply another form of Utopianism, and we have already discovered how flawed such ideology is; rather, it is the belief that through nonviolence human communities can flourish and model, albeit provisionally and imperfectly, what is to be hoped for when God brings peace to reign on a cosmic level. The nonviolent ethic and life of Jesus reveals a Way of Life together that pushes back against the zombie apocalypse of rivalry, collective violence, and inequality. It reveals the possibility of community that offers forgiveness as the most powerful weapon in the cosmos, a weapon of such significance whereby anything is possible. It is no easy path, and it will come at great cost, but through it we will discover our humanity, a humanity that can get lost beneath the pain of our violent ways.

Jesus shows us the Way to Truthfully Live, but will we be brave enough to follow him through our fears and into the pursuit of unconditional love?

Conclusion

The Power of Peace

Marty: Didn't you tell me . . . you used to make up stories about the stars?

Rust: Yeah, that was in Alaska, under the night skies.

Marty: And look up at the stars and make up stories. Like what?

Rust: . . . it's just one story. The oldest.

Marty: What's that?

Rust: Light versus dark.[1]

—*TRUE DETECTIVE*

A T THE TIME OF writing this book, America has experienced yet another school mass shooting. On February 14, 2018, Nikolas Cruz, a nineteen-year-old student from Florida, went into his former school, Marjory Stoneman Douglas High School, and killed seventeen people using his semi-automatic rifle—three teachers and fourteen students, all shot dead indiscriminately by Cruz. A few days later Emma Gonzalez, a student from the school where the shooting occurred, spoke at an anti-gun rally in Fort Lauderdale, a speech that has caught the imagination of many people

1. *True Detective*, Season 1, Episode 8, "Form and Void," Cary Joji Fukunaga, Parliament of Owls, 2014.

across the world for its passion, bravery, imagination, and determination that something needs to happen within American culture for the murder and mayhem to stop.[2] James Atwood, in his book, *Gundamentalism and Where It Is Taking America*, makes this powerful point:

> Gun violence has changed the character of our country . . . Children . . . fear going to school because other kids bring guns. How could it be otherwise when our Congress and too many clergy think the best thing they can do is keep the families of gun victims in their thoughts and prayers instead of turning heaven and earth in the name of God to stop such madness from happening again? While verbally scorning violence, our nation has accepted its escalation as inevitable . . . We psychologically inoculate ourselves against the presence of more powerful guns and the frequency of mass shootings.[3]

The speech by Gonzalez displayed a sense of "enough!" and that, for many young people especially, radical change is needed to heal America of its gun problem, and that change will only come from the voice and action of America's children, young people, and young adults. Emma Gonzalez and the millions who have watched her speech are not inoculated to the gun violence; rather, they are awake and alert, prepared to do whatever it takes in order to bring sense, hope, and real, practical, and lasting reforms to gun laws throughout America. Why do I mention this? Because in my introduction I highlighted that history is filled with violence—how able we have always been at killing one another, and how our world has always known the horrific, and that fear, violence, and power have always walked hand in hand together throughout our human story. This school mass shooting in Florida is once again a senseless tragedy, a lifelong sentence of heartache and horror to the friends, family, and fellow students of the victims. We have discovered together that horror texts, in their variety, are often prophetic works that speak with a foresight and power into our modern world, revealing in stark and brutal ways our fearful violence, and how immunized we are to the suffering around us, and how implicit and imbedded within that violence we are. I have argued throughout that horror wakes us up to our violence and offers us another way, a pathway to our betterment and flourishing, a flourishing that is witnessed within the life of Jesus of Nazareth. This "waking up"

---

2. At the time of writing, February 2018, there has been over 2,000 gun-related deaths in America during the first six weeks of 2018 alone. "Between 2014 and 2017, 56,755 Americans were killed by guns, including 2,710 children under the age of 12." See http://www.theweek.co.uk/91679/us-gun-violence-in-six-chilling-statistics.

3. Atwood, *Gundamentalism*, 18.

to the need for radical transformation has happened to many because of gun violence, yet so much more needs to be done.

Gonzalez directly challenged Donald Trump in her speech, asking,

> If the President wants to come up to me and tell me to my face
> that it was a terrible tragedy and how it should never have hap-
> pened and maintain telling us how nothing is going to be done
> about it, I'm going to happily ask him how much money he re-
> ceived from the National Rifle Association.

She goes on and says, "To every politician who is taking money directly from the NRA, shame on you."[4] From politicians and leaders, through to every realm of society, there is the struggle with desire for wealth, for power, for status, that the decisions we make can so often be about "me" rather than the greater "us," and how far-reaching those decisions can impact society as a whole.

Horror so often looks unflinchingly at the impact of our violence and fear, and how wide an influence our choices have upon others. This is why epidemic horror stories so often fascinate us, with "patient zero" the one who is the cause, the reason, the source of the violence and horror that now grips the entire planet. In Justin Cronin's *The Passage*, the character Timothy Fanning is patient zero, contracting a disease given to him through a government trial that is testing a drug intended to prolong life, a drug that transforms him into a vampire-type creature, a creature that will become known simply as "Zero." Zero's place within the arch of the story is almost deified as humanity reflects back on the "one" from whom its almost destruction occurred. Other examples of seeking to locate patient zero are Max Brooks's *World War Z*, with interviews of those who encountered the first diseased person; the 2011 film *Contagion*, ending with the reveal of patient zero and how they contracted the deadly virus that killed millions worldwide; and Stephen King's *The Stand*, opening with the government employee who flees the base through fear of an outbreak and so inadvertently spreads the disease to the entire world. Count Dracula is the classic patient zero, the one through whom vampirism begins—Satan too, the prince of demons, and characters like Bruce Banner, whose DNA spawns Hulk-like characters and villains. Not only this, but it is common within the horror genre to tell the "origin story," revealing where the evil came from that caused terror in the previous storyline. Often this is due more to the original film or book's success and the desire to capitalize on its success by making an "origins" story that gives viewers a "reason" behind the evil character. More often

4. For the full video of her speech, see https://edition.cnn.com/2018/02/17/us/florida-student-emma-gonzalez-speech/index.html.

THE POWER OF PEACE

than not the main evil character is the direct result of extreme violence directed toward them or their loved ones, returning from the dead to exact vengeance and pain on any who dare awaken them. So to begin with they are evil and violent because of violence inflicted upon them, and then they are simply consumed by evil to inflict pain for no reason whatsoever. While origin stories are appealing, there is also the power of allowing the reality of evil to simply be evil for no other reason than because it is evil—no cause, no backstory, simply horror. That is not to say that people who commit acts of evil do not have a story, that who they are and the acts they commit are sometimes as much do with acts committed against them as it is to do with something horrific going on inside them, but it is also to say that evil is meaningless, and by naming it as meaningless gives voice to the victims.

Commentators can silence the cry of the victim when they pay more attention to the reason why someone has committed an act of atrocious evil, and we must fight to not allow that to happen, for every voice of every victim needs to be heard. There is no doubt that young men from Pakistan whose family have been killed by bombs from Western drones will likely be radicalized, a radicalization that is a direct result of Western foreign policy, but when these young men detonate bombs that are strapped to themselves and kill other people's children and families, we must not hold them up as victims in the same way those dead young children are victims. Those young men have acted in an evil way, fueled by an understandable anger and hatred toward Western powers, but they have a choice, a choice to be driven by this hate, or to seek the way of peace and forgiveness. It is possible to pursue forgiveness in the face of monumental evil perpetrated against us, for history has proven this to be the case as woman and men, who have every right to demand blood and vengeance because of evil committed against them, have sought to end the cycle of hate, violence, and vengeance, and have pursued the way of peace—and let us be clear about this, every time a bomb is dropped an act of evil occurs, wherever it is dropped, whomever it is dropped upon. This way of peace enables the voice of the victim to be truly heard, that those who have been killed can be listened to and honored, those who have been abused and who have suffered great injustice can be listened to and learned from; the sound of revenge drowns out the power of the victim's voice, the call of forgiveness pays attention to the cry of the suffering.[5]

---

5. My friend, the Reverend Jeannie Kendall, is writing a book from the perspective of the unnamed women victims from the Bible, hearing their voice, and giving space to their stories, such as the unnamed concubine in Judges 19, as well as hearing the voice of modern victims, people whose voice have been silenced today. I hope that this book is published as it is a powerful, prophetic, and remarkable work that enables us to hear the voices of those women silenced through the centuries, as well as hearing the voices of

Patient Zero commands our fascination because we want to hear their voice, to know how this avalanche of evil has occurred, and this is where horror remains so deeply powerful and culturally prophetic, for it calls us to pay attention to those who have suffered at the hands of others. As has already been said, horror reminds us of the utter hopelessness and meaninglessness of evil and suffering; when a child dies of cancer there is no "hidden" meaning, no cosmic plan that we have to wait for to be revealed one day that will make sense of this great suffering, rather, the death of any child is an utter disgrace, a meaningless void of pain that hurts every part of what it means to be human, and any attempt to frame such tragedy as part of God's plan needs to be exorcised from all our thinking. To face horror full on calls us to pay attention, an attention that enables us to work out how we might move forward as human beings creating a world that is different to the violent narrative we have pursued since we crawled out of the mud and gathered in communities. Jesus has given us the ability to hear the cry of the victim, to pay attention to the horror of violence, the meaningless of suffering, and the evil that we can so often call good. Horror is an expression of this ability, for, as we have said, it calls us to pay attention to evil, fear, and suffering, an attention that has been made possible through the horror of the cross. The life of Jesus was lived in such beauty, in the overflow of divine love, grace, and forgiveness, that we know his death was unjust, that he was a victim to an unjust System that demanded blood to quench its violent wrath. In other words, we know Jesus was innocent and should never have died, and yet still he was crucified, subjected to torture and suffering, a life of unmistakable humanity, dehumanized through his murder. Yet from the cross Jesus calls out forgiveness, and that is why the blood of Jesus speaks a better word than the blood of Abel.[6]

Our crisis of violence is a deeply spiritual crisis that reveals itself through our actions; there is no sacred/secular divide, for who we are and our actions are the result of all that we are—heart, mind, soul, and strength. Horror has the power to reveal that crisis to us, to show us in the most brutal and disturbing ways the true scope and depth of our problems, and we become very afraid the more aware we become. That is why, perhaps, the woman I introduced you to in the introduction, the woman scared of demonic possession after watching a film, was so afraid because she was

women and men today who have been abused and suffered through the hands of others. For a sermon I preached on the unnamed concubine in Judges 19, go to Rev. Joe Haward, "Hearing a Silent Woman," preached November 29, 2015, at Barton Baptist Church, http://dynamic.livesiteadmin.com/podcast/odd56ed4-do1d-4a36-af93-09a326fd828f.

6. "Rather, you have come . . . to Jesus the mediator of a new covenant, and to a blood for sprinkling that bespeaks something better than that of Abel,," Heb 12:22–24.

becoming aware of the crisis of violence that we are faced with, a crisis that a horror film exposed her to and gave feeling and fear to. In essence, horror is the visualization, the expression of our violent crisis of the fear that this violence breeds within us, but that we so often have inoculated ourselves from, drowning out the voice of the victim through more shed blood, becoming numb to the sheer level and depth of our brutality against one another. Horror gives our fear a voice, an outlet that expresses all that we fear we are. But into that fear, into this crisis, the voice of the True Human is heard, a voice that declares, "peace," "forgiveness," a voice of hope that pushes back the despair, a voice of faith and love that casts out fear.

The voice of Jesus matters because our crisis, as I have already said, is a spiritual crisis, something that distorts our humanity and needs a divine/human cure; forgiveness is a spiritual act, a powerful action that is utterly transformative of all things. Horror shows us that violence simply breeds violence, that there is no path to peace through retribution, that no wound is healed through the act of wounding. Horror opens up the doorway to this understanding, and, as we have seen throughout this book, within each genre within horror that we have examined, it gives us the tools to make sense of where our fear comes from. We have traced throughout this book that our fear is a primal scream that horror gives voice to, that horror consistently shows us the reality of our violent struggles, and yet also, so often, gives revolutionary answers to the violence we are confronted with, answers, when interpreted through the life and gospel of Jesus of Nazareth, that can draw us into our true humanity and build communities of unconditionality that can ultimately not be overcome by the darkness of evil. Every community of unconditionality, every act of love in this life echoes out into eternity, never wasted, never forgotten by the God of all compassion and mercy. We have explored how horror, through the lens of the gospel, shows us the power of compassion, community, authentic speech, trust, the power of now, relationships, identity, and forgiveness.

If Jesus was made "into sin" (2 Cor 5:21) for our sake, if the Son of God "bore our sins upon the tree" (1 Pet 2:24) as the only One who is able to do so as God incarnate, the Creator crucified, then on the cross God takes upon God's Self the fullness of all evil, the totality of all sin, the suffering of all history; Jesus is made *into* sin to exhaust its power and overthrow it. The consequence of sin is death, the unnatural result of a world created "good" whose goal is to reach fullness within God's own life, everything held together in God, everything on a journey of "becoming," of being fully reconciled and at peace in and through Jesus. Sin brings death, and death has no place within a good God's good cosmos, and so Jesus takes everything—sin, death, suffering, pain, fear, loneliness—he takes it all fully upon himself and somehow experiences the full darkness of evil, allowing it to utterly consume him; on the cross God dies. Other people have died more painful physical deaths, have been tortured more in the body than Jesus, yet if all that we say above is true, then Jesus experiences ultimate horror, a horror by which all things are now to be interpreted through, for if life itself, the very source and goal of all things, *is made into the very antithesis of life and love*, then all human, cosmic, and divine events must be understood in the light of this darkest horror.

And so we come back to our own exploration of horror, and I hope you have been able to see how Jesus, in the context of all that has just been said, is the One through whom we interpret the text of horror, and how we are able to penetrate the depths of horror and find remarkable insights that cannot only speak directly into our human condition, but can call us toward gospel-orientated lives, toward lives that do not cower in fear, and do not succumb to the violence, vengeance, and wrath that such fear brings. When the disciples asked Jesus if they should bring down fire on the heads of those who would not accept him, Jesus rebuked them (Luke 9:54), for his way is peace, his way is the renunciation of violence, a life that seeks to pray for those who regard him an enemy,[7] to bless those who persecute him, cry forgiveness to those who would crucify him with their wrath, to speak peace to those who abandoned him; in other words, Jesus rejects of all violence toward *us*, for *we are those people*. Horror continually shows us that we are those people of violence, and yet the gospel offers us the hope of total reconciliation, a reconciliation that reaches beyond all boundaries and prejudices, beyond all creeds, beyond all racial and social barriers, a reconciliation where "all will be given life" (1 Cor 15:22b), united in the person of Jesus (Gal 3:28). In Genesis 4 we discover that Patient Zero of human violence, the archetype of violent desire is Cain, the one who kills his brother, and with whom the word "sin" is first used in scripture (Gen 4:7). Cain symbolizes our violent desires, the way "sin has walked within us; brother against brother, nation against nation, man against creation. We murdered each other, we broke the

---

7. God regards none as his enemy, for he has "effected reconciliation" (Col 1:22), "making peace by the blood of his cross" (Col 1:20). Psalm 23, some of the most famous verses in the whole Bible, declares that God will "prepare a table before me in the presence of my enemies," a sign of God's plan to bring enemies together in a meal of reconciliation. This meal of reconciliation is cosmic in scope as God invites all to "dine" with him (Rev 3:20) in this feast of peace. As Rublev's *Icon of the Trinity* expresses, there is always a place at the table for us with God. It is us who regard God as an enemy, never God who regard us as enemies. Indeed, God's love and peace are of such magnitude that when we encounter this God in ineffable glory all our God-concepts will be consumed, and that which we regard as enemy will be seen as love as we are seen to be regarded with such great love.

world; we did this, man did this. Everything that was good, everything that was beautiful, we shattered."[89] This whole book has sought to demonstrate in numerous ways how far the violent virus has spread, how resilient it is, and how destructive it has proven to be. So powerful is its contagion that we become numb to its effects, seemingly incapable of recognizing it for what it is, nor desiring to seek a way out of its grasp. There is a scene in *Predator* where the character Billy stops running, turns, and stands still ready to face the predator alien. Using his huge knife, he cuts his chest and waits for his death at the hands of the monster, deciding to give up and simply wait for inevitability to play out. The thought of resisting violence, especially in light of all that we have explored, can seem an impossible task, and, like Billy, many of us have simply decided that we will not bother trying to seek an alternative and allow the inevitability of violence within the world play itself out. Horror reminds us though that not everything will transpire as we imagine it to, that there are surprises in store, and incredible people who show us that the seemingly impossible can be made possible, that evil will not have the final say. Of course there are those nihilistic horror stories that have no redemption, where pain and suffering have the final word, and in some ways this is a very real truth for some in our world; some people do not experience a happy ending.[10] But if the gospel is to be believed, if who Jesus *is* who he is into all eternity, then hope and not despair is the final word. The good news is that the Great Physician has entered the violence and grit and beauty of existence and offered us a cure, an antidote to the violent contagion each of us is infected with:

> But he alone having reached our deep corruption, he alone having taken upon himself our labors, he alone having suffered the punishments due to our impieties, having recovered us who were not half dead merely, but were already in tombs and sepulchers, and altogether foul and offensive, saves us both anciently and now, by his beneficent zeal, beyond the expectation of any one, even of ourselves, and imparts liberally of the Father's benefits—he who is the giver of life and light, our great Physician and King and Lord, the Christ of God.[11]

8. *Noah*, Darren Aronofsky, Paramount Pictures, 2014.

9. *Noah*, 2014.

10. For me the film *Se7en* is the most terrifying, nihilistic, and unsettling movie I have ever experienced. For those that have never seen it, I recommend it as a brilliant piece of storytelling, and quite outstanding performances, but it may well leave you feeling utterly shell-shocked and reeling for a few days afterwards.

11. Eusebius, *Church History* X.IV.12, accessed via http://www.newadvent.org/fathers/250110.htm.

Humanity is in need of the One who gives life, not death, the One who has plumbed the depth of our violence, exhausted it, and overcome it through the power of love and forgiveness. Violence brings the "foul and offensive" stench of death, but forgiveness brings the aroma of life, the perfume of peace, hope, and restoration. Dr. Martin Luther King Jr. said, "Hatred and bitterness can never cure the disease of fear; only love can do that. Hatred paralyses life; love releases it. Hatred confuses life; love harmonizes it. Hatred darkens life; love illumines it."[12] The gospel is the declaration that love has entered into the fullness of our violence, fear, and horror in the Person of Jesus; love is the cosmic cure to the totality of death, not simply a soothing word when we are trembling, but the promise that one day all will be well. This is a wellness that will surge into the deepest and darkest recesses of our existence, draw out every trace of violent poison, and breathe into us, by the Spirit, a totality of healing and peace. It is the total eradication of all that has damaged us, an entering into a time where we know and are fully known as children of God. "God's gonna take care of you" Mother Pollard so confidently expressed to Dr. Martin Luther King Jr. one day, and so we face our fears, listening to the prophetic voice within horror, voices that expose our deepest violent desires, yet also reveal our striving for the way of peace, people of authentic speech, pursuers of compassion, committed to unconditional relationships and unlimited forgiveness, lives that seek to reflect the light, beauty, and love of Jesus, the One who reveals who God is, and who we are becoming,

> Jesus Christ . . . in his transcendent love, became what we are,
> that he might bring us to be even what he is himself.[13]

This *becoming* leads us beyond all that horror so wonderfully and powerfully shows us about ourselves, and promises, into the violence and confusion of the world, the brilliance and beauty of the kingdom of peace, a peace that will one day reign in the hearts of all and over every conceivable reality.

12. King, *Strength to Love*, 122.
13. Irenaeus, *Against Heresies*, V, Preface.

Bibliography

Antonello, Pierpaolo, and Paul Gifford, eds. *How We Became Human: Mimetic Theory and the Science of Evolutionary Origins*. East Lansing: Michigan State University Press, 2015.

Athanasius. *On the Incarnation*. Translated by A Religious. London: Mowbray, 1953.

Atwood, James, E. *Gundamentalism and Where It Is Taking America*. Eugene, OR: Wipf and Stock, 2017.

Augustine. *City of God*. Translated by H. Bettenson. New York: Penguin, 1997.

———. *Confessions*. Translated by R. S. Pinie-Coffin. Reading: Penguin, 1988.

———. *Earlier Writings*. Translated by J. S. Burleigh. Philadelphia: Westminster, 1953.

Bailey, Doug, et al. "Transhumanist Declaration." *Humanity+*, http://humanityplus.org/philosophy/transhumanist-declaration/.

Barker, Clive. *The Great and Secret Show*. Glasgow: Fontana, 1990.

———. *Weaveworld*. Glasgow: Fontana, 1988.

Barth, Karl. *Church Dogmatics*, vols. I–IV. Translated and edited by G. W. Bromiley and T. F. Torrance. Edinburgh: T. & T. Clark, 1956–75.

———. *God Here and Now*. London: Routledge, 2003

Bartholomew, Craig, and Thorsten Moritz, eds. *Christ and Consumerism*. Carlisle: Paternoster, 2000.

Bauman, Zygmunt. *Consuming Life*. Cambridge: Polity, 2007.

———. "Living in Utopia." *Repekt*, June 13, 2005, https://www.respekt.cz/respekt-in-english/living-in-utopia.

Bentley Hart, David. *Atheist Delusions*. London: Yale University Press, 2009.

———. *The Doors of the Sea*. Cambridge: Eerdmans, 2005.

———. *The Experience of God: Being, Consciousness, Bliss*. London: Yale University Press, 2013.

———. *The Story of Christianity*. London: Quercus, 2009.

Bernasconi, Robert, and Simon Critchley, eds. *Re-Reading Lévinas*. London: Athlone, 1991.

Bethge, Eberhard. *Dietrich Bonhoeffer*. Minneapolis: Fortress, 2000.

Blatty, William, Peter. *The Exorcist*. London: Transworld, 1972.

Bonhoeffer, Dietrich. "Christ and Peace." In *Berlin: 1932–1933*, edited by Larry L. Rasmussen, 258. Dietrich Bonhoeffer Works, Vol. 12. Minneapolis: Fortress, 2009.

———. "The Church and the Peoples of the World." In *London: 1933–1935*, Edited by Keith W. Clements, 307–9. Dietrich Bonhoeffer Works, Vol. 13. Minneapolis: Fortress, 2007.

————"The Confessing Church and the Ecumenical Movement." In *Testament to Freedom*, 140. New York: HarperCollins, 1995.

————. *The Cost of Discipleship*. Minneapolis: Fortress, 2000.

————. *Ecumenical, Academic, and Pastoral Work*. Minneapolis: Fortress, 2012.

————. *Ethics*. Minneapolis: Fortress, 2000.

————. *God Is in the Manger: Reflections on Advent and Christmas*. Louisville: Westminster John Knox, 2010.

————. *Life Together*. London: SCM, 1954.

————. *Meditations on the Psalms*. Grand Rapids: Zondervan, 2002.

Brooks, Max. *World War Z: An Oral History of the Zombie War*. Croydon: Duckworth, 2011.

Brueggemann, Walter. *The Prophetic Imagination*. Minneapolis: Fortress, 2001.

Calvin, John. *Institutes of the Christian Religion*. Edited by J. T. McNeill, translated by F. L. Battles. Philadelphia: Westminster, 1960.

Chardin, Teilhard de. *The Future of Man*. New York: Doubleday, 2004.

Clement. *The First Epistle of Clement*, in ANF, vol. 1, 5–21.

Coakley, Sarah. *God, Sexuality, and the Self*. Cambridge: University Press, 2013.

Colwell, John E. *Promise and Presence: An Exploration of Sacramental Theology*. Imprint Carlisle: Paternoster, 2005.

————. *Why Have You Forsaken Me?* Milton Keynes: Paternoster, 2010.

Chomsky, Noam. *Requiem for the American Dream: The 10 Principles of Concentration of Wealth & Power*. New York: Seven Stories, 2017.

Connolly, John. *The Unquiet*. London: Hodder, 2007.

Cronin, Justin. *The Passage*. London: Orion, 2010.

Dionysius. *The Works of Dionysius*. In *Ante-Nicene Fathers of the Christian Church*, vol. 6, 81–120. Edited by Alexander Roberts and James Donaldson. Edinburgh: T. & T. Clark, 1866–1895.

Dittmar, Linda, and Gene Michaud. *From Hanoi to Hollywood: The Vietnam War in American Film*. New Jersey: Rutgers University Press, 1990.

Ellul, Jacques. *Violence: Reflections from a Christian Perspective*. Eugene, OR: Wipf and Stock, 2012.

Engels, Friedrich, and Karl Marx. *The Communist Manifesto*. London: Penguin Random House, 2002.

Eusebius. *Church History*. http://www.newadvent.org/fathers/250110.htm.

Fahy, Thomas, ed. *The Philosophy of Horror*. Kentucky: The University Press of Kentucky, 2012.

Farrow, Douglas. "St Irenaeus of Lyons: The Church and the World." *Pro Ecclesia* IV/3 (1995) 333–55.

Girard, René. *Things Hidden Since the Foundation of the World*. London: Continuum, 2003.

————. *Violence and the Sacred*. Baltimore: John Hopkins University Press, 1977.

Gregory of Nyssa. *The Life of Moses*. Translated by A. J. Malherbe and E. Ferguson. New York: HarperOne, 2006.

Gregory Nazianzus. *Epistle to Cledonius the Priest Against Apollinarius*. Monachos.net, http://www.monachos.net/content/patristics/patristictexts/158.

Gunton, Colin E. *The Promise of Trinitarian Theology*. Edinburgh: T. & T. Clark, 1997.

Hardin, Michael. *Mimetic Theory and Biblical Interpretation: Reclaiming the Good News of the Gospel*. Eugene, OR: Cascade, 2017.

———. *The Jesus Driven Life.* Lancaster: JDL, 2010.

Hardin, Michael, ed. *Reading the Bible with René Girard: Conversations with Steven E. Berry.* Lancaster: JDL, 2015.

Harris, Thomas. *Hannibal.* London: Arrow, 2000.

———. *Red Dragon.* London: Corgi, 1983.

———. *The Silence of the Lambs.* London: Arrow, 2013.

Hauerwas, Stanley. *Approaching the End.* Grand Rapids: Eerdmans, 2013.

———. "McInerny Did It: Or, Should a Pacifist Read Murder Mysteries?" in *A Better Hope: Resources for a Church Confronting Capitalism, Democracy, and Postmodernity*, 201–10. Grand Rapids: Brazos, 2000.

———. *The Peaceable Kingdom.* London: Notra Dame, 1983.

Hauerwas, Stanley, and Jean Vanier. *Living Gently in a Violent World.* Downers Grove, IL: IVP, 2008.

Haward, Joseph. *The Ghost of Perfection: Searching for Humanity.* Eugene, OR: Resource, 2017.

Heaney, Seamus. *Beowulf.* London: Faber & Faber, 2000.

Hedges, Chris. *Empire of Illusion: The End of Literacy and the Triumph of Spectacle.* New York: Nation, 2009.

Helmreich, Ernst Christian. *The German Churches Under Hitler: Background, Struggle, and Epilogue.* Detroit: Wayne State University Press, 1979.

Hippolytus. *The Refutation of All Heresies.* In *Ante-Nicene Fathers of the Christian Church*, vol. 5, 9–162. Edited by Alexander Roberts and James Donaldson. Edinburgh: T. & T. Clark, 1866–1895.

Hitler, Adolf. *Mein Kampf.* Mumbai: Jaico, 2007.

Irenaeus. *Against Heresies.* In *Ante-Nicene Fathers of the Christian Church*,vol. 1, 315–567. Edited by Alexander Roberts and James Donaldson. Edinburgh: T. & T. Clark, 1866–1895.

Jameson, Frederic. "Historicism in 'The Shining.'" In *Signatures of the Visible.* London: Routledge, 1992.

Jones, Darryl. *Horror: A Thematic History in Fiction and Film.* London: Arnold, 2002.

Justin Martyr. *First Apology.* In *Ante-Nicene Fathers of the Christian Church*, vol. 1, 159–302. Edited by Alexander Roberts and James Donaldson. Edinburgh: T. & T. Clark, 1866–1895

Kierkegaard, Søren. *Fear and Trembling.* Reading: Penguin, 2005.

King, Martin Luther, Jr. "Nonviolence and Racial Justice." *Christian Century* (1957) 118–22.

———. *Strength to Love.* Glasgow: Fount, 1981.

———. *Where Do We Go From Here?: Chaos or Community?* Boston: Beacon, 2010.

King, Stephen. *Doctor Sleep.* London: Hodder, 2014.

———. *The Green Mile.* New York: Pocket, 1996.

———. *It.* London: Hodder, 2011.

———. *Mr. Mercedes.* London: Hodder, 2015.

———.'*Salem's Lot.* London: Hodder, 2011.

———. *The Shining.* London: Hodder, 2011.

———. *The Stand.* London: Hodder, 2011.

Kirkpatrick, Kate. *Sartre and Theology.* London: Bloomsbury T. & T. Clark, 2017.

Lacan, Jacques. *Écrits: A Selection.* New York: Routledge, 2001.

———. *The Seminar of Jacques Lacan XI.* New York: W. W. Norton & Company, 1998.

Long, Michael, ed. *Christian Peace and Nonviolence: A Documentary History*. New York: Orbis, 2011.

Lossky, Vladimir. *In the Image and Likeness of God*. Crestwood, NY: St Vladimir's Seminary Press, 1974.

MacIntyre, Alasdair. *Marxism and Christianity*. London: Duckworth, 1995.

Marx, Karl. *Capital: Volume 1*. London: Penguin Classics, 1990.

Masson, Jeffrey M. *The Assault on Truth*. London: Ballantine, 2003.

Matheson, Paul, ed. "New Guiding Principles of the German Christians, 16 May 1933." in *The Third Reich and the Christian Churches*, 23. Grand Rapids: Eerdmans, 1981.

Mathetes. *The Epistle to Diognetus*. In *Ante-Nicene Fathers of the Christian Church*, vol. 1, 23–30. Edited by Alexander Roberts and James Donaldson. Edinburgh: T. & T. Clark, 1866–1895.

Maximus the Confessor. *Ambiguum 7* [Eng. translation], edited by Andrew Louth. New York: Routledge, 1996.

McArthur, Neil, and Markie L. C. Twist. "The Rise of Digisexuality: Therapeutic Challenges and Possibilities, Sexual and Relationship Therapy." *Sexual and Relationship Therapy 32, no. 3–4* (2017) 334–44

McCarthy, Cormac. *The Road*. London: Picador, 2009.

Nation, Mark Thiessen, Anthony G. Siegrist, and Daniel P. Umbel. *Bonhoeffer the Assassin?: Challenging the Myth, Recovering His Call to Peacemaking*. Grand Rapids: Baker, 2013.

Newman, Kim. *Anno Dracula*. London: Titan, 2011.

Niebuhr, Richard H. *Christ and Culture*. San Francisco: Harper and Row, 1975.

Nietzsche, Friedrich. *Thus Spake Zarathustra*. London: Bibliophile, 1997.

O'Donovan, Oliver. *Begotten or Made?: Human Procreation and Medical Technique*. Oxford: Clarendon, 1984.

Parks, Rosa. *Rosa Parks: My Story*. New York: Puffin, 1992.

Pelikan, Jaroslav. *Christianity and Classical Culture*. London: Yale University Press, 1993.

Pound, Marcus. *Theology, Psychoanalysis and Trauma*. London: SCM, 2007.

Rice, Anne. *Interview with the Vampire*. London: Sphere, 2012.

Russell, Jamie. *Book of the Dead*. Surry: FAB, 2008.

Russell, Mary Doria. *Children of God*. London: Black Swan, 2009.

Sartre, John Paul. *Being and Nothingness: An Essay on Phenomenological Ontology*. London: Routledge, 2003.

———. *The War Diaries: November 1939–March 1940*. New York: Pantheon, 1984.

Schwager, Raymond S. J. *Must There Be Scapegoats?: Violence and Redemption in the Bible*. New York: The Crossroad, 1987.

Shakespeare, William. *The Tempest*. http://shakespeare.mit.edu/tempest/full.html.

Shelley, Mary. *Frankenstein*. Croydon: Alma Classics, 2010.

Solzhenitsyn, Aleksandr. *The Gulag Archipelago: 1918–1956, vol. 1*. London: Harper Perennial Modern Classics, 2007.

Stoker, Bram. *Dracula*. London: Wordsworth Classics, 2000.

Tertullian. *De Spectaculis*. In *Ante-Nicene Fathers of the Christian Church*, vol. 3, 79–91. Edited by Alexander Roberts and James Donaldson. Edinburgh: T. & T. Clark, 1866–1895.

Tillich, Paul. *The Essential Tillich*. New York: Collier, 1987.

Tolkien, J. R. R. *The Lord of the Rings*. London: HarperCollins, 2005.

Vanier, Jean. *From Brokenness to Community*. New Jersey: Paulist, 1992.

Weaver, Denny J. *The Nonviolent Atonement*. Grand Rapids: Eerdmans, 2001.

Webb, Lance. *Conquering the Seven Deadly Sins*. Nashville: Abingdon, 1955.

Wink, Walter. *Engaging the Powers*. Minneapolis: Fortress, 1992.

———. *The Powers That Be: Theology for a New Millennium*. London: Cassell, 1998.

Žižek, Slavoj, *Enjoy Your Symptom!: Jacques Lacan in Hollywood and Out*. New York: Routledge, 2008.

———. *God in Pain: Inversions of Apocalypse*. New York: Seven Stories, 2012.

———. *Living in the End Times*. London, Verso, 2010.

———. *Looking Awry: An Introduction to Jacques Lacan Through Popular Culture*. London: The MIT Press, 1992.

———. "A Perverts Guide to Family." http://www.lacan.com/zizfamily.htm.

———. *Puppet and the Dwarf: The Perverse Core of Christianity*. London: The MIT, 2003.

www.ingramcontent.com/pod-product-compliance
Lightning Source LLC
Chambersburg PA
CBHW061737270326
41928CB00011B/2279